# HOUSE OF PAIN

# House of Pain

## Through the Rooms
## of Mayo Football

# Keith Duggan

MAINSTREAM
PUBLISHING

EDINBURGH AND LONDON

First published in Great Britain in 2007 by
MAINSTREAM PUBLISHING COMPANY
(EDINBURGH) LTD
7 Albany Street
Edinburgh EH1 3UG

ISBN 9781845962975

A catalogue record for this book is available
from the British Library

Typeset in Sabon and Trajan

Printed in Great Britain by
Clays Ltd, St Ives plc

# CONTENTS

# PREFACE

Many years ago, my friend Frank Shovlin told me about standing on the Canal End and watching the 1993 All-Ireland semi-final between Mayo and Cork. It was an infamous day for Mayo football, and long before the match ended the Canal End was strewn with green-and-red flags abandoned by Mayo people who had left the old stadium in great despondency. Frank's father is a Donegal man, but the family lived for many years in Castlebar, and, like most people in the county, they were loyal to the complicated and quixotic attempts of generations of Mayo football teams to win the Sam Maguire Cup. On that black afternoon, an All-Ireland victory seemed further away than ever. Before leaving the stadium, Frank and his father collected armfuls of flags and, not knowing what else to do with them, placed them in the boot of the car and drove west.

In 2006, after Mayo and Dublin had illuminated the summer with a spellbinding All-Ireland semi-final, Frank senior went to the shed at the rear of the house and retrieved a green-and-red flag. It had been saved from that hoard collected more than a decade earlier. It was clean and well preserved and, of course, worth flying.

The story of that 1993 semi-final first stoked my curiosity as to what Gaelic football means to people in Mayo. In later years, I met many Mayo football people and found them to be admirably honest and brave in explaining the extremes of emotion that went with kicking ball for the county. It became clear that people there regard Mayo as an aristocratic football county, however down-at-heel the estate may have become over the years.

Through some mysterious process, the championship heritage of the Mayo teams of the early 1950s has been passed on through subsequent generations. Mayo football has gone quiet since that time, but it has never disappeared, because, if nothing else, Mayo football teams were something to talk about in letters dispatched across the Atlantic during the most furious years of emigration. More locally, the team remains the most potent force for uniting what is a big and lonesome county. And despite the absence of the big prize since 1951, the fact that Mayo has produced many fabulous football players since that time is undeniable. It is equally true that, while there is a great hunger for that grand success in Mayo, there has been a refusal to compromise the traditional county style – open, somewhat flamboyant, sometimes brilliant, frequently risky – in getting there. Mayo know only one way to play it, and to hell with the consequences.

Mayo football is a big subject and is, of course, deeply rooted in whatever qualities make that county and its people different from all the others in Ireland. I hope this book gives an impression of why Gaelic football means so much to Mayo and salutes the hundreds of men who tried, be it for a single season or several decades, to contribute something. So much of sport has been reduced to tidy little stories of redemption, of winning in the end. So much time and genuflection is afforded to the champions, to those who prevail and who make victory seem like the easiest thing in the world. But for most teams and sportspeople, the opposite is true. Losing is the universal sporting experience. In Gaelic games, Mayo stands at a strange and lonely impasse, in that it seems destined to be the county that almost always nearly wins. In the past twenty years, the fascinating and sometimes tortured relationship that Mayo has had with the All-Ireland football championship has made for a sometimes uncomfortable and voyeuristic spectacle. Several Mayo teams and many thousands of Mayo people have had their morale crushed on big days in Croke Park. They have dealt with those defeats with eloquence and dignity. And most importantly, they have always returned, with big-hearted, open, skilful teams and behind them the Mayo public – a chorus that is, when it comes down to it, incapable of true cynicism. It seems true to say that the next time Mayo qualify for an All-Ireland final, fear will grip the county as much as excitement. But they will turn up and they will honour the fixture. And some year they will win it all. The football men in this book and those whom they represent will know that they have played their part in whatever September Sunday it is that heaven reveals itself over Croke Park and Mayo become champions. Again.

# ONE

# THIS IS THE END

It was like breathing in ether. David Brady stood in the mellow autumn sunlight, solemn and resolute, about to enter his fourth All-Ireland senior football final. This one was over almost as soon as it began. On the field, the Kerry players were responding to their own private motivations with a performance of skill and power that was majestic and cruel. They were playing Gaelic football as if the Mayo men were just ghosts on the field instead of fifteen primed, finely tuned athletes. Kerry took command of the game with such killing and withering finality that they succeeded in largely silencing the crowd of some 80,000 people that had gathered on that gorgeous Indian-summer day hoping for drama and intrigue. Mayo people had dared to hope that this day would transport them back to the bonfire nights of 1951, when their team were last champions. Instead, they were treated to a frightening exposition of the inherent desire and ambition, the carnivorous need, that drives Kerry football men and of the shocking depth of paralysis and capacity for big-day misadventure that have haunted Mayo football teams for too long.

To make matters worse, the match echoed eerily what had happened when the counties met in the 2004 All-Ireland final.

11

It was a stroke of bold genius by the Kerry manager Jack O'Connor once again to present the Mayo team with their worst nightmares as soon as the cheering from the national anthem had finished. High, booming balls were rained down on the Mayo full-back line, and where two years earlier the green-and-red-shirted defenders had struggled to cope with the bulky wizardry of Kerry veteran Johnny Crowley, now they were helpless against the height and smart passing of Kieran Donaghy, the rangy young Tralee basketball star whose unorthodox, blue-collar full-forward instinct had made him the sensation of the championship. Declan O'Sullivan offered a portent of the afternoon to come with an early goal of supreme ease and confidence. Then Donaghy caught a ball and turned to find the net with a murderous shot. Colm Cooper, pale and lethal, was a torment. He too would find the net before the half was out. Further up the field, the Kerry lines were moving at speed and in harmony.

Billy Fitzpatrick, the veteran Mayo forward who now calls live matches with Midwest Radio, the flagship station in the county, was almost speechless with disbelief. Looking on from the godly heights of the upper Hogan Stand, it seemed as if the Ó Sé brothers and the totemic Séamus Moynihan and the black-haired Paul Galvin were just flowing through the Mayo rearguard at will. There seemed to be twice as many Kerry men as Mayo players on the field.

Fitzpatrick had been worried from the second Mayo had taken the field. He detected lifelessness in the way the players moved, as if they were burdened rather than inspired by the task ahead. It was so different to the melodramatic, anarchic scenes of three weeks earlier, when Mayo had outraged the Dublin fans and team by warming up in front of Hill 16 before the All-Ireland semi-final. The atmosphere had been revolutionary that day. Now, in the hazy afternoon warmth with the brass band sounding out tunes of triumph and excitement in the amphitheatre, Mayo looked meek. He watched Ciaran McDonald, probably the purest kicker of a football in the game, send two practice shots tailing lamely towards the old Nally Stand and he feared the worst. 'Something is not right here,' he said aloud, not speaking to anyone in particular.

Brady had become something of a shop steward to the Mayo team over the course of the season. Coaxing the Ballina midfield man out of retirement and resurrecting the career of Kevin O'Neill – the classy but forgotten Knockmore forward – had been two of the brightest moves made by the Mayo management team of Mickey Moran and John Morrison. The Ulstermen had used Brady as an impact substitute, and although he believed he could have started this final, he was at peace with the role. It was his habit to sit in the reserves' dugout with his boots unlaced, but four minutes into the All-Ireland final, he began to lace them tightly, his heart pounding.

Later, he would liken those minutes to an out-of-body experience. 'I remember feeling as though I was being sucked into a vacuum. It was as if the light went on. We suddenly realised where we were and what it meant. You would swear Kerry had never won a thing in their life. They were killing us. And they set out to beat us in the first ten minutes. We went six points down, eight points down, ten points down. We were in disbelief. It was all happening again. I had to keep telling myself that this was not some kind of f***ing joke.'

When Brady, inevitably, was called to go on, after just eleven minutes, the notion of the All-Ireland final as a contest was already a ruin. Of the four All-Ireland senior finals Mayo had lost in the past decade, this was the most spectacular implosion. Three weeks earlier, they had starred in a match against Dublin that drew immediate comparison with the finest of the last one hundred years. Now, just ten minutes into the GAA showpiece, a day of ritual importance not only in

Ireland but also in the emerald enclaves of the great American cities and throughout England and the far-flung reaches of the world, Mayo were a hunted thing.

On televisions across the world and to the crowd in Croke Park, the match seemed almost leisurely, with Kerry bossing proceedings so thoroughly that it no longer felt like a competition. But for Brady, it was still a live proposition, and the hour passed by in a blur. He remembers flashes. He was sent in to try to rein in Donaghy, and he made a pact with himself not be passive. They shook hands. There was no cheap talking. Kerry never resorted to goading. They just took care of business all afternoon. Brady clattered into the taller, younger man for the first three balls they contested and, somehow, he came away with them. Through the stunned quietness came the first tentative sounds of Mayo cheering. It was a small mercy, a brief moment of defiance on a day of staggering capitulation.

Brady heard no sounds, nor was he conscious of the terrible lull that fell over the ground when the match settled into a rut in the second half. After all, he was playing in an All-Ireland final and his last match for Mayo. He made deals with himself. He played clever and he played bullish. 'I had to gamble and play like it was midfield. I wanted to contest every ball. I decided to forget that the goalposts were behind me,' he would remember later.

Kevin O'Neill's heroic season continued as he manufactured a goal out of nothing shortly after Brady joined the game. There was a fleeting sense of optimism when Pat Harte hammered home a second goal on the half-hour mark, and when O'Neill found the net again, just seconds later, a brief shiver of fatalism passed through many Mayo people, a short-lived prayer that maybe this might be the day after all.

Brady felt gung-ho after Mayo's third goal. He distinctly remembers Donaghy looking across at Cooper and shouting,

'What the f\*\*\*?' It was the faintest scent of Kerry vulnerability. But just as he was beginning to make more personal deals, Paul Galvin sauntered in from the right side and landed a brilliant, almost arrogant point that seemed to say rebellion would be pointless.

Before the match began, there had been such singing hope. It must be remembered that scattered through that vast crowd of supporters were Mayo heroes from yesteryear. Pádraig Carney, the chiselled All-Ireland-winning centre-fielder from some fifty-five years earlier, had made his annual trip from the sunshine of California. He had been invited to sit in a corporate box, and although he was glad of the distraction of the wine as the day unravelled, he found the spectacle tough to watch. Carney is no sentimentalist when it comes to the old days. He believes the game has improved and reserves special praise for the unique skills of Ciaran McDonald. 'Oh, he is so talented,' he laments, 'but he needs to stay in his position or he is wasted. That day was a shock. Maybe we expected too much. I reckoned the Northern guys [Moran and Morrison] would put fire in their bellies. And then this collapse.'

Elsewhere, his old friend Paddy Prendergast, full-back on that last Mayo championship team, was trying to make the best of a bad situation. He had turned up in the lower Hogan Stand for a supposed unofficial reunion of the 1951 team. 'I don't know what happened, but there wasn't a shagging sinner there but myself. In the end, I had to go. I couldn't watch any more.'

Peter Ford, the raven-haired defender of the 1980s, was in the Cusack Stand sitting beside his wife. 'After ten minutes, the worst had happened. I was horrified and I was not expecting it. I know we got the few goals, but it was over after ten minutes. I felt sorry for the players, but I didn't feel humiliated as a Mayo person or anything like that.'

Sitting not too far away from Ford was Anthony Finnerty,

the chubby-faced forward of the same era, whose joviality had always masked a heartfelt ambition for his native county. Finnerty knew the treachery of these September days better than most. 'The fear was there,' he would admit, 'but nobody expected that. And it was hard to bear. You knew straight away it was going to be bad. Look, I left with ten minutes to go. Grainne, my wife, said, "You can't go." But I said I could not watch it. It was too hurtful. I won't apologise for it either. It was a very low point.'

Elsewhere, John Casey, whose form had illuminated Mayo's All-Ireland run ten years earlier, was seated in the lower Cusack Stand. The Charlestown player had been having a fine day, touring the pubs with his brother. He had swaggered up to the champion jockey Barry Geraghty with the amicable salute 'Howya, Ruby'. He greeted men he had played against years ago as they walked along a crowded Jones's Road. Although he was still young enough to be playing for Mayo, it felt liberating to attend a final as a fan, as a face in the crowd. The match brought the sensations of his own lingering disappointments rushing back. 'I just felt awful for the boys out there. Particularly Aidan Higgins, my own clubman.'

Jimmy Maughan, who had been part of a Mayo team badly beaten by Kerry in the summer of 1981, was with friends down at the old Canal End. 'A blind man up in the stands could have seen what was going to happen. I said it to the guy beside me, "This has the shape of a disaster. It'll be over in twenty minutes." The form Donaghy and those guys were in, they had to sacrifice someone for the first seven to ten minutes and play a sweeper role. My neighbour said, "You're talking through your hat. Were you in Barry's for pints?" I said, "I hope I'm wrong." And I was: it was over in ten.'

John O'Mahony, the man whom all Mayo people wanted to see leading the county team again, sat upright in his seat, holding his match programme like a holy scroll. 'I suppose my main thought was: "It shouldn't have to be this bad."'

Kevin McStay, the quicksilver forward who had played in the 1989 All-Ireland-final loss, sat in the cocoon of the RTÉ television studio. He would give his analysis of the match later that night. Sitting on the low table beside him was the gleaming Sam Maguire Cup. He could have reached out and touched it, but he hadn't the heart.

John Maughan, who had been Mayo manager when Kerry had gone on a similar rampage two years earlier, watched on, torn between admiration for the force of the conquering team and empathy with the many Mayo players he knew and cared for. 'You had to ask again if we were good enough. It comes down to that.'

Liam McHale, the convivial midfield giant who lost three senior All-Ireland finals, had been asked by RTÉ to do a half-time interview. He left his seat with ten minutes to spare, and as he hurried through the chilly tunnels underneath Croke Park, he twice heard the huge rumbling acoustics of the crowd roaring above him. When he was escorted to the side of the field, he saw that Mayo had scored two quick goals. 'I had been ready to put a brave face on things and talk about how brilliant Kerry were, and then the whole thing was confused. There was a very strange feeling in the stadium. I think I said that Mayo had a chance.'

Six points down at half-time, the Mayo team huddled together in the dressing-room and promised themselves that if they scored the next point, they would win the All-Ireland. Brady believed it. But they were spooked. The big electronic scoreboard flashed a strange and lopsided state of play: 3–08 to 3–02. There was something terribly lonely and incriminating about those two points.

After the break, Mayo were passive. Kerry just took up where they had left off. Not for the first time, several Mayo supporters left the game early. They fled the ground, in shame or heartbreak or whatever, an abandonment that was becoming a motif. Brady didn't notice them, nor would he have particularly cared.

'We didn't show the heart. We made a deal that if we got the first score of the half, we would win the All-Ireland. And we didn't. Why not? We didn't get possession in the middle. We were destroyed in the middle half of the pitch. It is the whole thing of taking responsibility. I don't know how any man – any human being – cannot give it their all in an All-Ireland final. But maybe, maybe, that's not fair to say either. Like, I know our lads were so physically fit, but they seemed to be genuinely drained of energy and motivation. If they were racehorses, you would be questioning if they were drugged. There was something preying on them.'

It was a strange, hollow conclusion to the All-Ireland championship. Mayo managed three points in the entire second half, all desultory frees from Conor Mortimer. Kerry were impressive and may have privately wished they were being given a better game. Brady kept on telling himself to keep going, to try to make something happen. But when Brian Crowe, the referee, told him there were two minutes left, he couldn't wait to escape the whole thing. 'I just said to myself, "I want to be out of here. Out of here."'

He had one pressing duty after the final whistle. He sought out Séamus Moynihan in the pandemonium. The great Glenflesk man was expected to retire after a glittering career and Brady wanted to shake his hand. 'Pleasure to have played against you.' Moynihan gave his open country smile but was too distracted to respond, and then Brady ran off the famous field.

In the coolness of the dressing-room, the Mayo boys gathered for the last time of the season. Brady realised, to his surprise, that he felt nothing. He still has keen phantom pains when he thinks about his first All-Ireland defeat in 1996, when he played as a cocksure twenty-two year old in a bizarre and gripping September series against Meath. 'Until they throw earth on top of me I will be hurting about that,' he will say to those who ask. But he was like a war veteran in these days of abject Mayo misery. He had company in players like Jimmy Nallen and Ciaran McDonald and David Heaney. Sitting there broken and even sobbing, however, was a group of players ten years younger.

Few people can know what it is like to play in an All-Ireland final, to know what it is like actually to be out there on that field with what might as well be the entire world watching you. Few people get to know those rarefied heights of emotion, the sense of experiencing a mortal version of heaven or of feeling absolutely alone. 'Like floating in the middle of the Atlantic Ocean' was how Ronan McGarrity described the sensation of being utterly consumed by the same Kerry team two years earlier. Now, many of them were back in the same bleak, inescapable place, handed a humiliation that the Kerry players had inflicted as respectfully as they could.

There was not much talking. For a half an hour, there was sanctuary in that crowded room. It would have been nice just to have locked the door and sat there until darkness fell and they could creep out of Croke Park and through the amber streets of north Dublin unnoticed. People were the last thing they needed. But they had to face the music.

Jack O'Connor came in and spoke with direct compassion about what had just happened on the field. He explained that the one, single year Kerry had been waiting since their All-Ireland-final loss to Tyrone had been more cutting and salty than the half-century of constant keening that accompanied Mayo teams. He explained that Kerry's need had been greater. Brady listened because he respected O'Connor, and his mind roamed back to the exchanges on the field, the uncompromising hardness of the Kerry tackling, as swift and clean and accurate as middleweight combination shots. 'Mean' was the word he would use to describe that Kerry performance, and he meant it as a compliment. But still, it didn't seem logical that those Kerry players, all of whom had All-Ireland medals in their cabinets at home, could summon up more hurt than his teammates and friends. And it certainly wasn't the case now. What had happened out there to those Mayo players was about as distressing and cruel as sport gets. It would have been no real surprise had they decided to quit en masse.

Brady went around and murmured words of consolation here and there and eventually delivered a muted valediction. 'I remember thinking, "These are the lads who have to carry this f***ing thing for the next ten years." Afterwards, the one thing I said was about this word "if". It has been embedded in Mayo football players for the last thirty years. If only this had happened in 1985 or that had happened. If only I could have got my hands to block Colm Coyle's point in 1996. Then it all might have been different. All the "if"s in the world would not have won that game. To lose an All-Ireland final by a point is agonising. But to lose it by thirteen points, well, there is no pain there.'

And yet he was hurting. It didn't matter that his own performance would see him exonerated from the criticism that would come in the following days. Outside the dressing-room, he flung his bag into the team coach and confirmed to waiting pressmen that he was retiring. He was dreading the trip home on the bus on Monday evening. After a sorry night in the Citywest Hotel on the outskirts of Dublin, they packed for home and drew the curtains across the windows of the bus as it rumbled down through the plains of Kildare. But, as it turned out, the mood was defiantly bright as they journeyed west. They drank beer and played cards and laughed. One player got turned over for about 500 quid in a blackly comic run of wicked cards. It was as though he was a cosmic example of the truth that there is no limit to the misfortune a Mayo footballer must endure. He was branded the unluckiest man on earth. They laughed a lot as they headed through the twinkling midlands and back to the beloved and bereft in Mayo. 'We knew it would be the last time we would be on our own,' Brady says. 'After that, it would go f\*\*\*ing mental.'

In Castlebar, a small but steadfast crowd was waiting in the heavy rain outside the Welcome Inn. Nothing official had been arranged, but these Mayo people stood vigil all the same. Their gesture choked Brady up in a way he hadn't felt in years. He didn't even know the faces of the people who moved forward to shake the hands of the beaten players, to stand in the squalid evening and offer their consolation. The atmosphere was as gentle and respectful as a country wake. He wished at that moment that they had opted for a homecoming, almost to give a two-finger salute to the embarrassment and humiliation they all felt.

When he sat down in the function room, he was overcome. That was when it hit him. Thirteen years of playing county football and this was how it ended. He had to lower his head, had to raise his hand to warn his friends away. 'The warmth of those people was incredible. It kind of dawned on me then. The whole thing hit me and in my heart and soul I shed a tear or two inside. That is what I had been doing this thing for – the thirteen years of breaking arms, legs, nose, jaw, the hundreds of training sessions, the whole lot – that is why. These were strangers standing in the pissing rain to greet a team that had been destroyed in the biggest football match of the year. I won't ever forget that.'

When he composed himself, he was D.B. again, gregarious and friendly and laughing. They began pounding drinks and the night splintered. At dawn, he woke in a pub belonging to a relative of Gerald Courell, the great Mayo football man who had trained the 1950 and '51 All-Ireland champions. He walked through downtown Castlebar feeling shattered. It was still dark and wintrily peaceful, and there wasn't a soul on the streets. He had the freedom of the town.

Back in the hotel, he lay down for a couple of hours, and when daylight pierced the room, he realised he wasn't ready to return to real life just yet. 'I was sharing a room with Trevor Mortimer, and I just said, "Trevor, let's go again." I was in a sorrowful, pitiful state, but there was nothing else to do. This is not a thing to be saying, but it felt like the choice was to either die or have another drink. That is a traditional football thing. You need it after a summer of training. You need to be with your own. Eventually, we made it back to Ballina. And we did it all again.'

Those few days were his goodbye. After all, he was only experiencing the same everlasting truth that every other Mayo football player of the last fifty years has learned at the end: it wasn't meant to be. Somehow, as the years after 1951 became decades, that became the proud, melancholy story of Mayo football. The county produced good ordinary players and hard men and exceptional stylists, and they all fell short in one game or another. It does not matter that Mayo has only ever won three All-Ireland senior titles in the history of the GAA. Mayo is nothing if not a football county. There is a deathless expectation running through its darks fields that the next period of grandeur, the next period of glory, is out there on the horizon. David Brady is one of a rich cast of men who have given a considerable chunk of their lives to chasing down that dream. And call it bad luck or call it innocence or put it down to some inexplicable fear at the heart of Mayo football people, but it just hasn't happened.

Brady is luckier than most. He has, after all, awoken on four September mornings wondering if this was the day he would win that precious cross, the medal that would unite him with the band of brothers from the 1950s. It was of little consequence to him that on one of the bleakest days for football in his county, Brady had stood out there as the chief flag-bearer of courage and integrity for whatever the green and the red represents. In his last hour, his bravery promised that Mayo would be back.

What a place to find himself, though – standing on the edge of this great tradition, the All-Ireland football final, waiting to enter a contest that had been flipped into a twilight world of embarrassment. It must have been the loneliest moment of his football life. 'To be honest,' says David Brady, thinking back to his last hour with Mayo, 'I felt like I was being sent in there to look for survivors.'

# TWO

# THE LAND OF LOST CONTENT

Paddy Prendergast leafs through a well-thumbed hardback copy of Raymond Smith's old book *The Football Immortals*. He is searching for the name of a Meath half-forward who played in the All-Ireland semi-final of 1949. He flicks through the pages like a man consulting a telephone directory while his wife, Irene, looks gravely through the kitchen window at the steady rain. The Prendergast home is located along the old bog road in the low hills outside Tralee. The house is completely obscured by spectacularly high trees, which make a verdant arch over the driveway, and the garden looks unbelievably tropical and well tended. But the rain has not let up in weeks and Irene, whom Paddy credits with the green touch, says in a light German accent, 'If this rain keeps up, the flowers cannot last.' It has been a sodden summer, even in the south. Friends of Paddy Prendergast always thought it amusing and typical of his contrary streak that he should be exiled in Kerry, the county of perpetual All-Ireland winning, through the long decades since Mayo last won the championship. When RTÉ made a documentary, *Bonfires in Bohola*, about the 1950 and '51 Mayo teams, Prendergast, the full-back in both years, described the journeys home or to Dublin to follow subsequent Mayo teams over the years as 'my via dolorosa'.

It is a peculiar kind of honour, being the full-back on the most famous team a county has produced, or possibly ever will produce, a football team whose energy and youth are locked into the middle part of the twentieth century. Gaelic football was always important to Paddy Prendergast without ever fully possessing him. The house is not crammed with mementos but on the wall above a writing desk in a cosy alcove by the kitchen hang several photographs that would alert a visitor to an extraordinary sporting past. There is a terrific action shot from the 1950 All-Ireland semi-final against Kerry. In another, Prendergast is larking around with the Flanagan boys, Seán Mulderrig and Eamonn Mongey in front of cricket wickets. They all took a passing interest in the colonial game and Seán Flanagan was downright knowledgeable about it, so they used to organise one-day classics on summer days in the late 1950s. It gave them an excuse to meet. In the most modern photograph, Pádraig Carney and Mongey are standing with their great Galway friends and rivals, Jack Mahon and Seán Purcell. Paddy stands in front of the other four men, a pair of sunglasses hanging from a beaded chain, his arms folded, and he is pleased as Punch. The photograph was taken about ten years ago, before a championship match, when the men just happened to encounter one another as they were taking their places in the stand in Pearse Stadium. It was a genuine gathering of greats and from the crowd came a murmuring of acknowledgement.

When the Mayo team of 1950 is mentioned now, it is as though they are in full bloom yet – hardy, Brylcreemed and self-assured young men in the white shirts and green crested emblems of their day, prevented from winning infinite All-Ireland finals for Mayo only by the ludicrous constraints of time. Of course, in the years since 1951, those champion footballers had to get on with the less heroic business of living. We forget that several lifetimes have passed and reached conclusion since those crowning years. Paddy remains remarkably fresh faced, as if he has just returned from a good tramp in the woods, and moves with startling agility when he goes to fetch a silver-embossed photograph of the All-Ireland-winning teams in order to fully account for the living and the dead. The faces of his teammates as they were on those days of permanent splendour in Croke Park stare back at him, stern, young, confident, anxious to burst free of the team pose and get on with the match. Paddy goes through them all in order, as if taking a roll call in national school, while the rain falls outside.

'[John] Forde is there. [Henry] Dixon gone. John McAndrew has been ill for a long time but he is still there. He is in England and unable to travel. Tom Langan is gone. Joe Gilvarry is gone. Tom Acton is still there. Billie Durkan is gone. Paddy Irwin is gone. Seán Wynne is gone. Mick Caulfield is gone. Tommy Byrne is gone. Seán Mulderrig is gone. Mongey and myself are here. Jimmy Currin is here. Mick Flanagan is dead. Peter Quinn is OK. Seán Flanagan is dead. Carney is all right. Mick Mulderrig is there. Billy Kenny is dead. And Peter Solan is dead. Liam Hastings is dead. Joe Staunton is still alive. Ah, a huge number are gone.'

And then, over a pot of tea and a plate of biscuits, the redoubtable number three proceeds to resurrect them all. It is not the fact of the medals that interests Paddy Prendergast fifty years on, or the remembered thrill of those two days of ultimate victory in Croke Park – although he still marvels at how many Mayo people made it to Dublin from the furthest reaches of Belmullet and Bangor Erris. What has carried through the years undimmed is the fantastic friendships that emanated from those All-Ireland-winning teams and the realisation that, as is so often the case in Gaelic games, they happened because a number of extraordinary men sat down in the same room and discovered that their creative instincts and energy were irrepressible. Paddy talks about those All-Ireland years as something that was thrust upon him. He was, after all, happily ensconced in north Donegal as a member of the Garda Síochána, something of an exoticism in the town of Dungloe, and deployed at midfield for the local derbies against Gweedore, games that consumed all the passions of those communities. It was like playing football in a foreign land, with a cacophony of strange and half-recognisable Irish ringing about the fields.

Prendergast was only vaguely aware that the Mayo team had written a letter of protest to the county board in 1948 and had little thought of ever trying to pursue a career with his county. He kicked some with Donegal and was happy enough with that. Then came a letter of invitation to a challenge match against Galway. It was signed by Liam Hastings, one of the senior Mayo players, and the game was to be a de facto trial. One night in the barracks, Prendergast showed the letter to Frankie White of Sligo. After word got around, the Donegal men he knew persuaded Prendergast that it would be treasonable not to turn out for his native county.

'Of course, there was no chance of a five-pound note to help me get there,' he says, throwing his eyes to heaven. 'I was working in the station in Ardara around the time of the match and took a bus to Sligo. And in those years, not many people could afford to be in the Guards, the pay was that bad. Tony Sheridan, who owned the Imperial Hotel, kindly took me in and gave me food and my bus fare. He didn't charge me – and if he had, I couldn't have paid him. Then I got a bus to Charlestown, which ended there. So I called into the barracks and Hugh O'Brien, the sergeant, managed to get hold of a taxi. The two of us went to Ballina and I am quite certain that the poor unfortunate taxi man never got paid either. Once we reached Ballina, we had to find out where to go. It was hellish just getting there.'

The only Mayo player that Prendergast knew personally was Mick Flanagan, but he understood that Mayo football was in a chaotic state and had heard the famous story about how Mayo had held Kerry, who had played in the All-Ireland final just two months earlier, to a draw in a tournament match, despite having just a bare team of fifteen. Finn Mongey, the county secretary, and a reluctant, hefty and mature car driver who had not run the length of a field in many years were pressed into acting as substitutes. Mayo earned an unlikely draw that afternoon, a result which provoked the extraordinary coup spearheaded by Eamonn Mongey, Seán Flanagan, Langan, Hastings and Carney, who all signed a letter that led to a spirit of cooperation and renewed ambition between the county board and the players. It was a radical communiqué that laid out in the starkest terms imaginable the future for Mayo football:

> Year after year we have seen the County Board bring to nought the hours of training which we have put in, but yet, believing it was outside our sphere as players, we have desisted from drawing your attention to the matter. Events in Tralee last Sunday have banished our indecision, however, and we feel the time has come when something must be done before football disappears completely in Mayo – unwept, unhonoured and unsung.

Acquiring new talent was an immediate requirement and Prendergast was on audition at full-back. He played with Flanagan on his left and John Forde on his right. Prendergast introduced himself to his teammates when it was time for the throw-in. He was still readjusting to the Mayo accent and the last time he had played the number-three position was as a schoolboy in St Jarlath's. He was marking Ned Keogh, who sensed an afternoon of fun against the new boy. Keogh ghosted around the back of Prendergast and scored a goal with his right. Then he repeated the trick finishing with his left. When he cleaned Prendergast out again, Flanagan lost patience and said in exasperation, 'Paddy, what in the name of Christ do you think you are doing here?'

'To be frank, Seán,' Paddy replied, with all the stiffness he could muster, 'I have no idea.'

Flanagan breathed deeply and said nothing more. But in the pub afterwards, he took the novice into a corner and produced a pencil and paper. For a full hour, he took Prendergast through the entire repertoire of Mayo defensive and attacking plays as he envisaged them. Prendergast had passed the test. Soon, he would be transferred from Donegal. In the weeks before the 1948 championship, the panel of new players and the senior kingmakers all stayed in Mrs Gaughan's guesthouse in Ballina. Given the impoverished time, they were an astonishingly well-educated and driven group of men: Flanagan the barrister, Mongey the barrister, Solan the engineer, Gilvarry the lawyer, Mick Flanagan the lawyer, Carney the doctor, Dixon the farmer, Quinn the curate. In the kitchen, they would sit at night-time drinking tea and taking turns standing before a blackboard to explain how they saw the Mayo alignment, how to react in any situation. They explored their strengths and weaknesses and became firm friends. Nicknames bloomed. Seán Flanagan was 'Theophilus', from the Bible. Dixon was 'Mixer'. Mongey was 'George'. 'Haven't the faintest idea why,' Prendergast admits now, 'but I don't believe I ever called him Eamonn.'

The trainers, Gerald Courell and Jackie Carney, provided a flesh-and-blood link to the original Mayo All-Ireland epoch. Both men were involved with the 1936 team. Carney was still as lean as a greyhound, an energetic man of fastidious habits. Their stewardship was almost paternal. Social gatherings were frowned upon; girls were out of the question. One night, a friend from Ballintubber hailed Prendergast as he walked with the team on an official outing to the cinema. The man was driving and was escorting his cousins, the Gilroy girls, to the pictures and offered Paddy a lift. No sooner had Prendergast closed the door than a rap came on the window and Jackie Carney was looking at him, shaking his head and pointing the road back towards Mrs Gaughan's. 'Get him home,' he warned, 'get him home.'

And that guesthouse felt like home. They trained twice a day with intent and ate heartily. The full-back line was Flanagan, Prendergast and Forde. There was no deviation. Prendergast learned his position and felt almost unassailable given the quality of the two men on either wing. He learned he could play full-back without fear of being exposed. The cover was fierce and constant. Perfection came with time. That night after his inauspicious debut was the first lesson, and he never stopped hearing Flanagan's clear instructions coming at him through the din. He probably half realised then that this preternaturally confident and charismatic young professional would become his friend of a lifetime. But the more immediate sensation was of having stumbled upon a wonderful secret. That night was when Paddy Prendergast realised he had chanced upon a group of men that was incomparable.

Pádraig Carney stands in the noonday heat reading a monument to lost fishermen. It is quiet along the main street in Fethard-on-Sea, although there is line of people waiting for whipped ice creams in the shop across the road because the heat is of a true, sultry summer quality. In a light pastel shirt, the Mayo man looks as cool as you like: fifty years of living in California have made him immune to heat. The sedate Wexford village has been a favourite haunt of the Carneys since the late 1960s, when they built a summer house here. The house is located around two miles outside the village, a bright bungalow with vast windows that frame one of the most breathtaking coastal sights of Ireland: Hook Head and its lighthouse. When their children were younger, the family would often walk the rough-hewn steps down the cliff face to swim on the beach below, a small cove with golden sand and choppy energetic waves. The place is an idyll. As Pádraig and his wife, Moira, lay the table for a lunch of smoked fish and cold meats and brown bread, it is hard not to marvel at their journey. From a childhood in pre-war Swinford to a lifetime working in the citadels of Californian medicine is quite a story. Pádraig Carney met Moira while they were students in Dublin and after graduating they bolted for the big continent. But somehow Carney managed to squeeze in the winning of two All-Ireland senior medals, and when he emigrated in 1954, he had proven his granite athleticism at the elite level. His football career seems at once terribly distant and at the very centre of what he represents. Carney is engaging and friendly and effortlessly accommodating. And it would be impossible for anyone to spend time talking to him and not understand that at the core of his calm, unflappable personality there is a furnace, a determination of the rarest kind.

'Perhaps I had that awful one-child-family syndrome. Moira tells me that I was spoiled, the classic little prince,' he says agreeably, thinking about his need to fly so high and so far. The nickname of 'The Flying Doctor', which he acquired during that extravagant season when he moonlighted as a Mayo footballer in the league play-offs of 1954 while furthering his medical expertise in New York, was appropriate in more ways than one. At the height of his sporting career, Carney had to make a choice between his profession and his football, between what he believed he could do in the field of medicine and what he knew he could do on the Gaelic fields of Ireland. He literally flew from the cheering and the prestige that went with being part of Mayo's gilded generation. He wanted more of the world.

'I guess I always had an inborn ambition to succeed in life. I don't know. For better or worse, I went to the school where my mother taught and she made sure I was diligent. I was never forced to do anything. I was encouraged. My father always made it easy for me to play sports and from an early age, I realised that I wanted to excel at studies. Even then, I knew there was something after sport. I passed that on to my kids: give yourself options. I don't know why I picked medicine other than I admired some of the dispensary doctors I would have seen around the infirmaries in Mayo. And after I qualified, I knew that if I wanted to do something in medicine, I had to go to America. That was where the action was. But the hardest thing in life for me was leaving athletics. The hardest decision I had to take was to stop playing for Mayo.'

In the autumn of 1959, the Carneys were ready to embark on a transcontinental journey from Detroit to California. Pádraig had spent four years studying in the Motor City and had been offered a position out west. They had three boys by then: Brian, Terence and Cormac, just six weeks old. Pádraig had bought a new Chevrolet Delray, the cheapest in the range. They had about $1,000 to their name. In addition, they had Pádraig's parents. The most remarkable aspect of the Carney emigration is that the parents followed their son. His father, Tom, had fought in the War of Independence and was wounded almost fatally in an ambush against the Black and Tans outside Kiltimagh. For two years, he lived the renegade life, darting from safe house to safe house. His mother, Ellen (née Groarke), had been in Cumann na mBan and was wrongly accused of carrying messages for the IRA, for which she spent a year in Kilmainham prison. They lived through extraordinary times and when they married and had a child, those days were rarely spoken of. Years later, Pádraig Carney encountered returnees from the Vietnam War who displayed a reticence, a closed-down silence, that reminded him of his father's. His parents had lived the great, traumatic adventure of the early twentieth century in Ireland: the strike for sovereignty. Their son was caught up in the pioneering cause of his day: of striking out for improvement, of heading west. His parents had already watched him win fame and praise in Croke Park, and in the home town of Swinford he was a genuine hero. He was also their only son, so at an age when most couples would have been locked into an unbreakable pattern of life, Tom and Ellen Carney simply quit Ireland. They lived in Detroit and when it was time to move to California, they packed their possessions into the Chevrolet.

It was a fabulous and arduous journey. They shared the driving and tried to cover 600 miles a day. Moira shakes her head when she thinks back to the haphazard feeding schedule they subjected Cormac to. One morning when they were staying in Yellowstone National Park, she found the baby's milk had frozen solid when she fetched it from the car. They stayed in motels in Oklahoma, Texas and New Mexico and drove along shimmering linear roads that appeared to plane off into infinity. They drove through arid heat. It would have been a nerve-wracking crossing for any young couple but for Pádraig's parents, it must have been the strangest trip imaginable. Tom Carney took in the heat and dust and vast space without ever saying very much about it. When the family established a home in California, Ellen promptly found a teaching post that kept her happily occupied for the next ten years. They passed away in the 1970s and are buried in a Long Beach cemetery. What they did to be with their son was astonishingly brave for people of their generation. It was both radical and highly sensible. And maybe that combination is at the core of the Carney make-up.

The Mayo county board's decision to fly Carney back for the 1954 league play-offs was lavish but it was not predicated on sentiment. He took a taxi to Idlewild Airport on Friday evening and tried to sleep on the twelve-hour flight to Shannon. When he got to Dublin, he rested again and met up with the team, before playing the semi-final on Sunday afternoon and flying back to New York that night. With the time difference, he was able to make it back to the hospital on Monday morning. Despite having played almost no football that season, he lined out at centre half-forward, took responsibility for kicking frees and scored ten points. His last match in Croke Park took place a few weeks later – the final proved to be a one-sided victory over Carlow. In the autumn of that year, he pulled on the Mayo jersey one final time for an exhibition match in New York. 'I knew that would be my last game. I was twenty-six years old and I was at the very peak of my career as a footballer. I do believe that Mayo would have won another two All-Irelands if I had stuck around. But I just had no time to dwell on it.'

Priorities were different then. Carney had seen his dear friend P.J. Duke, the esteemed Cavan footballer, perish of pneumatic fever while still in his twenties. Duke was studying dentistry in UCD and they just didn't have the correct drugs to administer. The tragedy left a deep impression on him. The football years were wonderful; it is the homecoming in Mayo after the lost final of 1948, when it seemed as though the entire county was illuminated by bonfires, that has stayed with Carney most vividly. He was imperious in the 1951 All-Ireland season and was honoured as man of the match in the final but remembers being bothered by a 'bittersweet' feeling because he was also graduating from medical school and knew that football, a passion and a pastime, could not continue indefinitely. He worked in Castlebar and Charlestown during 1952 and 1953, two years when Mayo failed to win the Connacht championship. Perhaps those quiet years hastened the decision to leave. Once he and Moira decided upon their course, there was no turning back. 'We did get lonely sometimes,' he admits, 'but we both fell in love with California and we were trying to create a lifestyle and raise a family. We worked hard.'

Carney applied the same combination of meticulousness and intensity to medicine as he had done to playing with Mayo. In his early days, he read everything about medical techniques and he practised developing his hand skills for operations. A doctor he knew from Detroit moved out west to become head of the pathology department, despite hating to do post-mortems, and Carney volunteered, to gain experience. Eventually, he specialised as an obstetrician and gynaecologist and built up a private practice. He joined the American College of O&G and got certified. He won plaudits and attained a national reputation within his field. In his career, he delivered over 10,000 babies and performed over 2,000 surgeries. Medicine consumed him and it replaced the sudden and severe elimination of Mayo football from his life.

'The same satisfaction was there but in a different way. Of course, nothing can ever compare to walking around Croke Park on All-Ireland-final day with your friends. That was one of the great thrills in my life. But if you have a really sick patient and bring them through a difficult surgery, that too is incomparable – a feeling you cannot get from money or anything else. It is knowing you did the right thing well.'

It was the early 1960s before Moira and he managed to visit Ireland again. The Mayo team had broken up. Lives had moved on. They all stayed in touch through letters and Christmas cards. California became, by gentle degrees, home. The Carneys seemed proof of the American dream. They were bright and industrious, good-hearted people and because of that the New World was implausibly good to them. They had four children who inherited their parents' hunger for academic and sporting excellence. Brian, the eldest, joined the air force and played varsity football there, then studied medicine in UCLA and now works at Dartmouth College in New Hampshire. Terence was probably the most versatile athlete and went to the University of the Pacific on a basketball scholarship, playing as a shooting guard. He studied law in Los Angeles' Loyola Law School and is now a partner in a firm in Orange County. Cormac went to UCLA and played division-one football as a wide receiver. He earned athletic and academic All-American honours and went on to play in the NFL for a year. Then he enrolled at Harvard Law School and he is now a federal judge in Los Angeles. Sheila, the youngest child, excelled as a student and now runs a library at Johns Hopkins University in Washington DC.

Carney laughs when he hears himself referring to his 'kids'. 'Brian is fifty-two now, he is no boy any more. But they did all right for themselves. And I guess watching them play sport almost gave us as much pleasure as the Mayo days. Funny, though, I never worried about getting injured myself. But it is always a concern with your children. One year, we were up in Wisconsin watching Cormac play. There was about 60,000 people in this football stadium and it was a hard game. So he went to catch this ball and two defensive tackles hit him at once, in the chest and back. And from where we sat, it looked as if he couldn't move his hands. So we had to make our way down from the stands without knowing. As it turned out, he was fine. But those are the moments you worry about.'

Moira and Pádraig are proud of their children without being boastful about them. What is truly remarkable, though, about listening to the star-spangled accomplishments of the Carney children is to imagine their grandfather Tom Carney lying bleeding on a dead road outside Kiltimagh with the fumes of gun smoke around him. It is hard to believe he belonged to the same century as his grandchildren.

The Carneys maintained their Irish heritage without moving in green-tinted circles. The Kennedy dazzle was at its most blinding when they were establishing themselves in the early

1960s, but although Pádraig admired JFK's articulacy and dash and was half proud of the Irish connection, he found himself voting for Nixon and the Republican manifesto. By coincidence, the home the Carneys built in Wexford is just a short drive from the original Kennedy farmstead. After Pádraig was secure in his practice, the family began visiting Ireland more frequently. The decades rolled by and there were several Mayo reunions and functions, which Pádraig attended, astonished to find that they had all become a little whiter and stiffer, that they were no longer footballers. Most of all, he was surprised and disturbed that the county had not won more All-Irelands since 1951. He had simply never imagined that the teams he played on would become magnified in importance with every decade. When he visited home, he understood that people had begun to romanticise the feats of 1950 and 1951. In their mature years, he and his teammates became truly invincible. He was symbolic of a brief period when anything seemed possible in Mayo football, swooping in from America to win titles – Pádraig Carney, The Flying Doctor. 'It was flattering. But it was also kind of sad. We all had our day in the sun and we would have been happy if our team had been put back on the shelf.'

One night in the winter of 1953, Prendergast and Carney attended a hunt ball outside Castlebar together. It was a dress affair, and Paddy offered to drive, as Carney was on duty in the local hospital at seven the next day. The dancing went on late, and when they left the ballroom, the county was under snow and it was falling thickly. It was after five by the time they reached Carney's house in Swinford. Mrs Carney had waited up for the boys and she produced tea, sandwiches and, extraordinarily, bowls of ice cream. They sat talking at the kitchen table until it was time to head to the hospital. As they crawled through the ghostly countryside, Paddy wondered how his friend was going to last the day. No sooner had Carney signed in than Paddy Bresnihan, the Limerick hurler who was county surgeon in Mayo, was looking for him to assist in an emergency operation. He worked until six o'clock that evening. Later that night, Prendergast heard in the pub that Carney had been seen out running alone in the snow after work.

'That was Carney. Look, the man was a powerhouse. He was indestructible. He was fifteen stone and close to a ten-seconds man. At training, when I saw Carney coming hammering at me, I would honestly stand aside. I would weigh up the options and decide on 'no' fairly fast. I remember against Meath in the 1951 All-Ireland final, at half-time Carney was sitting down and he was saying, "Look, we have to get serious about these fellas. This lad Taffe is causing us problems." Mick and Pat Flanagan were in digs in Dublin with a Meath crowd who were rabid supporters. They were full of confidence before the game. They were hell-bent on quietening Carney. So Carney was there speaking quietly about Taffe. Des Taffe was a fine player. At the beginning of the second half, the very first ball that hopped a yard off Taffe, Carney took off and en route he ran through Taffe. He demolished him. Now, Pauric was by no means a dirty player. Everything he did had a purpose. He was ruthless and rigorously logical.'

It took Mayo a few seasons to achieve that certainty of champions. The 1948 All-Ireland final was probably the strongest case of grave injustice and misfortune to befall any Mayo football team. The following year, 1949, was to be the season of atonement. The consensus in the county was that they would beat Meath in the All-Ireland semi-final with ten points to spare. Each half was thirty minutes long that year, and after twenty-four minutes the Mayo full-back line had hardly seen a ball. John Forde was beginning to complain of being bored. Flanagan and Prendergast headed about forty yards out, like a scouting party in search of a war tribe. 'You know, Theo,' Prendergast said, 'we will not handle a football today.'

They proved fateful words. Prendergast is still baffled at the decision of the selectors to play Billy Kenny and Seán Mulderrig in the wing half-back positions: both were fine footballers but not natural defenders. Gradually, Meath worked out where the weaknesses were. Paddy Meegan clipped a point from the right wing. That provoked another three quick points and the teams were level at 0–04 apiece at half-time. Mayo controlled the second half. When a long, high ball came in, the Mayo goalkeeper, Tommy Byrne, raced out to claim it, changed his mind and got caught in no-man's-land as the ball hopped into the net. Ten minutes later, Prendergast stood back for a ball that was claimed by Seán Mulderrig and watched aghast as a Meath poacher knocked it free as Mulderrig was about to release a kick and scored another goal. Mayo lost by 3–10 to 1–10.

That disappointment may have steeled their resolve for the following summer. The odd thing about Mayo's 1950 All-Ireland was how easily it seemed to snowball: a forgettable 1–07 to 0–04 Connacht final win against Roscommon on a filthy day in Tuam Stadium and then a comprehensive All-Ireland semi-final win against Armagh by 3–09 to 0–06. Louth awaited them in the final and, despite playing a laboured game for most of the afternoon, Mayo had simply too much craft and strength, with Mick Flanagan scoring the definitive goal in a 2–05 to 1–06 victory.

The following year was a much tougher campaign. Meath had the Indian sign over Mayo around then. In April of 1951, the counties met in Croke Park for a league final weighted with the prize of a trip to America. The match followed the same pattern as their last meeting. Peter McDermott was wandering around the Mayo half of the field like a lost soul, looking extremely unhappy. He stopped near where Forde and Prendergast were and said, 'Lads, how much will you beat us by?' Forde said, 'Peter, take a look at the scoreboard and you might get your answer.' There was nothing in it.

For all their possession, Mayo could not buy a score. Peter Solan missed a penalty and the team ended up scoring just six points. Afterwards, Seán Flanagan sat on the steps of Barry's Hotel and said mournfully, 'We have lost the only chance we will ever have of seeing our friends in America.'

The teams were matched again in the All-Ireland final that September. It had taken Mayo two matches to overcome Kerry in an absorbing semi-final distinguished by the full-back play of Paddy Brosnan for Kerry in the drawn match. It took a late goal-from-the-blue by Tom Langan, who directed a long, measured ball from Eamonn Mongey to the net, to keep Mayo alive. With time almost up, Paddy Irwin snapped over a point to earn the western side a replay. Over 53,000 made it back to Croke Park for a replay that was remembered for two feathery goals taken by Mick Flanagan. In the final, everything fell into place. The match was less a contest than a coronation: the final score was to 2–08 to 0–09 and the report in the *Western People* had the luxury of wishing for a better contest. Tom Langan scored another memorable goal and Carney was imperious, moving from centre-half to midfield, the dominant figure in the tableau.

'We never actually spoke about winning a three-in-a-row,' says Prendergast, 'because we never placed any limitations on our thinking.' But perhaps that September was their natural peak. Shortly after the victory, Father Peter Quinn left for the missions in the Philippines. Seán Flanagan and Carney travelled with him to Shannon, stopping in St Jarlath's along the way to meet the students and drink tea with the priests. That was one link broken. Flanagan was elected to Dáil Éireann in 1951, which placed further constraints on his time.

Carney had to limit his enjoyment of the 1951 homecoming to just two days before he took up his very first posting in Cavan General Hospital. Paddy Prendergast was beginning to conclude that he would owe the bank a fortune if he remained a guard (he would later take up a position with Shell).

The champions still met in Mrs Gaughan's guesthouse but the novelty had gone. In earlier years, Henry Dixon and Mongey had always delighted in quizzing Peter Quinn about religion, alarming the poor man by pretending to fret over their faith. Now, Quinn was at the other end of the world and they missed him. Perhaps they were not as robust or enthusiastic now that they had won the All-Ireland for two years running. In the back of their minds, they were probably thinking of Kerry as potential opponents the following September. And perhaps they were imbued with a sense of their own invincibility. Even today, Prendergast still sees Carney hurtling forward with the ball in a challenge match against Armagh to open Breffni Park; a defender drew his arm across his head, smashing and breaking Carney's nose. It was a sickening wallop but Carney behaved as if he hadn't even noticed it, driving forward. And he laughs about the day that a garda appeared in the dressing-room at McHale Park to tell Seán Flanagan that a phone call had come through for him at the barracks. His wife, Pat, was in labour in the hospital and Flanagan was alarmed that something might be wrong. The TD put on a heavy mackintosh coat and hurried out of the ground still in his football boots. Near the exit, he met a supporter who said, 'Seán, what are you going to do about my allowance?'

'F*** your allowance,' Flanagan growled and hurried to the barracks to learn that the news was good. Almost a quarter of a century later, Flanagan and Prendergast were on the streets when Seán was running for the European Parliament and Seán put the arm on a man whose face they both knew.

'Can I count on you?' Seán said. The man smiled back at him, slowly and deliberately. 'F*** my allowance, is it?' The story encapsulates Flanagan: impatient, in a hurry, charming, unorthodox, remembered. 'He could not be beaten,' Paddy marvels. 'That was the sense he gave. He was extraordinary, really. You could not beat the man.'

But in 1952, they were all beaten. Roscommon crept in stealthily to Castlebar. Prendergast was distracted by a lingering injury to his left leg. Minutes before the throw-in, he had suggested that he shouldn't play. Jackie Carney laughed and said, 'You'll be grand.' Afterwards, Prendergast lamented that they might as well have picked a ten year old at full-back. Mayo were flat and deservedly beaten, and perhaps, secretly, after four years of striving towards excellence, they were relieved.

The dissolution of the team was slow. They were good enough to win the league in 1954 and reached the All-Ireland semi-final of 1955. But the original potency was gone. Carney's decision to leave Ireland stunned them. For a while, the Carneys had been working and living in Charlestown, where Carney worked closely with Nora Healy, the mother of the journalist and provocateur John Healy. On his evenings off, Paddy Prendergast would drive over with Mick Flanagan to visit Carney and they would talk football. Paddy knew that his friend was restless and eager to move into consultancy. Prendergast had always assumed that the GAA could open those kinds of doors for a young, bright professional who had distinguished himself in Croke Park. 'The GAA owned Ireland in those days,' Paddy says now. 'I don't know what happened. But whatever the hell it was, they left. And we missed him and Moira terribly. And Mayo football missed him.'

One by one, the championship players left. Prendergast decided to stop one afternoon when he was driving Mickey Stewart and a few of the younger players from UCG to a match and one of them called him 'sir'. He took that as the sign. Other men had careers to build. At Christmas and on special anniversary occasions, letters and cards arrived bearing exotic stamps from the west coast of America. One hot August day in 1960, Mick Flanagan rang Paddy from Castlebar to arrange a bank-holiday visit to Galway. 'I'll have the cailíní lined up for ya,' Paddy said. A few days before their rendezvous, Mick cried off with a cold. Then he was rushed to St Luke's Hospital in Dublin. Prendergast headed to Dublin and saw his friend was distracted with worry. 'How do I look, P?' Flanagan asked.

'Sure, Jesus, you look grand,' Prendergast said. 'Sure, what the hell is wrong with you?'

They were footballers; neither of them much knew what cancer was. Prendergast visited the hospital most weekends for the next six months. Mick Flanagan died in January of 1961, the first of the gang to go. Mick was a laugh-a-minute merchant, but sitting by his hospital bed during those weekends, he and Paddy had talked and talked about the serious stuff. 'His innermost thoughts. He was a very special human being and it was a ferocious wrench for me. When I first came to live in Tralee, I was sitting in Benner's Hotel and Séamus Henchey, the chief justice, happened to be there. He came over to me and said, "Michael was one of the brightest and best I ever came across."'

Seasons passed. Paddy settled into life in Kerry. Paddy Brosnan became a great drinking pal of his. He saw Seán Flanagan regularly and seemed to spend half his life on the phone to Eamonn Mongey. In 1966, Jack Lynch made Flanagan the Minister for Health, the first of two cabinet appointments for the former footballer. Two years after he lost his seat in the general election of 1977, Flanagan decided to run for Europe. He called on many of the old brigade to canvas for him. Old footballers along the Connacht and Ulster coast put the word out for the great corner-back. Prendergast ended up roaming the old haunts near where Flanagan had been born in Aughamore, near Ballyhaunis. He was accompanied by the great Offaly footballer, Paddy 'The Iron Man from Rhode' McCormack. After several afternoons of knocking on doors, both men were astonished by the affection in which Flanagan was held and equally alarmed at the number of people who declared themselves mystified that they'd sent letters to Flanagan without ever receiving a reply.

'If you had only written a few bloody letters, Flanagan,' scolded The Iron Man when they met up in Ballaghaderreen that evening, 'you could be running for Taoiseach.'

Teams do not break up. They splinter into a million pieces. The Mayo football team of 1950s Ireland was united by friendships as much as football. None of them could have realised when they stood in Croke Park in September of 1951 that even as their finest hour beckoned, so too did their dissolution. What they achieved was down to a magical cohesion of energy and talent and ambition and diligence and laughter. Football was the chief reason that they stood shoulder to shoulder that day. Once that finished, the reasons to meet became less compelling and they saw one another less often. For many, that photograph and that day marked the most exciting passage that life could offer. In retirement, they became like other Mayo football supporters. But they also became like holy men, men who had unlocked the formula to winning, men who were living, warm-blooded proof of that time when Mayo were the All-Ireland champions.

It was not an honour they wanted. A few days after the 1989 All-Ireland-final loss, Paddy visited Seán Flanagan at his home in Dublin. His friend was in the living room, still brooding over the defeat. Paddy said nothing and eventually Seán simply exploded in frustration, issuing a series of oaths and curses that made them both feel better. The fact that it had taken Mayo thirty-eight years simply to reach another All-Ireland final seemed to nullify the power of what they had achieved. The reason why Flanagan and Liam Hastings and Mongey and Carney had been so adamant about change in the late 1940s had a dual edge. 'Winning the All-Ireland was paramount in their thoughts,' Prendergast says, 'but they also wanted to pick Mayo up off its bloody knees.'

Becoming champions was supposed to be a liberating legacy that future Mayo teams would draw inspiration from. Instead, through the luckless 1960s and meandering 1970s, that glittering double achievement seemed almost prohibitive and daunting. It shone more brightly as year followed year of failure. In 1992, Prendergast and Flanagan sat down together in the Hogan Stand to watch Mayo play Donegal in what was a terrible All-Ireland semi-final. 'I've counted eleven hand passes in a row,' Flanagan said in a resigned voice at one point, 'that started in their half and ended up in our half.'

Prendergast just smiled. He sometimes feared that they would end up as cranks, superior old men who could chide and scold in the knowledge that their victories made them infallible. But it was never about that. He watched as his younger brother Ray endured a succession of disappointments both as a player and manager with the county. On championship days, he would go to Ray's pub in Castlebar and listen to theories about Mayo football until he was worn out. He reckons that if he had walked in with Ger Power and John O'Keeffe, there would have been Mayo lads ready to tell them how to win All-Irelands. Talking football became a penance but when he observed how hard his brother and others like him were trying, he wanted more than ever to see another All-Ireland going to the county.

Paddy always believed Ray was the more natural footballer in the house; but because of his older brother's reputation,

Ray was shaped into a full-back. Ray put his soul into the Mayo game and then he was taken away young. A random check-up led to appointments with specialists that Ray blithely ignored. He didn't want to know about it. The illness was cruel and arbitrary. In the years after Ray passed away, habit made Paddy keep attending Mayo matches, but on jaunts around the pubs, he found himself making a customary vow: 'I'll talk about politics or horses or women or anything. But no football.' It had come to feel as though he'd been having the same conversation for years.

Time pushed on. Seán Flanagan died in February of 1993. The funeral marked a huge day in Ballaghaderreen and among the mourners were many of his former teammates, the boys who had spent many midnights plotting and planning in Mrs Gaughan's guest house. Pádraig Carney did not make it home to say goodbye. 'Seán and I would have drifted apart,' he says solemnly as the Wexford sun streams in through the window and Carney remembers the forceful TD, the captain of them all. 'I felt that Seán's life was a tragedy in many ways. He could be a very, very likeable guy, so charming and bright. He was a good leader and he built up loyalty in a tremendous number of people. But he lost me when he became obnoxious with drink. And he did. If Seán didn't like a guy, he could fling the contents of his pint at him. He could be so funny and so generous and he was such a clever man that I believe he would have ended up leading Fianna Fáil had he been more careful. I had tremendous respect for Pat, his wife, a really lovely woman. And [his son] Dermot, too, I met when he was playing football with Mayo and he was very different, very balanced and a really fine young man. Seán was complicated. He could get so many people of different political persuasions to go out and canvas for him. He had so much brilliance. Seán made me sad.'

Carney's voice is just ever so lightly dusted with a Californian twang after half a century of living there. Since the 1970s, he and Moira have made frequent trips across the Atlantic, and they attended the five All-Ireland finals Mayo have appeared in since 1951. He has retained a deep affinity for Mayo but he is not sentimental about his past. It has been many years since he walked through his home town of Swinford, and although he knows that his parents' house is still there, he has no idea who lives there and is genuinely amused to consider that it might be adorned with a plaque to mark his birth there. 'No! God. No, I don't think so.'

He is not prone to speculating on what might have happened had he remained in Ireland, beyond missing the football that he did not play. Fleetingly, he has imagined that politics would have attracted him had he stayed. But he never indulges that parallel life for very long. As Prendergast says, 'Carney was always going forward.'

The pair remain fast friends. When Paddy's son Mark ended up living in San Diego, he and Irene began flying out annually and they would always stop off to stay with the Carneys, enjoying the balmy weather and the good wine. Sometimes, they wouldn't talk about Mayo football at all. They had no plans to meet in the summer of 2007, and both Pádraig and Moira were amused at just how unpredictable Paddy can be in his whereabouts, travelling to his daughter's house in South Africa as casually as he would head out to buy a newspaper. Paddy is as spontaneous as Pádraig is composed and deliberate. It is only after you meet them separately that you realise what they have in common. These are men in their eighties but they stride on unburdened.

They wear their years lightly and carelessly and talk of one another as though certain that there are plenty of good dinners ahead, plenty of future All-Ireland finals in which to cheer on and agonise over Mayo. When they get together, Paddy, the raconteur, will get excited about those best of times. You think of him in his kitchen on a drenched afternoon imitating Flanagan when the team stopped in Foxford during the night of the 1951 homecoming. The sky was navy blue and clear and the player's knuckles red from the cold and from shaking hands. Flanagan raised the cup, as he did in all the other towns, and then addressed the microphone with the flamboyance of a showman politician and the authority of a natural captain. 'The one thing warmer than a Foxford blanket,' he shouted, 'is a Foxford welcome.' The people roared in appreciation. The Mayo countryside flickered with bonfires and on the stage the young footballers laughed. It felt like they would be champions forever.

# THREE

# ELECTION

It was just after half past three on a Saturday morning in May 2007 when John O'Mahony was elected to Dáil Éireann. His actual ascension to the ranks of Ireland's political army was a formality by that hour. But when the announcement went out that O'Mahony had received over 4,000 transfers from fellow Fine Gael candidate Michelle Mulherin, there was bedlam on the concert floor of the Traveller's Friend Hotel and Theatre, Castlebar. Regardless of how things were panning out on the national scene, this felt like a glory night in Mayo politics. Earlier in the evening, the Fine Gael leader and putative Taoiseach Enda Kenny had been returned as TD for Mayo with a whopping 14,000 votes. Shortly before the announcement of the first count, Kenny was ushered into the main hall to primal whoops and shouts. The likelihood of his becoming Taoiseach had already dissolved, but however deep his disappointments, he masked them beautifully with the veteran political man's talent for simultaneously blending in and standing out among a crowd of hundreds.

From the balcony above, we watched him as he moved through the mob, the copper hair shining, that slightly terse smile, cheek pecks for the ladies, handshakes for the men, waving to the old faces with movements not quite so robotic as they had appeared on television throughout the long campaign. The thought must have occurred to many in that hall that never had Henry Kenny's son looked as statesmanlike or plausible as a leader of Ireland as in those manic minutes of his homecoming, when he walked among the Mayo people knowing that his best shot had, in all probability, vanished in the night.

O'Mahony's car had pulled into Castlebar at just after eight o'clock that night. All day long, the atmosphere in the bar and hotel foyer above the count centre had been jubilant. Because Mayo had a chance to elect a Taoiseach, the county had become engaged by the election to an astonishing degree. The gathering had the slightly dreamy feel of a young wedding and the raucous energy of a championship Sunday. Elderly men wore their suits out of respect for the day. From noon, the chefs were standing behind the sweltering deep pans, serving beef and turkey dinners and cold-meat salads from the iced display case. The bar staff struggled to replenish the shelves with glasses. Outside, smokers stood in the mellow evening and there was an instant round of applause when O'Mahony emerged from a saloon car, looking immaculate and fresh in a navy suit and pale-blue shirt. One man moved forward and shook O'Mahony's hand with the intensity of emotion that comes with being good and tipsy. He said something low and urgent to O'Mahony, who listened as though he had all the time in the world. But he was being prompted and cajoled forward by the electioneers, along with his wife, Ger, and his daughters, Niamh and Cliodhna.

O'Mahony is an expert practitioner in these environments of passion and drink and sentimentality and local pride, having experienced them during his triumphs on the GAA field. Composure had long been identified as his abiding characteristic as a manager and he was equally unruffled through this remarkable hour. There is something innately moving and innocent about the way that elected politicians are championed and sometimes carried aloft like prizefighters on the night when the nation's votes are ordered and stacked. To trumpet O'Mahony's arrival in the count centre, a Fine Gael stalwart ran ahead and entered the hall hollering like a Hollywood Apache. It was enough to draw the general attention, and when O'Mahony walked in, warm, loud sustained applause quickly blossomed into a familiar chant: 'Johnno, Johnno, Johnno.' He moved leisurely, comfortable in the body heat and the excitement. People struggled to get near him: they had words that needed to be spoken at that instant and O'Mahony has the natural communicator's gift for knowing when to pause, when to dip his head so confidences can be passed.

Soon, he was presented in front of the wooden barricades where over a dozen photographers and television cameramen were throwing sly elbows for the best angles. Enda Kenny was there and he held aloft the hands of his two deputies elect, Michael Ring and O'Mahony. In a five-seat constituency, Fine Gael looked set to land the first three places, a fine local coup. Watching O'Mahony that night, one was struck by how completely at home he looked in this new arena – arguably more treacherous and devious than anything he would have encountered on the Gaelic fields.

'To be honest about it, I was dumbstruck,' he smiles on a damp autumn lunch hour as he sits on a couch in his constituency office in Claremorris. 'It was the first time I was ever at a count. I had always imagined it differently, in that once the votes were cast the night before, the die was cast, so there was no nervousness. My eyes were opened by the tallymen, these experts who can just read the transfers and have been at numerous elections. They all said that I was sound.

'When I took on the challenge, I thought that as long as I

did everything that could be done, I would be happy. But I had a fair indication from early in the day [that I would be elected]. And I couldn't believe the energy that was in that hall. It was almost like professional boxing where everyone was around their own man. I didn't realise when I started out that it would be like that on election night. It is almost a sport.'

As Seán O'Rourke noted on RTÉ radio, O'Mahony was the only 'celebrity candidate' to gain a seat. 'Celebrity' seems like a strange word to use in connection with John O'Mahony. He has never been a showman, and whether buying a newspaper in a shop or talking after an All-Ireland victory, the manner – measured and innately courteous – has never changed. Yet O'Rourke was perfectly right, in that John O'Mahony comes as close as one can to being genuinely and legitimately famous in Ireland, having acquired a public profile through work that means a tremendous amount to local communities, all the while adopting no airs and graces. In the west, he is a folk hero and he matters greatly. Regarded as having a slender chance at best when his candidature was announced, the O'Mahony campaign was a triumph of organisation and thoroughness and humility, of communication and rigid planning. His election bid was run, in other words, along the same lines as the football teams he managed down the years.

Nonetheless, the tale of O'Mahony's electoral appeal is the most vivid proof of the truth in the cliché about a week being a long time in politics. On the Sunday before election night, O'Mahony had endured a mortifying championship beginning with Mayo. The 2–10 to 0–09 defeat by Galway in the Connacht championship quarter-finals shook the county faithful. Because of the optimism that had been generated by his return after a sixteen-year exile, many supporters regarded the lesson Galway inflicted as more dismaying than the All-Ireland-final humiliation of the previous season. Through the disappointments of the 1990s, Mayo people could console themselves that it would be different on O'Mahony's watch. It was as though they regarded him as a shaman, a magic worker.

Now, his team had been outplayed, and up in the press-box on that billowy Sunday, they were arguing that the master had been tactically outfoxed by Peter Ford, his former Mayo full-back. It was the performance that the Galway football public had been hankering after. For Mayo, it was the hardest provincial defeat for years because it shattered the deeply held conviction that, in addition to being a great manager, O'Mahony had access to some celestial power that he could call down from the sky to return the county to glory. The fans realised that John O'Mahony, for all his talents, was mortal. Nothing worked for Mayo. One unforgettable passage of play illuminated that. Ciaran McDonald, racked by injury throughout the league, had come into the match with less than half an hour left to play. As the Crossmolina man took a pass near the halfway line, Galway defender Damien Burke came thundering through and shouldered McDonald on the blind side. The challenge floored the Mayo man, and as Burke came dashing clear with the ball, roars of approval came from the stand in Pearse Stadium. McDonald was Mayo's conjurer. Inspirational though the tackle had been, it demanded immediate retribution. Instead, Mayo let Burke run for twenty yards and raise the roof before Conor Mortimer, their slenderest player, dragged him down. They had no fire that afternoon.

'I could not see that coming,' O'Mahony says. 'Maybe there were small signs that we were tired coming into the match. But the most disappointing thing was that we decided with twenty minutes to go that it wasn't our day.'

Outside the dressing-room, a crowd gathered as O'Mahony prepared to give a live television interview in the grim grey-bricked anteroom. He mustered a bleak smile when the technician asked him to count to ten for the volume reading. Afterwards, he admitted that he was 'bewildered' by how meek and almost uninterested his team had looked on the field. On Monday morning, he took a phone call from Tommy Marren's show on Midwest Radio and heard the first voices of dissent since he had returned to the job.

That evening, the Mayo panel and management met up in Claremorris to discuss the match, and by nightfall the bar talk was of honest, provocative exchanges, of real anger. 'It was frank. The players were devastated and angry. Regardless of the qualifying system, the championship has never escaped the absolute hurt of the first-round defeat, and losing to Galway is such a public thing. There were harsh words spoken that night. Anyone who wanted had the floor and it was therapy. The idea was that we would clear the air and look ahead to the qualifiers.'

So it was over for seven weeks. It was a popular assumption that a rollicking victory over Galway was required to give O'Mahony's election bid the necessary voltage. Plans to hand out his campaign literature to Mayo people outside Pearse Stadium had been hastily scrapped. None of the political pundits gave him much of a shout. And yet here he was on election night, a success story in one of the most heated political barns in the country. It was as though the Mayo public had backed him in spite of the loss of the match. Mayo football players past glittered in the crowd. Ford was there, John Maughan and Willie Joe Padden too. They drank to him. It was an incredibly giddy and optimistic evening. Outside the foyer, O'Mahony's friend and canvasser Tommy Goonan spoke excitedly on a mobile phone: 'It's like the old days, but you've never seen a crowd like it. It's wonderful. There's a buzz you couldn't leave.'

Three months earlier, I met with O'Mahony on a rainy Wednesday lunchtime in Ballaghaderreen. In Durkin's, he insists on paying for two roast-pork meals. 'You're in my town now,' he says, with mock suavity. The O'Mahony family live in the old stationmaster's house, a handsome, grey-stone towered building on the edge of town, directly across the road from St Nathy's College, which John attended as a boarder and to which he returned to teach for thirty-odd years. As we sit in the living room after lunch, O'Mahony produces an old press pack he has saved from the 1989 All-Ireland final, preserved in a plastic folder and bearing the names and details of the players in a fancy font. He happened upon it when clearing out a box of football memorabilia a few days ago and was amused by the simplicity of it. 'We always tried to do everything right and this was the best we could manage at the time.'

Mayo people place such faith and trust in O'Mahony because of 1989 and what happened afterwards. Although the season ended with an All-Ireland-final defeat, it was one that Mayo accepted with something approaching valour and optimism. One night before Christmas last year, O'Mahony was pottering around the house when he received a text from Tony Davis, the former Cork defender, who played against Mayo in the 1989 final and who became friendly with O'Mahony when they worked together on *The Sunday Game*. The match was being replayed on the *All-Ireland Gold* series on TG4 and Davis took delight in messaging O'Mahony about the tracksuit he had worn that day, a sky-blue number made of the chintzy, inflammable material that was in vogue in those times. 'The old shell tracksuit,' O'Mahony smiles in admission.

'So I turned it on and watched the last part of it then. I hadn't seen it for a long time. And the thing that struck me was how physical that Mayo team was. And, in fact, watching it, if you hadn't known the result, you would have imagined we were going to win it. Cork were poxed lucky in a way. I knew they were on the cliff. We missed four easy point-scoring chances. But we just couldn't push them off.'

In late September 1989, it did not matter. The popular belief was that Mayo would be back, and during the emotional and drink-sodden week-long homecoming, the squad promised as much. It just never happened. In the days of the old knockout system, one bad afternoon could kill an entire year, and Mayo were ordinary in the semi-final against Galway in 1990, losing by 1–12 to 2–11. A summer later, they were drawn into a lionhearted fight for the provincial championship with Roscommon in Castlebar, and a young St Jarlath's graduate named Derek Duggan dispatched a monstrous sixty-metre free to earn a draw for the primrose county. A week later, Mayo were beaten by 1–09 to 0–13 in Hyde Park. It all went sour. 'There were people hammering at our dressing-room door in anger and real disgust after that display,' O'Mahony remembers.

By then, the manager's relationship with the county board had grown strained. O'Mahony was annoyed that he had been overlooked for one of the two managerial positions on the 1990 All-Star tour. It was traditional that the managers whose teams contested the All-Ireland final travelled but, along with Cork's Billy Morgan, Mick O'Dwyer was selected. Before the 1989 All-Ireland final, O'Mahony had been subtly pressurised by a county-board official to free some players for interviews with the new Midwest Radio station. O'Mahony was instinctively dubious about the exposure and the hype but, reluctantly, he agreed to send Jimmy Browne and one or two other senior players along for a half-hour. The inference was that a good word would be put in for him ahead of the All-Star tour, which at that time was in May. Six Mayo players were selected, but their manager was passed over. O'Mahony was angered at what he believed to be a slight and let his feelings be known at the next county-board meeting. 'I really saw red. I kicked up a stink about it and I knew that was the death knell. I felt, leaving that meeting, that the attitude was this boy is trouble and he is going as soon as Mayo are out of the championship. I knew there was bad feeling towards me.'

His exit following the Roscommon defeat was not straightforward. Before he was due to meet with the board to discuss his future, O'Mahony made it known that he would return only if he had the freedom to choose his own selectors. He had just come in from school when Mick Higgins, the county chairman, phoned him out of courtesy. 'Look, John, don't go looking for your own selectors. You won't get them.' O'Mahony walked into the meeting and repeated what Higgins had told him. 'I just said, "In that case, I am resigning." I felt it was constructive dismissal but they interpreted it as a resignation. I was hurt that they didn't really think I was up to the job. A few club delegates nominated me again for the vacancy. I was hurt, but it wasn't in my psyche to say, "Right, I'll get some other county and f***ing show ye." That was never in my mind.'

O'Mahony was gone. It should be acknowledged that the Mayo executive could not have guessed they had such an alchemist on their hands. At that time, O'Mahony had a reputation for being thorough and disciplined and durable. His playing career suggested that he would always be around and, while his had not been a magnetic name on the playing field, he always looked like one of the smart lads who seem destined for management. Rushed through with a handful of other young Mayo footballers after the Under-21 All-Ireland success of 1974, O'Mahony's senior career was a chastening experience. He played through to the 1975 championship and was withdrawn after eight minutes in the Connacht-final replay against Sligo. Even though he remained on the periphery of the panel in the following years and enjoyed a late renaissance moonlighting as a forward for Ballaghaderreen in the 1981 championship, he was never able persuade the selectors to see him as part of the solution. If he complained, it was never publicly and he continued to contribute to Mayo GAA, managing a gifted Under-21 team to the 1983 All-Ireland title. He wrote the Ballaghaderreen notes for the *Roscommon Herald*. He was Young Referee for Connacht in 1987. And by 1989, he was wearing that blue tracksuit on the third Sunday in September.

The convenient conclusion is that the frustration O'Mahony felt as a football player facilitated his patience and fastidiousness as a manager. But he reviews his athletic life unsentimentally. 'Look it, I was a corner-back. I was never the most stylish. In 1975, well, Séamus Reilly was marking Mickey Kearins that day, but I had a poor enough game in the drawn match, and I think the selectors had misgivings about starting me again. So the disastrous start made their minds up.

'I may never have made it anyway, but I kept trying. I would get called into league panels but could never really break into it. I remember, in 1976, one of the regular corner-backs got injured and I still didn't get a game. I knew I was pushing myself to the limit. So I went to Johnny Carey about it. He was one of the guys in charge, and he said, "Look, John, I think you are good enough but the other two boys don't." Then I spoke to one of the others and was told the same thing. So someone was lying. They did ask me in as a forward but I never really had it in that position. I hung around playing club football so they knew I was available. And that was it.'

In 1989, O'Mahony was younger than his most senior player, Martin Carney. He was still learning his craft but he was a manager of extraordinary potential. After his departure, Mayo football foundered under the regimes of Jack O'Shea, Brian McDonald and Anthony Egan, who honourably agreed to take up the position when nobody else really wanted it. When O'Mahony was approached about managing Leitrim, he held long conversations with Carney, Seamie Daly and T.J. Kilgallon before agreeing. He was effectively looking for assurances that it would be an acceptable move. And when he guided Leitrim to the 1994 Connacht championship, their first since 1927, he took phone calls from sympathetic Mayo people telling him to shake the cup in the faces of his adversaries on the county board. 'But absolutely not. There was never a negative motivation for managing. It was for Leitrim.'

The stunning impact that John Maughan made on Mayo football in the two seasons of 1996 and 1997 made people forget about O'Mahony. It could be considered unfortunate for Mayo that O'Mahony and Maughan came to managerial prominence in the same era. The men had history. Maughan had shone as a football player, easily achieving at all inter-county grades, and he was a part of O'Mahony's Under-21 team. A serious knee injury destroyed his prospects of playing in the 1989 senior championship, but he was such a big presence that O'Mahony kept him on the panel.

'He was a good link between myself and the players. I remember that, coming up to the All-Ireland final, John and Frank Noone were both injured and they did a television interview for the RTÉ news in Knock Airport. John was fiercely ambitious and he was really into his training. Like, he organised circuit training and weights and did some winter training. But when he was approached about going to take the Clare job in 1991, someone tipped me off. His knee was bucked and he probably had ambitions down the line. I phoned him to wish him well but he probably felt or knew he had made a mistake in not telling me himself. Things went great for him in Clare and I was delighted to see it. But as the success got higher, he wasn't returning my phone calls. And I suppose I got ticked off with that. Like, I felt that I had given him a leg up a few years earlier. And by 1996 and 1997, it felt like John didn't want to know me.'

Maughan's instinctive combination of setting gladiatorial physical challenges for his players with his breezy, confident optimism brightened up Mayo football. Maughan was a persuasive figure, well liked by the players and bold enough to make smiling, confident predictions. He was unafraid and, as Mayo swept through to an All-Ireland final in 1996, the public loved him for it. O'Mahony, out in the cold, came to the conclusion that Mayo wouldn't be looking for him any time soon, and when he was asked to join Galway after the 1997 championship season, it seemed foolish not to accept.

'And things took a turn of their own after that. Again, I sought permission from the people I respected before I took the job. I wasn't doing anything disloyal. I could have spent my life whingeing about what had happened me in Mayo. I could have turned bitter about it. But that wasn't the way I felt. I wanted a challenge. So I went to Galway.'

Hideous luck and familiar team failings came between John Maughan and football immortality in 1996 and 1997. The following summer, O'Mahony and Maughan patrolled the sidelines and O'Mahony's team prevailed on a scoreline of 1–13 to 2–06. It was one of those early-summer classics, with Ciaran McDonald in irrepressible form, landing one sumptuous goal and slamming a great shot off the crossbar in the last few minutes of the encounter. The trajectory carried the ball downwards – it was desperately close. Mayo might have won. For two summers, Mayo football people had embarked upon long and emotionally draining journeys under Maughan. Both had ended in the exquisite disappointment of All-Ireland-final defeat. Now they were out. That it was O'Mahony who masterminded this abrupt early exit seemed like karma.

Mayo people watched with a mixture of dread, fascination and pride as O'Mahony and Galway kept on winning, suddenly empowered with the maroon verve of old, overwhelming Kildare in the All-Ireland final with a performance that was lauded as a vindication of class and old-fashioned football, as a spiritual return to the old days. Mayo had come close and Galway delivered. The following year, the counties met in the Connacht final. Galway scored 1–10 in the first half, came out after the break and, in a freakish half-hour, failed to register a single score. Mayo won by 1–14 to 1–10, and immediately Maughan was swamped and chaired off the field by the rampant Mayo fans. If the question of Maughan or O'Mahony had entered the minds of Mayo football people before, it was crystallised on this afternoon.

By the time O'Mahony finished in Galway after their 2004 season was over, he had delivered another All-Ireland title (in 2001) and established himself as a giant figure in the modern game. Mayo pined for him and leaned on the consolation that things would finally fall into place if and when O'Mahony would take the post again. And yet in 2004 Maughan led Mayo back to an All-Ireland final against the odds. O'Mahony had a low-key few months, writing a newspaper column and hosting a sports show on Midwest Radio, sitting on the *Sunday Game* couch. It meant he had ample time to dissect and comment on what Maughan was doing. When Kerry overpowered Mayo in that year's final, Maughan announced he was stepping down and there was an immediate clamour for O'Mahony to succeed him.

Maughan could have been forgiven for feeling haunted by his former manager and resentful at the public acclaim he received. It seemed as though the longer O'Mahony stayed away from the county, the greater his reputation became. Even the former Galway manager himself was surprised by the vociferousness of public opinion. One night on his radio show, Paddy Prendergast, the 1951 full-back, surprised him by making a direct on-air plea for him to take the vacant position. Prendergast reminded O'Mahony of seeing his wife Ger crying after the 1989 disappointment and suggested he had an obligation to give it another go.

O'Mahony hesitated. 'I remember ringing Ger one day and

asking her to book us a holiday, anywhere, just to get the hell out of it for a while. I was exhausted after leaving Galway and I didn't know if I had energy to go back into the game. I suppose John Maughan felt that maybe I was hanging around waiting for his job. Once he resigned, he immediately more or less said, "Give it to O'Mahony, he wants it." At one point, he would have said I was the man for the job. And there was that upsurge of opinion. And maybe from John's perspective I was fuelling it by doing the column and *The Sunday Game*. John and I would have very different styles of managing. But he was unlucky. He deserved to win an All-Ireland with Mayo in 1996. And I will always think it was very big of him to admit that the one thing he hadn't factored on was being six points up with fifteen minutes to go. I think I got a few breaks along the way that John didn't. But in 2004, I was never trying to undermine him. Maybe he got the wrong impression from some of the stuff I was writing. But hand on heart, it was never meant that way. It was meant to provoke a bit of discussion or interest. That was it. And, in fact, I could have made that blossom more if I had been more controversial, but that is not my nature. I stayed very neutral when it came to Mayo –the television people would have preferred it had I kicked up a bit more. So I suppose when the job came up, I did want to prove to people that I wasn't just hanging around waiting for it. And I genuinely did feel I needed more time off as well.'

But when the post became available in autumn 2006 after Mayo's latest All-Ireland dream was vaporised, O'Mahony must have known that he had no choice but to take it. John Maughan had been approached to manage Roscommon and had found it impossible to say no. But with Roscommon and Mayo playing in different league divisions, Maughan would still be free to voice his opinion on the Mayo radio sports shows. The wheel always comes full circle. It would be wrong to characterise John O'Mahony and John Maughan as enemies. They see each other regularly and are cordial, but the phone calls have stopped. That is as it should be. Although the two men are different, they are not radically so, sharing a fundamental belief in hard work and an immense ambition and pride in Mayo football. Mayo is a roomy county but it is hardly big enough for the two of them.

And yet on a huge night for O'Mahony, a night of tremendous personal achievement and pride, a night that affirmed his lasting popularity within Mayo, John Maughan turned up at the hotel in Castlebar to tip his hat. It was well into the early hours of Saturday morning when the football men actually saw one another. O'Mahony stopped in his tracks and Maughan gave him that magnanimous grin of his. 'What in the name of Jaysus are you doing here?' O'Mahony demanded, exhausted and happy and pleased to see an old comrade from the football fields. But he knew.

Thirty-one years is a long time to devote to a classroom. O'Mahony taught geography. For three generations of St Nathy's boys, he brought the Inca tribes and the monsoon seasons into the boarding school on the Mayo–Roscommon border on those fresh and timeless west-of-Ireland afternoons when the clouds move fast and the classrooms smell of Juicy Fruit. He had the reputation of being an excellent teacher, interested and organised and dedicated. His two brothers, Dan and Stephen, chose priesthood as their vocation. For John, it was education. From the living room of his house, he could see the square, stoic outline of the school after dark, lights burning from the study rooms and dormitories, nightly reminders of his own teenage years. He would joke that he was part of the furniture. Teaching taught him about how to talk to young people and how to manage time and how to advise and convince without being coercive. He brought many of his classroom practices to the training field. In school, kids felt they could trust O'Mahony and knew he was no pushover. The same rules applied in the Ballaghaderreen club and later with Mayo and Leitrim and then Galway.

It has often been claimed that O'Mahony has been meticulous and scrupulous in planning his managerial career. But if anything, his triumphs have been so cavalier and exceptional that they defied planning. It would have seemed delusional to have anticipated that he could lead Leitrim to a first Connacht title in sixty-seven years. And it would have been bold in the extreme to bank on returning Galway to glory in his maiden season. In both instances, he was shouldering against a significant chunk of negative history. O'Mahony unlocked both those enigmas and made them appear fairly simple. It is strange now to watch the archive footage of those manic seconds after Leitrim became champions of Connacht. That film looks like what it is: snatched moments from a departed century, when people looked slightly scrawnier and slightly scruffier, less carefully groomed, than they do today. As Leitrim fans stormed the field, Mayo football players stood around dazed and stunned. That turbulent day marked – some might say fittingly – Ciaran McDonald's championship debut. O'Mahony was subdued and awkward even as he accepted the handshakes. The last thing he wanted to look was cock-a-hoop, because that was the last thing he felt. He operated with extraordinary stealth through those Leitrim years and defused what could have become an awkward and personal situation. It was the same when he moved to Galway.

When O'Mahony was still a player, he was fond of studying the great managers as they stood in the dugout seconds before the final whistle. In the 1970s, when he went to All-Ireland finals, he kept his eyes fixed on Mick O'Dwyer and Kevin Heffernan. A few years later, he watched the Longford charismatic Eugene McGee. 'You had all this energy and hype and the movement on the field and the hits and the referee's decisions and the scores, and then it all comes down to those last two minutes when the whole thing is decided but it is not quite over. That gap, I suppose, is where I always dreamed of being. And standing there was amazing.'

Galway enjoyed a close to perfect football season in 1998. Those last seconds of the All-Ireland final against Kildare were when O'Mahony felt that sense of completion. He had transformed a very promising and predominantly young group of football players into a great team. In the following years, he used to remind the players that once he left he would be a Mayo man, but that while he was coaching Galway he would put his soul into it. The worst hour of his Galway years was when he left Tuam Stadium after Roscommon ran riot against them in the first round of the 2001 championship. O'Mahony went for a pint in Loftus's of Tuam town convinced that day was the end. Four months later, Galway were All-Ireland champions again, rampant against Meath in the All-Ireland final. That victory confirmed his place among the great GAA managers.

He was in charge of his neighbouring county for six years. The end came against Tyrone in Croke Park. During that defeat, Seán O'Domhnaill, the veteran midfielder, had kicked a long, booming point that was redolent of his famous distance score in the 1998 All-Ireland final. Croke Park was deserted quickly after the qualifier and O'Mahony stole out of the changing-rooms for a private walk on the field. When he made his way up the steps, he saw O'Domhnaill out on the field alone, standing at the place where he had kicked his point. O'Mahony realised that the player was saying his own goodbyes. 'I don't know what he was thinking but I have no doubt that retiring was on his mind. When I came back into the dressing-room, I went to say a few words but, ah, I just broke down. I got very emotional because I knew that this was it. I don't think I actually formally announced it to the boys, but if they were listening intently, they would have known. A few days later, I met the county board in the Sacre Coeur Hotel and that was it.'

Through those years, teaching was reliable and familiar territory. O'Mahony had become one of the most recognisable figures in Gaelic games, but St Nathy's was his job and it was an escape. Sometimes, the boys would joke with him after league Sundays but ultimately they did not need him to be a football man. When he decided to retire, he might have been expected to rest easy. But there was always the nagging sense of unfinished business with Mayo. And then the men from the party came knocking. His father, Stephen, had always been a Fine Gael man and Ballaghaderreen was keen Blueshirt country. It was, in retrospect, an incredibly brave and ambitious and radical act to run in a general election even as he returned to Mayo football. All last winter, local and national polls had O'Mahony listed as an outsider. John read them and absorbed whatever lessons he could and then went around preparing as best he could, as he would have done for an honours geography class or a championship training session.

He knocked on doors the day after Mayo lost the league final to Donegal in Croke Park and he was out again the morning after his team had been knocked out of the Connacht championship. 'There was no abuse. The games came up in conversation and there would be a bit of banter. But it was on those two days that I began to think that maybe people were willing to look at me as someone other than a football manager.'

Old colleagues and friends helped. John Prenty, the long-serving Mayo county-board man, worked as his director of elections. O'Mahony has always been happy to listen, always open to following guidance. For months, they scoured their Mayo constituency. The constant question was how he could combine running for the Dáil with running the county football team. There was no pat answer. He simply made the time. 'It was said that my eye was off the ball around election time. I didn't see it that way. I remember on the Saturday before the Galway game Enda Kenny was giving a rally in Castlebar and I was up at the pitch when he was down talking. Now, it would have been advantageous for me to have been down there with him, but training was scheduled and I wasn't going to miss it. The one thing I am delighted about now is that the election happened after that match. At least the cards were all on the table.'

It was bright when the O'Mahonys left the election celebrations in Castlebar. He sat in the passenger seat as they drove across the countryside at dawn, numb with tiredness. Even during the cheering, O'Mahony had been conscious of just how new and innocent he was in the slippery world of politics. He had watched enthralled as her team ushered the independent TD Beverly Flynn into the theatre sometime after one o'clock, the flashbulbs popping and the family supporters crowing and jubilant. He knew from football that people were clannish, that Irish loyalties were more complex than mere parish boundaries, but the faith and energy that people placed in their political allegiances that night took him aback. It took him a while to get used to the idea of being a TD. He was a teacher. He was a football man. Old habits stayed with him. On his first morning in the Dáil, he left home so early that he was standing on Kildare Street at ten to seven in the morning. He found a breakfast place around Duke Street and listened to *Morning Ireland* on the radio. That first day was ceremonial, but in the polished floorboards and the oil portraits on the walls and the realisation that statesmen, great and otherwise, had walked these same halls, he was caught up in the sense of history of the house. After matches in Croke Park, when the stands were vast and silent and the field had darkened, he had occasionally experienced a chill transcendent appreciation of the great moments gone and those to come, the overwhelming impression of merely passing through an institution defiant of time. Great people had stood in these rooms, brimming with ideas and energy. Seán Flanagan had stood in these rooms when O'Mahony was carrying his lunch across to St Nathy's.

In his first few days in the Dáil, he sat watching and listening, fascinated and conscious of his novice status – even though the other politicians knew him from football. 'I suppose I was astonished. There is a formality and a protocol to the whole thing, but then you see people insulting each other across the chamber and then at lunchtime they would be talking perfectly reasonably outside. In the GAA, if you have a row, there would be a bit of a cool for a while. With this, I suppose there is an acceptance that it is performance. And then there are people there who are clearly excellent at their trade.

'When I was out knocking on doors, I never once dreamt of what the Dáil might be like. I had no time. Those two weeks before recess taught me a lot about what lies ahead. I suppose I am more streetwise about the political game now, but I have so much to learn and I am fascinated by it. Being a TD, you become an incredibly public person, you have to be available to everyone, and that added to the football is a lot. But that is what I chose.'

Three days after the Dáil went into recess, Mayo beat Cavan in their first qualifying game of the championship. Then they recorded good challenge-match victories over Laois and Cork. On the day of the Cavan game, Ronan McGarrity made his comeback after an exhausting battle with illness and O'Mahony was in high spirits heading home. He began to entertain the idea that they might squeeze through the qualifying games and get into the quarter-finals with a fully fit panel. Then he heard on a radio bulletin that Keith Higgins, the sniping young corner-back who also plays hurling for Mayo, had been injured in a match in Kerry. He made a phone call and was informed that Higgins had broken his arm. It was another setback. In mid-July, Mayo travelled to play Derry in Celtic Park. They were well beaten in the end. The match was not televised, which made it a quiet and almost obscure exit for a county whose championships are more often characterised by extreme dramas.

It was odd territory for the players and also for O'Mahony, who had become accustomed to August football. 'It is lonely. That is the feeling. And that day, you all of a sudden realised that there is a massive task to be tackled here in Mayo. You are in the dressing-room and it is the end of the year and there are flashbacks to all the previous games – the league, the Galway match. There was a sense of finality about it all. But I do remember one of the younger lads talking about next season and asking about weights programmes. Youth is magnificent in times like that. It keeps you going. We had to think of it as a beginning as well as an end.'

Soon, O'Mahony will move among the paperwork and expensive suits and the whispers and chicanery in Dublin. Through the most wretched nights of the coming winter, the best football players in Mayo will run and suffer and hope to the sound of O'Mahony's voice. There will be nights when he will drive across the midlands for morning meetings in the Dáil, wishing Val Joyce was still on the radio. He cannot guess as to what next year will be like. Mayo are starting over again in an unwritten season. In a way, O'Mahony is starting out again as well, back to where he was in the late 1980s. The abiding wish has not changed: 'Look, if I could ever lead Mayo to an All-Ireland, then I would die a happy man.'

# FOUR

# IN THE SHADOW

It is venomously cold for mid-April and Joe Corcoran keeps his jacket zipped tight as he watches the Ardnaree boys trot in slow, silent procession around the field. In Mayo, those who remember football in the 1960s speak wistfully of the clean and lyrical brilliance with which Corcoran played the game. He was fast and expressive and skilful, and although his career coincided with a magnificent period for Galway football, Corcoran made the years of narrow losses more tolerable. In Ballina in the 1960s, Joe Corcoran was a school caretaker from Monday to Friday and then on championship Sundays he bloomed into a kind of god.

Like the rest of Ballina, Ardnaree is fiercely territorial and, with a kingly wave of his hand, Joe Corcoran plots the townscape of his childhood across the inky evening sky. 'There was a factory across the way there that used to make hosiery and that. A local guy called Larry Ruane married one of the girls there and he gave my mother, who used to work there, a pair of football boots to get me to play. He must have known I had something, because he would come around watching me when I started playing. I went to the boys' school in Ballina, but for years I just watched the football team. When we were playing, there were no dressing-rooms here. We would tog out behind the wall across the field there. I went into football as a minor in 1958. And I went up awful fast.'

Corcoran played with Mayo for fifteen years and won two Connacht championships, in 1967 and 1969. Throughout the prime of his football career, he played on teams that came close to breaking the Galway three-in-a-row side but ultimately sent those maroon teams out of the province reassured of their own invincibility. In those two years that Mayo travelled to Dublin, they were not so iron-clad in their mentality. In 1967, Mayo played Meath in the All-Ireland semi-final. The first live television broadcast had taken place the summer previously and any Mayo person who was not at Croke Park had found their way to a TV set. The game was finely balanced early in the second half when there was a national blackout. The picture was restored after twenty minutes but by then Meath had scored two goals. Jaws dropped across Mayo. The fact that they were unseen made them all the more vivid. They seemed like phantom goals, some conceit of television, inflicted by the gods in the machine as a joke on Mayo. But they stood bold and true on the scoreboard. Two years later, Mayo made it back to Croke Park and lost to Kerry by a single point.

Corcoran speaks about those games with the slight impatience of those who found football easy to master. He attaches no mystery to Mayo not winning since 1951: even on the days when his Mayo teams shone, there was another county just that little bit better. 'I was certain we would win an All-Ireland,' he says quietly, keeping his eyes trained on the progress of the footballers. 'We had a good spread of lads from around the county and plenty of leaders, men like John Morley and Tom Langan, Ray Prendergast, Johnny Carey and P.J. Loftus. These were all serious footballers. I would have been up around the top in scoring the whole time then. I loved the space in Croke Park because I was a terror for the solo run. I kicked points with two feet and I never had any fear about taking frees. I think we might have been a bit unlucky. Those Meath goals should not have happened. Our goalkeeper went up with one of the defenders for the ball and next thing it was in the net. The same thing happened after they got a fifty. It was a bit of misfortune. And that was a very good Galway team in the 1960s. There were games when there was nothing between us but they just sneaked by us. They were grand people, too. You never minded seeing Galway winning.'

Three years after Mayo had confirmed their reputation as the best team in Ireland, Galway beat them in the 1954 championship in Tuam on a score of 2–03 to 1–05. It was such an extraordinary turnaround in fortunes that ecstatic Galway fans chaired the local boys off the field. The Mayo mystique, glittering in the middle part of the century, was already beginning to fade. Two years later, Galway won the All-Ireland championship, playing with panache and a sense of entitlement against Cork. It was an October final because of a polio outbreak in Cork and was all the more eagerly anticipated for that. Frank Stockwell scored 2–05 and Seán Purcell – who had been supreme at full-back in that landmark defeat of Mayo two years earlier – was hailed as a peerless centre half-forward. The two formed a unique Tuam double act within the Galway side. The final score was 2–13 to 3–07: it was a joy of a game for neutrals. That Galway team went on to record five Connacht titles in a row, and when that side began to break up a fresh wave of talent from the exceptional minor team which won the 1960 All-Ireland provided players like Enda Colleran, Séamus Leydon, Christy Tyrell and Johnny Geraghty. In less than a decade, Galway football had got its act together to the extent that Mayo would win just three Connacht titles between their crowning season of 1951 and 1981.

It might have been different had Galway been just a little

less dominant in the '60s. While Joe Corcoran was Mayo's maestro in that decade, the performances of a tall young Claremorris man named Michael Connaughton had begun to excite close observers of the game. Connaughton was an athletic, ball-playing midfielder who grew up at Farmhill and was just old enough to feel the tingles from the distant heroism of the 1950 team. He went to the Callaghans', the neighbours' house, to listen to that All-Ireland final, but the living room was full so the window was opened and he sat with others outside listening to the names – Henry Dixon, Seán Flanagan, Pauric Carney – floating away in the afternoon air. A few days later, his father took him cycling into town to see the cup on show in Hanley's Bar. That was enough for him to vow that he would wear a Mayo jersey.

These days, Connaughton lives in Galway city, within a short walk of Pearse Stadium. His Mayo career was brief and eventful. He was sixteen years old when he played in the All-Ireland minor final of 1961. A record crowd of 90,000 descended upon Croke Park for the senior match between Down and Offaly. Mayo faced Cork in the curtain-raiser. What he remembers is an abiding sense of innocence. In the dark dressing-room, county-board man Paddy Waldron made an impassioned speech about playing the game correctly, about avoiding dishonour at all costs. Shortly after the throw-in, Connaughton took a neat smack on the nose from a passing Cork player. 'I didn't know how to react. Paddy Waldron was a brilliant, brilliant man and he was ahead of his time in many ways, but he had this belief about how you conducted yourself on the field. That killer instinct was maybe lacking. Anyway, Cork beat us easily.'

He lost another minor final to Kerry the following September and was still underage when the 1963 minor team fell to Kerry in the semi-final. A year later, he was selected on a Mayo senior team to play in the league away to Meath.

He had yet to play a senior game for Claremorris. When he thinks back, everything happened just a little too quickly. He was a little too naive for the realities of senior football. In his first Connacht final, against Galway in 1964, he was playing at left half-forward in the company of John Donnellan and was certain that he could expose the Dunmore man with his pace. 'But I kept getting this little tug of the jersey and it meant I was behind him every time. I remember complaining to [teammate] Johnny Farragher about it and he looked at me and said, "Why didn't you let back the elbow?" I think now that a manager should always take any young player coming out of minor and have a long chat with him. My greatest fear was that my man would have a good game. With Claremorris, I would cover every blade of grass; I had Cormac Hanley to cover me so I knew I could roam. But with Mayo, in the beginning, I was tentative. If I could do it again, it would be different.'

By 1966, Connaughton was beginning to find his voice. Mayo were still comfortably the second-best team in Connacht, although they were weakened when Johnny Farragher decided to go to London for seasonal work. There was a month between their facile defeat of Sligo and what was to be the definitive clash with Galway. Farragher reappeared a week before the final and Connaughton made a personal entreaty to Seamie Daly, the team trainer, stressing the importance of including Farragher. He said that if Farragher was not included, then they might as well strike him off too. Farragher was named on the team in the half-forward line, along with Joe Langan and Connaughton. But on the day of the match, wholesale changes were made, with John Morley dropping to centre-back and Connaughton forming the midfield with Langan. Farragher was a substitute.

It was the classic Connacht match of that decade, distinguished by an indomitable display at full-back by Ray

Prendergast and the bloody tenacity of the twice All-Ireland champions. At one stage, after M.J. Ruddy from Achill hit the game's only goal, Galway trailed by five points and were looking weary in comparison to the younger Mayo men. But by the last five minutes, they had patiently and calmly regained the lead. Mayo were a point down and were awarded a free from an attack that resulted in an injury to Mick Ruane. The referee, Jackie Martin, warned the Mayo men surrounding the stricken player that time was almost up and they had better convert the free. But Joe Corcoran was adamant that he wouldn't kick a ball until his teammate had been treated. Connaughton headed over to the bench, knackered from the game, and, in a last desperate gamble, suggested he be taken off for Farragher. The selectors rejected the idea and sent him back in.

'I was feeling the pinch at this stage. So the kick-out came and Mattie McDonagh, the Lord have mercy on him, and John Morley, the Lord have mercy on him, they went up and the ball broke straight into my hands. This was our chance. The next thing, Joe Corcoran came around behind and Séamus Leydon made a great interception.' John Donnellan delivered a long ball towards the Mayo square and Liam Sammon rose to fist the winning point. The final score was 0–12 to 1–08. Galway had shown the poise of two-time All-Ireland champions, and by the time they clinched the three-in-a-row over Meath, the Connacht final was forgotten. Connaughton, though, can still hear the crucifying shrillness of the final whistle when the ball was kicked out. The team had togged out in the Imperial Hotel and then headed down to McHale Park in cars. Connaughton was so dismayed that he found himself walking out the gate with the supporters in his Mayo jersey and boots, oblivious to the murmured consolations and claps on the back.

He was obsessive about training, and a few weeks later he was trying to perfect the art of catching the ball and turning in one motion. In a challenge match with Mayo shortly afterwards, he felt his knee jarring. Soon, the pain was intense. When he visited a specialist, he was informed that he had damaged cartilage and that Pat Donnellan of Galway and Paul Earley of Roscommon had successfully recovered from the same injury. Connaughton had surgery and was back on the panel the following summer but his knee never felt secure. Running in straight lines was fine but it felt weak and vulnerable whenever he turned sharply. He was picked for a first-round game against Sligo in the 1967 championship and fired a goal fifteen minutes in. His knee felt as if it had exploded as he made contact with the ball and he was in acute pain by the time the score had registered. It was the last ball Mike Connaughton ever kicked for Mayo. He was twenty-two.

In wintertime, the pretty town of Louisburgh all but hunches away from the great Atlantic through the dark months of gales and buffeting. For decades, it was one of the most isolated communities in Mayo, but the commercial crossroads in the heart of the town now has a ribbon of summer dwellings around it. All journeys are circular, and after serving for many decades in Galway, Father Leo Morahan came back to the town of his childhood. Louisburgh has a phenomenal tradition of sending young men to the seminary at Maynooth. Out of curiosity, a few years ago, Leo took a record of all the extant priests who came from Louisburgh, and there were more than forty dotted across Ireland and remoter Catholic outposts in the world. It made him smile, because as a young curate, he had looked on with some envy as classmates who were ordained in the same year spoke of the tremendous shout-outs that awaited them when they went home, with bunting on the telegraphs poles and their local street looking spruce for the occasion. 'Here in Louisburgh, you were just another priest,' he smiles. 'Its hard to fathom why so many came from here. I suppose some people would say there was an economic impulse behind it. I think I was just following in a tradition.'

These days, Father Leo lives alone in a modern bungalow on the edge of town, and from his doorway you can feel the clean saltiness of the ocean air. It was four o'clock and fading light when we met one February afternoon. In his living room, the priest had prepared a tray bearing tins of stout, a choice of whiskeys and some soft drinks and chocolates. Although he is over eighty now and likes to nap in the afternoon, he has prodigious energy and the voice of a newscaster.

Morahan was a Mayo county-board lifer and is one of the few men left in the county whose experience ranges from the sepia world of Paddy Moclair to the tattooism of Ciaran McDonald. He does not particularly care for a strict division of football by decades and speaks of the 1930s generation and the modern team as though they somehow mingle and are interchangeable. He can see Purty Kelly as vividly as the contemporary crowd sees McDonald.

One of his favourite Mayo football stories concerns the funeral of Henry Kenny. At the graveside oration, Johnny Walsh from Kerry remembered a 1938 league match between the counties being played in Castlebar. Kenny was in his prime then and the Kerry man had received blunt instructions to put manners on him. He badgered Kenny as they raced towards a high ball and as the Mayo man began to jump, Walsh let fly with his fist. Kenny duly hit the turf. The play was stopped and the Kerry man kept an anxious watch to see if any of the other Mayo players would seek retribution. But they were more concerned with the health of Kenny. After being doused with water, Kenny walked around gingerly and made his way back to Walsh. 'Johnny,' he said reproachfully. 'Why did you do that to me? Don't you know I would never do that to you?' The Kerry man told the funeral gathering that he felt so guilty about what had happened that he was unable to perform for the rest of the match and followed the action miserably as Kenny happily went about playing up a storm.

The 1930s players roamed freely through Morahan's boyhood imagination. He listened to the 1936 All-Ireland victory over Laois on the radio, and the next morning in school, his father set the class a composition to write on the story of the victory. He heard many years afterwards that although it felt like a seismic event, captain Séamus O'Malley had travelled down on the Sunday evening of the victory with the Sam Maguire in the back of the car and appeared before his class at the school where he taught the following morning.

The notion of Mayo as an elite football county surely has its origins in the consistency of the 1930s teams. Mayo won six league titles in a row between 1933 and 1939, losing just five matches out of forty-four. They opted out of the league in 1940 as a mark of respect to Patsy Flannelly, the popular Castlebar midfielder who was killed in a hunting accident. No football was played and Galway took the league honours. The following year, Mayo reclaimed them.

'I often heard it said that Mayo were the best "untrained" team in Ireland,' Morahan says. 'But Dick Hearns, an army man at the time and an Irish champion boxer, did train them. They probably should have won more All-Irelands, but they were a great team. Purty Kelly was the folk hero for us all. He actually worked cleaning the streets in Westport and wouldn't entertain the idea of a better job, even though his football profile would have made that easy. Dick Burke was my own hero. I thought he was outstanding. They were a hugely influential team with Gerald Courell and Jackie Carney, obviously. I got to know a lot of them after I became involved with the county board. I would call in to Paddy Moclair, who ran his pub in Ballina. I had a real gra for Henry Kenny. And

Josie Munnelly of course was a huge figure in Mayo football, as was Séamus O'Malley, who lived into his nineties.'

There was a period when the Mayo county board was considered to be an empire run by Father Morahan and Johnny Mulvey, as they were the only two board members not attached to clubs. For years, the priest taught and trained hurling and football teams in St Mary's College in Galway city and toiled in junior administrative roles in Mayo football. The sheer level of organisation required to run Gaelic games in a county fascinated him. Even when stationed in Gort in the far south of Galway, he thought nothing of driving after evening Mass to attend disciplinary hearings or monthly meetings in Ballina or Foxford. He served as Mayo chairman from 1966 to 1978 and then sat on the Central Council for a further decade.

He knows that it seemed an odd compulsion, dedicating his free time to the paperwork and thousand rows that come with governing games in all counties. In the parish house, the other priests were often amused by his rambles. Morahan actually seemed to like heading across the provincial interior on black, soaking nights for complicated meetings held in the boardrooms of hotels. On tricky nights, they told him he was driving into a nest of hornets. Those meetings, though, felt like a form of refereeing to Leo Morahan. 'Driving back to Gort, I would think about the meeting all the way home. On contrary nights when we had to suspend someone, I would wonder, "Did we do what was right? Did we get the truth?" And there was criticism. There was always a bit of a "them and us" between the players and the county board. It was a form of therapy to blame us when things went wrong. But I wasn't daunted. I enjoyed it tremendously and I got such happiness out of it.'

Over the years, as the 1950 and '51 successes became more remote and splendid-looking, Morahan often pondered what

Mayo and football was all about. As a long-serving county official, he watched as talented players came and went. In that period, the chairman sat in the dugout at matches and had a considerable say in selection. Sometimes, he would give a speech in the dressing-room. Over the years, Father Morahan visited the dressing-rooms in Croke Park more frequently than many players. He was there for the significant triumphs – the minor teams that won in 1966 and 1971 and the famous 1967 Under-21 final in which Willie McGee banged home four goals. Privately, he sometimes worried that Mayo would not replace the cast-iron leaders like Carney and Flanagan. He sometimes fretted over the fragile nature of the mood that governed Mayo football. On the sweet days, people were excitable and almost bombastic in their predictions for the next season. But the big disappointments seemed particularly crushing for Mayo people. That was especially true in the weeks after the 1969 All-Ireland semi-final defeat. It was as though the county brooded on what might have been.

When he was a boy, his mother had a saying if she ever saw him being in any way wasteful with food. Even if he did something as innocent as throwing a crust of bread to a dog, his mother would scold, 'If you were in it in '47, you would pick that up.' This would have been ninety years after the Famine, but it always struck him that his mother spoke about the Hunger as an occurrence that had only recently passed. It stayed with him through his adult life. Even nowadays, driving towards the bright lights of Westport, the road passes the National Famine Memorial at the foot of Croagh Patrick. It is a wrought-iron coffin ship with writhing skeletons in rags looking at visitors with hollows for eyes, and when lit on the heavy winter evenings and set against the sea, it is a disquieting apparition for passing motorists. 'Maybe we make too much of the football,' Leo says. 'Mayo has the whole Celtic thing of being either ecstatic or absolutely down in the depths of despair. Maybe it is common to all the coastal counties, I don't know. It is something I ask myself. Kerry and Mayo are similar in topography, but obviously in terms of football the success rate is different. I was struck by the time that Meath gave Kerry a real hammering in the All-Ireland semi-final a few years ago. They were down in the dumps, but they didn't seem to make a big, public thing about it. Maybe there is a social thing here. Take the old saying "Mayo, God help us". My belief is that it originates from the Famine when a lot of people fled the land and crowded the port towns like Sligo and Dublin and Galway to get away. And when people were asked where they came from, the reply was "Mayo, God help us" and it stuck. But, in a way, I am kind of proud of that. You carry your wounds with honour.'

Some afternoons were hard to take, though. Mayo responded to losing the 1969 semi-final in wonderful fashion, winning the league the following year. They promised themselves that 1970 would be their season for atonement. And then came a wet and windy May day and a Roscommon team with no fear and plenty of know-how and the year was wasted.

Morahan kept busy, immersing himself in the affairs of Central Council. Although he was never a radical, he was an instrumental figure in facilitating the removal of Rule 27, which banned GAA members from playing 'foreign' games. He formed his conviction that the ban should be revoked while coaching students in St Mary's, where he obeyed the rule that boys who played soccer would simply not be considered for the Gaelic football team. He was rigid about enforcing the censure, but privately it bothered him. In November 1968, he brought a motion from Louisburgh with the support of the Kiltimagh delegates. The basic proposal was that the GAA would explain the contemporary reasons for retaining the ban. Getting the motion passed through the Mayo fiefdom was tricky, but after that the mood for change quickly gained momentum. Morahan has always remained impressed by how honourably and fairly the GAA president, Pat Fanning, behaved during the approach to the 1971 Annual Congress in Belfast, even though he was absolutely against any such repeal of the rule. In the end, the matter did not even go to a vote. It was a notable shout from Mayo, and it ended years of misery and subterfuge for many young sportsmen in Ireland. But it did nothing to help Mayo football. The ban was a half-forgotten anachronism when a Mayo senior football team next kicked a championship football in Croke Park.

Gay Nevin was a wraith of a wing half-back on the Mayo minor team of 1966, and before the All-Ireland final against Down, he sat on the crowded bench in the dressing-room beneath the Hogan Stand. The room was stuffy and poorly lit and had a mildewed atmosphere, but the boys felt that they were at the epicentre of the most glamorous sporting event in the world. There were so many people in the room that someone turned a plastic C&C case upside down so the mentors would have a platform from which to give their speeches. Father Leo spoke first, and in his clear, sonorous voice, he told the boys about what the green-and-red colours meant and proceeded to give a rousing address about the importance of playing clean, honourable football. Then he gave the floor to Paddy Waldron. It was chill weather for September, and Paddy wore a long black coat of de Valerean import. He smoked heavily, and that may have added to the effect; certainly, he had absolute silence as he delivered his own words of inspiration, which were brief: 'Lads, go out and hit every effin' thing above the grass.' His attitude had evidently changed over the course of the decade.

Ninety minutes later, Mayo had won the Tommy Markham Cup for the first time since 1953. Forty years on, Gay Nevin can remember that game as though he played it yesterday.

Snowy-haired and immaculately tidy, Nevin often bumps into Mayo football players from yesteryear in Breaffy House Hotel, where he is general manager. The Breaffy is a Castlebar social institution. On the morning we meet, staff are preparing for a local wedding, and we move through the vast, silent dining room as Nevin runs an eye across the linen and silverware to satisfy himself that everything is perfect. He has spent all of his adult life in the hospitality industry and has the cordial, courteous manner of a successful hotelier. He can see now that there were years when the business consumed his time and energy so completely that he could afford only a flickering interest in football. He left the game a long time ago but the game never left him. Nevin was one of the generation of Mayo players whose senior careers were slightly eclipsed by the brilliance of the Galway era. Even now, he can hear the voice of John 'Tull' Dunne, the captain of Galway's 1938 All-Ireland vintage and the trainer of the '60s team, ringing with authority and defiance on championship days in Tuam. The dressing-rooms were located side by side, and Dunne knew that his words carried to Mayo ears as he demanded, 'Who do they think they are, thinking they can come into our sacred home and beat us?' It was fearful stuff, and it added to the mystique.

When Nevin went to school at St Gerard's in Castlebar, he lived in town with his older brother and had such a natural aptitude for the game that he ended up playing minor for Castlebar Mitchels when he was still thirteen. He was fast and light and fearless. He was still a teenager when he was selected for the senior team, and his first opponent was Mickey Kearins of Sligo. Nevin wasn't sure whether to hit him a shoulder or ask for an autograph, but he always treasured the hour of learning from him, of watching the way the Sligo man would use now his strength and now his guile as the situation demanded. Nevin allows that he survived the test.

In the Connacht final of 1969, he was introduced early in the match after Ray Niland got injured. When he made his way to Liam Sammon, he offered his hand to the Galway man, a little bit dazed at the prospect of marking him. Sammon cleared his head by responding with a firm handshake followed by an even firmer thump.

'There was nothing malicious in it,' Nevin says, as we sit down on a cool June morning on the veranda where guests are having coffee and reading newspapers. Gay lays down his folder and pen and allows himself to melt back into the fiery days of big-time football. 'Liam just saw this little fella running towards him. It was just to let me know where I was. But Galway were magnificent. Séamus Leydon was the toughest forward I ever marked. He beat the socks off me above in Tuam one day – absolutely trounced me! And Martin Newell was the guy I tried to emulate, an attacking half-back who would venture up past the halfway line. Galway had so many big names that I think the maroon jersey was worth two or three points to them in those years. And that was a great Connacht final that could have went the way of so many previously in the 1960s. Galway were attacking late on and there was a miraculous save. All that Liam Sammon had to do was tap the ball into the net, but it skewed sideways or someone stood on the ball – and we had won!'

Three years after his All-Ireland minor success, Nevin was back in Croke Park for the All-Ireland semi-final. He was a substitute but was sent in early in the first half to mark Mick O'Dwyer. They clashed near the Hogan Stand during a chase for the first ball sent in towards the Waterville man, and as Nevin picked himself up from the grass, O'Dwyer flashed a grin at him and said, 'For a small lad, you're not bad.'

That match boiled down to a late free from no more than twenty-one yards out. The dead-ball duties were being shared between Joe Corcoran and Séamus O'Dowd, who had captained the champion minor teams of just three years earlier. This particular kick fell on O'Dowd's side, but Corcoran had been kicking smoothly all afternoon and it would have seemed more sensible to have the senior man in line for such a crucial kick. It was an unbearably tense moment: in his match report, Paddy Downey of the *Irish Times* declared the game 'the cliffhanger to end them all'. And he noted that the angle facing O'Dowd was tricky. He caught it wrong and it curled dramatically and tailed wide. It was desperate luck on the young Ballina man, who had already achieved more than most in his sporting life. The match ended 0–14 to 1–10. The Kerry players were relieved at this gift. A replay had seemed inevitable. Instead, Mayo trooped back in through the tunnel and closed the door in on themselves.

'Seamie blamed himself. He was hard on himself,' Nevin says sympathetically. 'I don't know why the ball didn't go over, because Seamie was good that day. But it was severe pressure. I used to visualise it from my point of view. If I had missed that free, it would have had a very serious effect on me. We rallied around him in the dressing-room afterwards. But I am sure there were plenty of club games when he was reminded of it. That comes with the territory when you are taking frees. And Séamus was a tremendous free-taker. I don't think he played for Mayo for many years after that.'

As it transpired, neither did Nevin. In what was a humdrum league match against Down in 1972, he wrenched his back and, to his astonishment, he never fully recovered from it. The pain was sometimes searing and sometimes intermittent, and he had to content himself with winning county championships with a superb Castlebar team jewelled with talented interlopers. Nevin had no regrets. He had breathed the same air as the modern greats on the field at Croke Park. He had set a strange record by winning a provincial club medal against Dunmore McHales on a Saturday night and an Under-21 medal with

Mayo the following afternoon. As far as he knows, no player has won two Connacht medals in twenty-four hours since then.

By 1976, he and his wife, Carmel, had opened The Beaten Path hotel and entertainment centre on the road between Claremorris and Balla, not far from his childhood home. In 1979, they opened a nightclub. What The Beaten Path specialised in was escape. This was a stagnant time in Ireland, and on busy nights up to 2,000 young people came from all over the county. Buses were organised, but mostly they came in cars. The Beaten Path was designed to have different levels, with a dance area and a disco area and a plush penthouse floor. It was extravagant and different, and it worked. Throughout the first half of the 1980s, Nevin was struck and saddened by the number of farewell parties that were held there, drunken nights of forced gaiety for a young son or daughter who had decided to get out for good. From the beginning, it was demanding and successful and became the metropolis of nightclubs in south Mayo in the 1980s, a vast emporium of live bands and new-wave music located along a country road. Mayo football people were good customers, and Nevin sponsored the county team during a period when it wasn't necessarily fashionable to do so. In the photograph of the 1985 minor team in Croke Park, the lads with Big Country hair cuts and the selectors wearing skinny ties, John Prenty, the county secretary, is on his hunkers holding a leather bag bearing the name of The Beaten Path. The place offered something for everyone. The big ballroom acts all visited. Nanci Griffith was a favourite turn. A post-Diana Ross incarnation of the Supremes rolled in regularly. There were teary nights when Mayo folks listened to Don McLean singing 'Vincent' and the rousing finale of 'American Pie'. The tills were busy and the hours were late. Nights often tumbled into grey mornings. 'It became my life,' Nevin says with a shrug. 'We worked very hard at it, and, at that time, it was something. And it was like an industry, because a lot of young people we employed went on to make their careers in hotels, which was nice to see.'

By 1984, Nevin had bought Breaffy House with two business partners. As if that wasn't demanding enough, he found himself elected as president of the Vintners' Federation of Ireland at the turn of the decade. One sunny morning in 1992, he was driving to Dublin to meet Ray Burke, then the Minister for Justice. As usual, traffic was at a crawl in Enfield. Someone in the opposite lane lost patience and came thundering out of the other lane, trying to jump the line. Nevin saw the car speeding towards him but could do little other than grip the wheel and brace himself. He was in a big, sturdy Volvo 240 and the rogue car was a Fiesta. At first, there didn't appear to be much damage, but Nevin spent 150 days in hospital afterwards. The surgeon told him that the tautness of his body on impact had caused deep and complicated damage. He required spinal surgery and operations on his tendons and elbows. He was in deep pain. 'But from my neck up, I was perfect. And I drove everyone mad. I was looking for phones and faxes and trying to stay on top of the business, and I was a nightmare to deal with. Then I was put on this drug that did me more damage. I was in hospital in Galway one day and my girls, Niamh and Saoirse, came in and they just said, "Enough."'

It was the year 2000 by the time Nevin had recovered sufficiently to do a full day's work. Hotels worked differently by then. The world worked differently. He had to do a computer-training course before he could even check his guests in at reception. When he first came back, he was exhausted after an hour of answering the telephone. The business was sold and the hotel was expanded. In the last few years, the Breaffy has opened up a sports wing, and the elite GAA teams regularly visit for training weekends. It keeps Nevin involved in the game. And during the most wretched times of his lost decade, the sport was a great comfort. He watched Mayo on television, went to McHale Park with his son Michael when he had sufficient energy. Old teammates dropped in to say hello. Nevin was always the smallest of the Mayo backs, and when he got in a scrape, it was only ever a matter of seconds before John Morley or Ray Prendergast or Johnny Carey was over beside him, big strapping men. Those that were left stayed in touch and that mattered greatly. Occasionally, he would see Enda Colleran or Mattie McDonagh or others of that great Galway era at a match or among the flushed faces on Shop Street during the Christmas rush. 'You see and meet these men, and it may not even be spoken of, but you can associate them with a certain day, a particular match and a moment in that match. It comes flooding back to you. And you know. There is this look.'

Some of the brightest of that generation of footballers have already disappeared. These are fast and affluent days in the hotel business, but Nevin is happy to be working again and watching his health. After the upset and trauma of that insane moment in Enfield, his life is calm. Hundreds upon hundreds of guests visit Breaffy House and encounter Gay Nevin, the diminutive and polished facilitator of their every whim and need. Although he suffers back trouble still from that injury against Down, he has the light, fast step of a man accustomed to spending long days on his feet. And if you look beyond the crisp shirts, the polished shoes and the silver hair, it is in the walk that you can still detect the darting teenage hopeful locked away inside. But few of the guests ever learn of this past or imagine the general manager as a young man chasing and kicking under the deafening thunder of Croke Park voices. Gay Nevin never claimed to rank among the Mayo football players who stride across the western skyline impervious to death and to everything. He has never made any claims at all. But he moved through and belonged to a rich chapter of football in the west of Ireland, and he has the satisfaction of remembering that he shared a team with men like Corcoran and Morley, that he combated football players who seemed more like presences than mere men.

His mobile phone has been ringing throughout the morning, and Nevin delicately places his coffee cup upon its saucer and prepares himself to work through an interminable list of chores. The hotel life resembles football in so far as you never stand still. But as Gay Nevin stands up and replaces the garden chair, he offers a half-sad smile of acknowledgement when asked what it is that he is, beneath everything. 'Oh, in my heart, I am a footballer,' he says briskly, as though there could never be any debate. 'Oh, yeah. You are always a footballer.'

After any team in any sport breaks up, life pulls its participants in different directions. Joe Corcoran left football as abruptly as he had taken it up. He was always an unflinching critic of his own game, and once he felt his speed diminishing, he bowed out. 'You have to be wise,' he told himself. 'Time to get out when you see the young fellas passing you.'

He was an automatic selection for Mayo for fifteen seasons, apart for a few months in 1963 when he quit the county panel, hurt that he had been inexplicably overlooked for a tour of America. A number of teammates and county-board men paid visits to his house before he was persuaded to come back. As a teenager, Corcoran had excelled at golf. During his Mayo years, he scarcely swung a club, but twenty years later, he resumed his passion for golf and enjoyed Mayo football as a spectator. When Liam O'Neill, who used to mark him in the Galway–Mayo matches, took over the county team, Corcoran sometimes sat beside him on the bench. Even now, he occasionally pays a visit to the dressing-room and speaks highly of the present generation of Mayo players. It annoys him to hear people in the stands moaning and rubbishing their efforts. 'Unless you are out there, you don't know how much of a step up it is. No bad player gets to play ball for his county for very long. Sure, people do be talking and they don't know what they're saying.'

John Forde, the corner-back on the 1951 team, lived three doors down from him in Ardnaree, and they would meet regularly to talk about the game. Just last summer, he had the pleasure of meeting Pádraig Carney for the first time, in McHale Park. It was strange: they could so easily have played on the same team and known the same people, but their paths had never crossed. But then Corcoran was always a home bird. He is passionate about Ardnaree and is deeply fond of the young team that his son Joseph manages. And he enjoys hanging around and tutoring them. It keeps him young. 'This is a tough time for youngsters. I don't care how much money is going about or what they say. Every door around here used to be left open day and night. You couldn't do that now. But I would never leave Ardnaree. The auld street never dies.'

Mike Connaughton did not feel bereft when football was taken out of the equation. It never occurred to him to feel sorry for himself. Instead, he got involved with the Mayo Under-21 team. He was serious about it and independent minded, and the joy of helping the 1967 generation win an All-Ireland made him forget about what might have been for himself. But he could never fully come to terms with the machinations of the county board. During that season, the first-choice Mayo Under-21 full-back would have been Tom Cafferkey from Achill, who had been a strong force on the 1966 All-Ireland-winning minor team. Cafferkey fished for a living and wasn't able to make training regularly. Connaughton was asked to go out to Achill and have a word with him. It was agreed that Cafferkey would try to put an hour or two in himself. During one of the early matches, Connaughton saw Séamus Daly and Willie Casey and Father Leo in conference in the dressing-room. They had their own ideas about who should play full-back and Connaughton could not agree with them. 'That was the day I was finished as a popular man in the system. The following year, I missed a trial match, and a letter was sent with a motion to replace me.'

So he took up refereeing and established himself as fair and composed relatively quickly. He was related to Seán Fallon of Tuam through marriage, and one evening the pair of them were having a drink when Fallon said to him, 'You'll referee an All-Ireland final some day. But row in with the system.' Mike asked the older man what he meant. 'Don't ruffle feathers,' was the reply.

In 1971, he was chosen to referee the championship match between Galway and Roscommon. Shortly after the throw-in, there was an incident between Pat Lindsay and Jimmy Duggan, and the Galway man ended up on the ground. 'I should probably have sent Pat off, but I looked at Duggan and he was all right, so, because there was only five minutes gone, I let it go. At half-time, Roscommon were leading by about ten points and it looked like it was going to be a one-sided match.'

But in the second half, Galway gradually came back into contention, and among the spectators, the mood turned from anxiety to outright anger at the perception that Connaughton was favouring Galway in his decision-making. It was a drawn match at the final whistle, and almost immediately, dozens and then hundreds of supporters came onto the field in protest. In the bedlam, Connaughton was attacked. He remembers Seán Purcell of Galway running over to try to prevent it. Dr Donal Keenan, later president of the GAA, was shouting at people to stop. Connaughton was knocked to the ground and became genuinely fearful. John Morley was on duty as a guard that afternoon, and he forced his way through to Connaughton, and, with the help of other guards and some players, a circle was formed around the referee. They made their way to the narrow gate at the bottom of the field through a deeply hostile crowd. There was particular bitterness over a late free he had awarded; the Roscommon fans believed that the ball was still rolling when the Galway men took it. Connaughton is adamant that he whistled the match fairly and was shocked and frightened that afternoon. He took asylum in the Galway dressing-room and sat in there as the shouting went on and fists beat at the door.

A few days later, Eamonn Mongey wrote about the incident in the *Irish Press*. Connaughton wrote an unflinching report of what had happened for the Connacht Council, and there was a hearing. But nobody was ever suspended. And Connaughton never did referee an All-Ireland final. He felt lonely and let down by what had happened. But life kept moving on. Many decades later, he met Dr Keenan by chance in a hotel in Athlone on the way home from the 1996 All-Ireland final. The Roscommon man had actually secured tickets for mutual friends, and they sat down together. The poisonous day in 1970 was never spoken about, but Connaughton was glad they had met and had shaken hands.

It was only in later years, when the children had grown up and he had more time on his hands, that he began to feel the pangs of regret about the brevity of his own football life. 'When you are young and busy, you don't have time to wonder about it. It sometimes hits me now. I was just gone 21 and had always looked after myself. It just wasn't to be.'

That could be the epitaph for Mayo football in the 1960s.

# FIVE

# TED WEBB

Thirty years on, the name of Ted Webb still holds luminosity across Mayo.

It was not just that he was the most complete and forceful football player ever to emerge from his home town of Ballyhaunis or that he possessed a likeable sunny confidence. You can see it in the brimming energy evident in the black-and-white photograph of him accepting the inaugural trophy for Ballyhaunis Footballer of the Year in 1974, in the winsome smile and dark, glittering eyes, the touch of Travolta in the wavy brown locks and flamboyant collars. It wasn't just that Edward Webb's youngest boy seemed to be singled out and groomed for the manageable glories and acclaim that came with being the star turn of his day. Ballyhaunis is a parish that has always been conscious of its geographical place, flush against Roscommon and on the edge of the Mayo interior; having Ted Webb made it seem as though the bigger towns looked east in envy for once. But it wasn't simply that he was special. The thing was that Ted Webb lived his twenty-one years without ever becoming spoilt or aloof. He knew that his athleticism and the dark flashing looks gave him a distinct allure when it came to summer championship afternoons or the Sunday night dances in Ballinlough or Castlerea. But he handled it with grace and appreciation and somehow managed to make people feel as if they were part of his good fortune rather than harbour any misplaced envy towards him. And then, suddenly, in a bizarre accident on a humdrum Thursday night not a fortnight after Valentine's, Ted Webb was killed and the handsome, bustling butcher's boy with the naturally quick smile and the easy word was gone. In a low-wattage, decent town like Ballyhaunis, that sort of incandescence is not easily replaced. Or forgotten.

'Ted had it all,' sighs his brother Mike, one February evening as we sit in the family kitchen sorting through old newspaper clippings and photographs starring his younger brother. Mike Webb is in his early fifties now, a bustling and diminutive man who has maintained the family victualler's business, which dates back to his grandfather. Although Mike was a nimble and talented forward in his own right, he realised in his early teenage years that the game – of football and life – seemed to come that bit easier to his younger brother. Where Ted operated on charm, Mike tended to be feisty. While Mike was athletic in a slender, ordinary kind of way, Ted was, as he recalls, 'well over six feet tall and built like a bull'. Ted had presence. Mike remembers a moment from the day of the All-Ireland minor final in 1971, when Mayo beat Cork. Mike had been injured in the Connacht championship and was a substitute on that September day in Croke Park. Ted was just sixteen and had gone on what was a desperately exotic adventure that summer, across to London to work in the Shakespeare's Head, a pub on Carnaby Street owned by their aunt. He returned shortly before the final and was spotted in casual clothes as the team headed into the great stadium, all smiles and good wishes for his brother. 'I would give anything to have that fella in here with us today,' said Paddy Waldron, the county secretary, in a wistful voice.

Ted Webb's greatest national accomplishment was the goal he scored in Croke Park in the 1974 All-Ireland Under-21 final against Antrim. It actually mirrored a goal he produced from nothing in Mayo's win against Brian Mullins' Dublin team in the semi-final. But the strike in the Antrim replay stays vivid to those who witnessed it and was caught on film that lies lost and unlabelled in the RTÉ vaults at Montrose. It was one of those signature Mayo goals, presaging the thunderbolt that Pádraig Brogan would deliver some eleven years later in the Jones's Road cathedral. Racing onto a pass from Richie Bell, Webb came thundering through the Antrim defence towards the Hill 16 goal and let fly. 'From thirty yards out and at an angle, he cracked in a blistering shot,' enthused Terry Reilly in the *Western People* match report. 'It was one of his specials with plenty of backspin and it flashed in under the crossbar to send the supporters wild.'

Afterwards, Michael O'Hehir ambled down from his commentary box to the tumult of the Mayo dressing-room and, in that mellifluous voice, assured Edward Webb that his son had produced one of the best goals he had ever witnessed in Croke Park. That 1974 team was supposed to transform what was threatening to be a woebegone decade for Mayo senior football. For Ted Webb, it was supposed to be the beginning. 'He had tremendous faith in that team. He was quite clear that his ambition was to win an All-Ireland senior championship with Mayo. And he believed they could do it,' Mike says now.

Ted Webb was always serious about football. Once he'd finished school, he decided to cut loose and took up employment with Wicklow County Council; but after several months, he returned home one Friday night and gravely announced that he was ready to set down in Ballyhaunis and work in the family business. Edward Webb was privately delighted but somewhat dubious about the idea. The care that Ted took in his appearance was something of a family joke. He was meticulous about his clothes and liked to be well turned out. 'Do you think you'll mind getting a bit dirty the odd time?'

his father quizzed. Ted assured him he'd be fine and with that the deal was settled.

Working at home meant Ted could practise his football whenever he pleased. He kept eccentric hours, regularly coming in from work at ten at night and phoning to persuade his cousin, another Michael Webb, to come up to the pitch so he could blast his high-velocity swerving shots at him, often pointing the car headlights at the goalposts during winter sessions. One night, he borrowed his father's new white Peugeot 405 and drained the battery up at the field. Those solitary sessions did Mayo no harm: by the mid-1970s, Michael Webb had ascended to the position of first-choice county goalkeeper.

'I would have to say that if he had lived, Ted might have become one of the best number elevens in Ireland,' Mike declares. 'He had the speed and strength to knock people off. He had vision. He could give a ball left or right and he would put it into your chest. He was in motion all the time.'

Ted practised with Ballyhaunis and Mayo, and the days of shifting heavy cuts of meat enhanced his natural strength. He did not drink, which was convenient for his brother and their friends when it came to travelling to dances. One story that became fabled in the months and years after Ted's accident concerned a dance at Ballinlough. Mike had taken the car and was having a few drams, which was the common practice then. With the group was a friend, Mickey Keegan, whose lack of height meant that drink sometimes got the better of him. On this night, it was decided to let Mickey sleep off his fill in the back of the car. During a routine Garda patrol, one of the guards glanced into the car and was disturbed to see what appeared to be a child, fast asleep and abandoned. The guard headed into the dance and, after several frustrated enquiries, it was announced from the stage that the owner of the registration number in question should appear outside.

By this point, Mickey Keegan's pals had removed him from the back of the car and smuggled him to a safer destination. When the guard came back out, he was alarmed to return to what appeared to have developed into a missing child case. Ted Webb, there for the dancing but indifferent to the drink, assumed responsibility for the car. The guard insisted that there had been a child in the car. Ted was sympathetic but assured him that there had to have been an error. 'Were you drinking, Ted?' the guard finally asked, vexed. 'Guard, you must have been drinking yourself if you think there was a child in that car,' Ted replied angelically.

Mike Webb was bursting with laughter as he stood tipsy beside the car, and sitting now at the kitchen table thirty years later, he guffaws anew. For the most part, it does not pain him to talk about his brother. Mainly, he associates Ted with good memories. Mike was absent for that 1974 All-Ireland-final victory because he was in the midst of a personal feud with the county board. Three years earlier, he had been excluded from the medal ceremony even though he had been a part of that minor panel that won the All-Ireland championship. He was smarting after the slight, to the extent that two years later he declined an invitation to trials for the Under-21 team. After scoring 1–04 while being shadowed by Aughamore's highly reputed defender Adrian Durkin in a club match, he listened to the overtures from the Under-21 representatives, who promised a guaranteed corner-forward spot in the upcoming 1973 final against Kerry. Whether it would have materialised or not remains unknown. 'Get me my minor medal and I'll play,' Mike Webb said. He was asking the impossible. Mayo played without him and lost that match in Ennis to a team of young Kerry players who hardly knew that day that they were on the cusp of an extraordinary decade. It was a match Mayo controlled, leading all the way until the last ten minutes. Then, in the closing quarter, a burly forward named John Egan made ground, cantering along the right wing before delivering a perfectly weighted pass for Mike Sheehy to fist a goal past Stephen Langan. With Mayo shaken, the Kerry boys kicked a series of demoralising points and then Egan conjured another goal from close range, so that Mayo trailed by two clear goals, 2–13 to 0–13, when it ended. Mike Webb watched that game from the stands as Ted led the Mayo scoring with five points. He never really did resolve the dispute with the county board and thus passed on the chance to win an All-Ireland Under-21 medal with his brother when Mayo delivered in thrilling style a year later. 'Ah, sure, everyone has principles,' he shrugs. 'There is no regret. Mayo won it and I was happy for them. It was simple as that.' As far as he was concerned, there would be other years.

Ted was already an established player on the senior panel. He played at centre field in the 1975 championship and was devastated after the famous provincial-championship-final defeat to Sligo in a replay defined by the bulky wizardry of Mickey Kearins, the Sligo virtuoso who landed a Connacht championship medal after some eighteen years of trying. Ted Webb was dumbstruck by that loss, which brought to an abrupt halt the hair-raising adventures of the previous year. But it didn't matter. They were young. By the following year, Mike had been invited to join the Mayo senior squad and through the winter a bunch of them would drive over to Castlebar in a crowded car, young men who were kings of their domain, full of mischief and plans to turn around a miserable period for Mayo football.

'Ted always had great time for Mick Flynn, the groundsman in McHale Park, Lord have mercy on him now. Mick was a great character. The night that Billy Fitzpatrick came back into the Mayo panel after a long absence, Ted went up to Mick and put the arm around his shoulder. Billy Fitz must have been about the age of thirty then and everyone was delighted to see him back. And Ted said, "Sure, Mick, we'll head off now and come back here when we're thirty and we'll walk onto the Mayo panel." We were all laughing. And that was his last night. That was the night he was killed.'

The Webbs have thought about that night, 26 February 1976, thousands of times. As the years have passed, the smallest details have become magnified. The family business is located in the heart of Ballyhaunis, a classic Irish butcher's shop with sawdust on the floor, a carefully dressed presentation counter, cheerful lighting and whistling staff in white coats. Mike Webb's family still live in the handsome townhouse above the shop. The kitchen has always been the gathering point, with a pleasant range and busy mantelpiece and high ceilings. Above the table where Mike's sons, Eddie and Michael, are sitting finishing dinner hangs a striking photograph of Ted leaping to claim the ball in some stilled instant from the 1975 Connacht senior final. The boys were not yet born when their uncle died but they speak of Ted as though they know him and they can recall the hours before his death with almost the same clarity as can their father or Cait, their mother.

Like so many of these things, it happened mainly as a result of terrible luck. Ted and Mike had returned from Mayo training in Castlebar and were settling down for the evening. *Kojak* was on television and Ted was eating a bowl of Ambrosia Creamed Rice. Word came that their uncle, Pat Lyons, was in a pub across the road and needed a lift out to the home place in Scahard. Ted volunteered and left immediately. It was only a couple of miles from Ballyhaunis but the road to the house is dissected by the main Dublin–Westport railway line. Strict observance of the rules for crossing the line meant unlocking both gates, driving the car across and then getting out to relock the gates. But nobody really did that. All the Webbs and Lyons knew the scheduled train times by heart, and anyway Ted was simply going to drop his Uncle Pat at the door and hightail it back in the road. He may have left the gates unlocked so that he wouldn't have to get out of the car and reopen them on the return journey.

'Ted had this habit of flicking off his headlights when he was coming onto a main road, so he could be sure nothing was coming,' Mike says. 'And I can honestly say he must have done that on the night.' The family can only piece together the likely sequence of events. The lone certainty is that as Ted approached the crossing line on his way back home, an unscheduled goods train was moving remorselessly towards the west. Ted was driving the white Peugeot that night. He probably had the radio on. He probably snapped off the lights but because it was not a passenger train, there were no carriage lights to warn him, just two low headlights on the front of the engine, obscured by the grass banks. There was nothing to be seen other than the dark peace of the countryside. Ted moved on. The engine bulldozed the car 500 yards down the track before it could be halted.

The next morning, up in Ballaghaderreen, John O'Mahony woke up to hear on the eight o'clock news that a Mayo football player had been killed. He was shocked and frightened but remembers thinking, 'Well, it's definitely not Ted Webb,' because he had dropped the Webb boys to the front door of their house the previous evening. Then he learned that it had been Ted after all. He left his parents' house to try to teach in St Nathy's but lasted about ten minutes before he broke down in tears.

Mike Webb often dwells on that journey home from training that night, the Webb brothers with Johnno driving and Jimmy Browne chatting away. They came upon a sharp bend somewhere and for an instant it felt as though they were going to skid into an open field, but Johnno managed to correct the car and they motored onwards, full of nervous laughter and banter, kidding O'Mahony about his driving. In

the months and years afterwards, Mike Webb found himself
wishing they had sailed into that heather and scrub grass,
because they would surely have been fine, except for a few
bruises. And that would have meant time would have been
altered. Ted would have driven his uncle home much later and
would have missed that infernal, malevolent train, cloaked by
night. The sequence of events would have been changed and
therefore rendered harmless.

'Those are the kind of little things you wonder about,' Cait
says. 'What if he had finished the dessert he was having? Those
few seconds could have made a difference.'

Mike cannot recall much of the immediate hours and days
following the accident but he does remember walking up
through Ballyhaunis behind the hearse and spotting Cait,
although the street was thick with mourners. 'That girl was a
girlfriend of Ted's,' he told his father. Cait had gone out with
Ted for some months the previous year and knew the family.
She takes the photograph of the 1975 final down from the wall
and points to the blurred background image of a blonde girl in
large sunglasses seated near the front of the crowd. 'That's me.
I was looking at this shortly after Mike and I got married and
there I was.' She picks out a young man further along in the
crowd, with unruly brown hair, intently concentrating on the
aerial contest for the football, the players soaring through the
open sky. 'And that is Mike in the crowd as well. We weren't
together then but I always thought it odd that we should be in
the photograph. They all thought it amusing in this house.'

She continues, 'It was the year after Ted died that I met up
with Mike. And I suppose all our initial conversations would
have been about Ted. But I am glad that I knew him because
he was a lovely fella and he had a good way about him. And it
was important because I heard so much about him, coming to
live here for the last thirty years. If I never knew Ted, I would
have always wondered how Mike and the others were never

jealous. Mike was a great footballer too but he was five foot seven and he hadn't the diplomacy that Ted had. Like, Ted was a bit of a charmer. He was only twenty-one and yet he made such an impact on everybody and made such an impression on people that to this day he is talked about. People talk about him in a way that means his personality never really left. Just at the weekend, I was up the street visiting with Mike's sister Helen. And an old school friend of hers called in. This woman left Ballyhaunis long ago but Ted came up in conversation. And she was recalling how, when she was at school, all the girls would just be praying that this footballer would even say hello to them. And how on the night of the removal, she took a flower from one of the wreaths and pressed it into a diary. She said she still has the diary.'

In the immediate aftermath, there was the consolation of the association. The GAA president, Dr Donal Keenan, headed a distinguished list of officials. A special float, draped in the Ballyhaunis colours, was constructed to hold the floral tributes that began to arrive at the Webb household from Friday morning. Ted Webb's casket was draped in the green-and-red Mayo flag. The removal took place on Saturday night and the main street in the town was dimmed and silent while the cortège moved up towards the church. That night went late and in the houses and the pubs Ted Webb – not for the first time – was the talk of the town. They remembered his best matches, and which was his finest hour was open to debate.

In a tribute that appeared in the *Western People* the following week, Ivan Neill wrote:

> In match reporting throughout the county, I had watched this young Ballyhaunis player in practically all major club and championship games and have many memories of his fine performances. But one performance which will always hold strong memories for me was in a senior championship game against Kiltane last season. On that very warm

Sunday Ted Webb was the inspiration of his side's great victory when he kicked over four frees in succession from distances ranging between fifty and sixty yards. That's a feat I had not seen accomplished before nor since.

Official estimates were that 4,000 people were present for the Monday morning funeral, but it felt like many, many more. The Reverend Father John Lyons, an uncle of Ted's from Youngstown, Ohio, was the principal celebrant of the funeral. The Mayo football team and the club boys formed a guard of honour. It was all very quiet and poignant and hard to reconcile with reality. After all, he had just been dropping his uncle out the road. And then it was over.

'My mother died the night Ted was killed,' Mike says suddenly. 'She never really recovered from it. It was desperately hard on the family and there was probably a bit of bitterness at first because Uncle Pat had told Ted to hold on until he finished his pint before they left. And Ted probably wanted to get back for the end of *Kojak*. I felt there should be no blame attached. My poor uncle was devastated too. He actually passed away himself a couple of years later through complications in a surgical procedure. And that was what he wanted, to be honest. The poor man didn't want to live. It was a terrible burden. And my parents were heartbroken. In a way, I didn't really absorb what had happened for a while because I felt someone had to stay strong. I do remember playing a challenge match for Mayo against Clare a couple of weeks afterwards. And that was tough. Being in that dressing-room was tough. But it was the best thing that I could have done.'

To the disbelief of all the Webbs, the weeks and months kept changing. Summer bloomed even though Ted was gone. Everyday life responded to the rhythms of work and Gaelic football. Surprisingly, Ted had shown a real aptitude for the family trade and had caught the eye of the distinguished cattlemen Peter and Larry Goodman at a mart in Dundalk, where they observed him shrewdly following the animals he had sold up the line as they were killed to see how much money they were making. They spoke to Edward Webb about taking him on. Larry Goodman turned up at the funeral, and a few months later he told Edward, 'He was a big loss to us as well.'

Letters and seraphic cards and Mass cards continued to arrive. All those small consolations amounted to a considerable comfort. One night, the doorbell rang and Paddy Waldron came in with a proposition. He wondered if the Webbs might consider donating a cup for the new Under-16 Connacht championship. It became the Ted Webb Cup. Edward Webb was thrilled with that.

Mike and Cait married; the kids were born. Mike continued to kick ball with Ballyhaunis and Mayo. The club lost four Mayo senior semi-finals by a point during Mike's career. On the day his daughter Elaine was born, he kicked 1–07 out of 1–10 on a misty, heavy day, but he still winces at a particular point that went astray during that semi-final. 'Of course, I was castigated for that one. That was the one people remember,' he laughs now.

Every third Sunday in September, Edward Webb would sit down and watch the autumn rivalry between the gilded Kerry footballers and the charismatic Dublin boys, names against whom his son had once sparred. Any aspirations of Mayo winning an All-Ireland title seemed to have departed with Ted. The county was in the doldrums. In idle conversation, they wondered at the difference Ted would have made. The 1980s arrived. Edward Webb was not ordinarily a betting man but when Mayo made it to the 1989 All-Ireland final, he placed a wager of £100. He died a week before the match was played. Strangely, his wife died a week before the 1996 All-Ireland final between Mayo and Meath. At least by then they had the consolation of knowing their son's name was perpetuated in the Under-16 championship and of seeing glimpses of Ted in the two boys, Michael and Eddie.

'We were kind of educated on stories about Ted,' Eddie jokes. When he was a boy, Eddie liked tramping the damp fields with his grandfather and hearing stories about this invisible uncle who was a mythical figure on the football fields of Mayo. The episode his grandfather was most fond of telling involved Brian Mullins, the long-haired Dublin midfield player who became the totemic figure on Kevin Heffernan's great metropolitan team. 'Grandad took particular pride because, apparently, Uncle Ted buckled Brian Mullins in some match,' Eddie laughs. They believe it might have been the Under-21 All-Ireland semi-final of 1975 – Mike has a distinct memory of Ted showing up for a seven-a-side tournament in Kiltimagh and provoking some booing from spectators because the county team had lost the Under-21 match earlier in the day. But in any event, the game didn't really matter, nor did the incident. It was the fact that Ted Webb had, however temporarily, grounded one of the most accomplished midfielders of his generation that was of significance. Like the brave, thrilling goal in Croke Park, it served as an exciting and comprehensible testament to the achievements of his short life. For Eddie and Michael, who heard these stories through the unfiltered imaginations of young boys, their uncle seemed like an impossibly fortunate and enviable character. He was there all about them, his name constantly on the lips of their aunts and his pictures in old newspapers and his feats shining in the trophies that sat on the dresser. It was just that he never showed up at dinner time.

Eddie recalls getting frustrated and upset as a youngster because he believed that being named after his uncle would bestow supernova football powers upon him. He was a skilful, tidy young player but easy-going by nature. Although he followed his uncle to boarding school in the Carmelite College in Moate, it was only in his senior year that he realised that hard, diligent work was part of the deal. He made a glittering senior squad containing a group of Westmeath youngsters who would go on to claim All-Ireland minor medals. 'Grandad was mad into high catching. In this house, you weren't a footballer unless you could catch a ball overhead. So he came up to Moate to see me playing and I think he was crying afterwards. Because I caught a ball.'

Michael, though, was a leaper. From when he was a toddler, it seemed as if Michael was the reincarnation of Ted. As a teenager, he was long and rangy and turned on the melting smile to skip out of trouble, and he had irrepressible potential as a football player. It was just a matter of his coordination catching up with his athleticism and while he missed out on the Mayo selection for the Ted Webb Cup, he had come to prominence by his minor year. Closure of the boarding school at Moate meant that he opted for St Jarlath's College in Tuam. At the boys' grandmother's funeral, Father Cremin gave Michael the same advice as he had given Ted years before at the Carmelite College. Measure your run before you jump for the ball, he told him. Improve your weak foot by kicking at a tyre. It was all practical, valuable advice. In the All-Ireland Colleges final of 1999, Michael excelled for St Jarlath's, kicking two points from wing-back as they fell by 1–11 to 1–07 to Good Counsel of Wexford. He became an established player on the Mayo minor and Under-21 teams, and when John Maughan returned as Mayo manager in the autumn of 2003, he was keen to groom the latest Webb from Ballyhaunis for the new squad.

Then, with unthinkable cruelty, bad luck descended on the Webb family again. Michael attended just one senior Mayo training session before he pulled a hamstring; after he had successfully recuperated from that, his knee caved in, denying him a summer of football. The injured knee was only the beginning. Michael Webb grins widely as he catalogues the misery of the following years. What began as vague stomach pains quickly escalated, requiring a series of tests and then surgery. When Michael was rehabilitating, John Maughan called him regularly, encouraging him to use the gym at Breaffy House whenever he felt like it, making him feel part of things, talking up his prospects. He promised Michael he would be back better than ever. The medical staff thought differently and when Michael fell ill again, he was told he would need a more serious operation, one that would involve the removal of a part of his stomach – and end his football career. By this time, he was a student in Galway and his life was almost completely sports oriented. He shared a house with a hurler from Clare and Gavin Duffy, the Mayo footballer who would go on to make it as a professional rugby player with Connacht, Harlequins and Ireland. When Michael thinks back to those days, he realises they were all borderline obsessed with sport. But his illness required immediate attention. He was gowned and headed for theatre before he had time to brood on a life without football.

Almost inevitably, his erstwhile Mayo colleagues were in Croke Park to play Armagh in the league semi-final on the weekend when Michael was convalescing and adjusting to this new reality. On that Sunday morning, he was reading newspaper previews of the match when, out of the blue, John Maughan materialised, tanned and good humoured and saying all the right things. He came carrying a card bearing the signatures of the entire Mayo panel and he sat down with the Ballyhaunis lad for half an hour. It wasn't as though Webb had yet blossomed into Maughan's key player. Webb was promising but he was only starting out. A simple phone call from Maughan would have sufficed. Maybe it was a schools thing (Maughan is a Carmelite College old boy). But on a Sunday when Mayo were involved in a league semi-final, John Maughan made time to come and visit a youngster who was hurting. And although none of the Webbs can remember the score of that match, they will never forget the simplicity and the class of John Maughan's gesture. They will never forget the pure good manners of it.

Even then, Ted's presence was about them. Mike and Cait sat with their son day after day in St James's Hospital, and one afternoon in the café, they noticed Michael O'Muircheartaigh alone at a table. Mike, never prone to shyness, went over for a chat. The great radioman's eyes lit up when he heard the name. He remembered seeing Ted Webb play. He could picture him. They could hardly bring themselves to explain that another Webb had been robbed of what might have been a fine and rewarding sporting career with Mayo.

In his prime, Michael Webb was fourteen stone of lean muscle. Sitting at the dinner table now, his face looks much the same but the frame is skinnier. Cait produces another photograph of Michael, wearing the St Jarlath's shirt and claiming a ball, knees up and face set in concentration, brimming with strength and confidence. 'It is uncanny the similarities, you know, between Michael and Ted and the fact that his football career was cut short,' she says, looking fondly across the table at her son. Michael, though, is utterly unsentimental about what might have been, shrugging it away through black jokes at his own expense. He quips that he might be able to line out as corner-forward for Mayo in a few years time. When he was getting well again in Ballyhaunis, he started coaching local children. It never even occurred to him to walk away from the game.

At the very least, he had maintained an exalted family tradition. Edward Webb and his brother Joe had both played minor for the county. An uncle of Ted and Mike's named Joe Regan, from Ballaghaderreen, had played for Mayo in the disputed All-Ireland championship of 1925, which was awarded to Galway. Then came Ted and Mike. Michael continued that pattern. 'There were blood lines there,' says Mike.

In Ballyhaunis, they still hold functions to honour Ted's

memory. They held a golf classic at the beginning of 2007, won by a Meath man named Brendan Murphy who had marked Ted in a league match shortly before the accident. In early February, Michael O'Muircheartaigh was the guest of honour at a function to honour Johnny Biesty, one of those towering figures in the local GAA. Michael introduced the pair of them and, later, O'Muircheartaigh commented on the similarities between this engaging young man and his long departed uncle. What Michael finds most strange now when he thinks about Ted is that he has become the older relation: 'Like, I am twenty-five now. Ted was just twenty-one when he died. He had another two lifetimes ahead of him,' he marvels.

Cait offers more tea and we talk of Ballyhaunis for a while. The place has not changed greatly in the decades since Ted Webb died, although since the main Sligo-to-Galway road was bypassed, it has lost a little of its vitality. For people accustomed to driving that route in the 1970s and '80s, arriving in Ballyhaunis now is disconcerting. For regular motorists on the N17, the town always seemed like a landmark in the journey south, with its ambling main street and the sharply winding road under the stone railway bridge at the bottom of the town. Seeing that bridge again is like being transported back in time, although the townscape has been altered in other ways. The Central Hotel, the heartbeat of Friday night socialising a couple of decades back, has become a fast-food restaurant. The Manor House Hotel has also vanished. Gribben's butcher shop, just three doors up from the Webb's premises and an institution in the town, as well as being the home place of the long-serving county footballers Father J.J. Gribben and Tony Gribben, is now closed. It went up for sale late last year and on the night I visited, the windows were whitewashed, a swirling pattern left by the brush; a pale statue of Our Lady loomed from an upstairs window and the green-and-red flag of Mayo was wrapped around a flagpole.

'Ballyhaunis was a great town,' Mike says passionately, 'but we were hurt by the bypass and not getting tax-designation status. This town has gone down a lot but I think it will come back again. Even in the football, we are intermediate now. But we won't give in.'

As we say goodbye, Mike presents the family scrapbook dedicated to Ted, its brown-leather binding crammed with photographs and those precious yellowed newspaper clippings. Cait puts it in a carrier bag for safekeeping. 'You wonder why things happen,' she says absently. 'Like I said, I knew Ted and then Mike. And we have our family now. Sometimes you wonder why he was the one to die and why we met up and lived on and were lucky enough to have four wonderful children. Of course you think about that. Ted's girlfriend at the time, Mary, ended up marrying a surgeon. And when they are visiting here from their home in Kuwait in the summer, they go up to the church and Mary would say a prayer for Ted at the grave. And she would always have called in to say hello to Ted's parents when they were alive. He touched people in that way. He was never going to be forgotten about.'

By eight o'clock, the main street is quiet and the pubs are doing brisk business. Images from the big European soccer match between Liverpool and Barcelona flicker through the pub windows and look attractive from the street, full of bright, compelling scenes of contemporary sporting glamour. Ted Webb was a George Best fan. He idolised the Belfast Boy and maybe, in a naive way, modelled himself upon him. Best had yet to quit Manchester United when Ted Webb died. Driving down past The Oak Bar and across the stone bridge and past the stately Ulster Bank, past Delaney's bar and Cunningham's shop and then around the bad bend under the bridge, it is easy to imagine how deeply Ted Webb must have loved this town, the source of all his triumphs and his cares. Ballyhaunis was his kingdom. It is yet.

# Six

# The Big Nothing

During the Christmas holidays of 1979, John P. Kean opened the *Western People* newspaper. In the usual way of Mayo newspapers, there was a comprehensive sports review of the decade, and Kean had to smile in resignation when he discovered himself in the centrepiece photograph. The transfixing image was of his goal chance against Sligo towards the conclusion of the drawn 1975 Connacht final. The Claremorris forward had been in full command of a considerable array of tricks that day, a consummate ball player who was supposed to epitomise a new brigade of Mayo footballers. And this moment of the game, now frozen on negative, had been an opportunity to alter history. That was undeniable. Kean was clean through and only Tom Cummins, the Sligo goalkeeper, stood in his path. The forward had already proved his ability to perform under pressure, and as he struck a hard, clean shot, he had no reason to suppose it wouldn't finish in the net. Instead, it struck the crossbar. Sligo survived and the replay would, of course, transpire to be Mayo's blackest hour. To sum up an empty decade for Mayo football, the newspaper had fished out this goal that never was. It was the quintessential Mayo allusion: wistful, agonising, vaguely recriminatory and haunted.

'I felt that I hit it perfectly,' Kean smiles, some thirty years on. 'Three inches below, and it was the perfect goal. But, of course, that was the only decade that Mayo did not win a provincial title, and I suppose a lot of the blame for that lay on my shoulders.'

These days, John P. Kean has a solicitors' firm with offices in his home town of Claremorris and in Tuam. He has a placid, likeable manner and wears a neat greying beard and a well-cut suit; beyond the professional attire, though, he has changed little from the wraithlike, busy young forward who enjoyed a sensational underage career. The good days came early for Kean, and had fate been different, had he boxed a little more shrewdly, he could well have become a powerful operator within the superstructure of Mayo football. But although Kean is gently spoken and polite, he has the soul of an agitator and a steadfast view of what he believes to be the rights and wrongs of Mayo football. His opinions have been shaped by his experiences as a county player and later as Mayo minor manager, and he has never been afraid to express them publicly. They have made him, to some extent, an outsider.

When we meet one afternoon in a café in Tuam, Kean hardly touches his coffee as he speaks about the way Mayo football has woven itself into his life. It made him as a young person and nearly broke him afterwards, and now, as a middle-aged man, he knows it preoccupies his thoughts much too frequently. 'My belief is that Mayo people and Mayo football teams have the potential to be as successful as those of any other county,' he explains. 'There is no innate negativity. With any Mayo minor team I took charge of, I believed we were going to win the All-Ireland. I love Mayo football. I had some wonderful times and I had some bad times. I think I am generally a level-headed person, but with football, it is all consuming. I do dwell a lot on the wrongs in Mayo football. I have been involved with the game here for thirty-five years, and it bothers me that Mayo has not won a senior All-Ireland in over fifty years. That bothers me. I don't think it should be the case. And I think it is very explicable.'

Kean was an elemental member of the 1974 Mayo Under-21 team that won an All-Ireland title. He had versatility, the nerve of a dependable free-taker and the stylist's appreciation of the big occasion. Although nominally a number eleven, he was selected at midfield for the All-Ireland semi-final against Dublin and matched up against Brian Mullins, a duel he now describes as 'a privilege' (a privilege that he marked by scoring four points). In the drawn final against Antrim, he clipped four points, and in the replay he fell into a groove, striking six of eight points from play. Even that moment of triumph was darkened by ambivalent feelings that Kean had towards an element within Mayo county. In the dressing-room afterwards, he told the mentor, John Kelly, that he wasn't going to travel home on the bus. He had already been seduced by the sensation of being feted as a champion on the Mayo minor team he had captained to the 1971 All-Ireland. He knew what it was to walk through Claremorris and have youngsters looking at him worshipfully.

Austin Garvin, the phenomenal Claremorris trainer who helped make Mayo a powerhouse in minor football, had nurtured Kean. Garvin had the eye. J.P. was slight as a boy, and at national school he was usually the last to be picked in casual games or for local matches. But he worked diligently on the fundamentals, and by the time he reached the age of fifteen, the speed and wiry strength and flair appeared in abundance. Garvin had quietly assembled a young team for whom the 1970s ought to have been a walk along the red carpet: Séamus Reilly from Lacken was at full-back; John O'Mahony was in the right corner; his Ballaghaderreen clubmate Connie Moynihan was number six and they had supreme forward talent in the Claremorris trinity of Mick Maloney, Michael 'Tick' Higgins and Kean. They could afford to shoot thirteen wides against a Tyrone team featuring the renowned Frank McGuigan and still they won the match. Cork were regarded as the sure thing in the final, but Mayo just overwhelmed them with the green-and-red panache game. They simply clicked, running up a score of 2–15. Kean raised the Tom Markham Cup and came back to his home county lauded. 'You would have felt like a little god in your own local environment – boys looking at you as though you could walk on water.'

Just three years later, that had changed. Mayo put on another champagne show in Croke Park, and the Under-21-final victory was crimson streaked with Ted Webb's comet of a goal. Many of Kean's 1971 minor teammates featured in this victory also, and there was no reason not to think that they had it all ahead of them as seniors. But now, the thought of going home to the cheering and back clapping bothered Kean. He had received plenty of the opposite in the previous few years. With his precocious reputation came the early knocks. Like many young players of that generation, Kean was pushed through to the senior ranks early, playing his first match in 1972. The following July, he played at centre field with John Morley and felt like a spectator as the towering Ballaghaderreen man almost rescued a failing Mayo effort on his own. Because he was involved with the Mayo seniors and studying law at UCD and training the Claremorris team, he hadn't been showing up for Under-21 training. The Tuesday after that senior game, Kean was announced as tenth substitute on the Under-21 team. He found out about it in the newspaper. Stung, he didn't attend the game. He refused to play with the Under-21 team for the remainder of the campaign, and, spurred on by a sense of injustice, he turned in the best performances of his life for Claremorris. The Under-21 team made it to an All-Ireland semi-final, and one of the selectors, Christy O'Hehir, visited Kean to see if the differences couldn't be ironed out. But Kean was still seething. He felt badly treated. He told Christy: 'As long as my arse is looking down, I won't be playing for Mayo this year.'

Some saw it as pique, others as principle. It was enough to earn J.P. a reputation. After that, he began to hear the criticism from over the wire. It was the usual stuff: that he was grand with the club but couldn't get it done for Mayo. Perhaps he was too sensitive. But he was twenty years old and looking for guidance. At UCD, he fell under the spell of Eugene McGee. At an early training session, the Longford man scrutinised Kean, lightly bearded and slightly scruffy, all feints and shimmies, and he grunted just loud enough for the new boy to hear, 'Typical f***en Mayo footballer.'

'I knew what he meant: probably a very stylish player who doesn't put himself about in the physical sense,' Kean laughs now. 'A purist. A fancy Dan. The thing is, I think plenty of hard men have played for Mayo down the years. But there is a culture of playing the game clean. Why that should be is a mystery to me, but that is how I played it. And growing up with the Mayo minors, we liked to turn on the style when we could. I suppose that is what McGee was alluding to.'

However, this was simply McGee's opening gambit. Kean studied in UCD from 1970 to 1978, long enough to become footballer-in-residence on the greatest college team, gaining two All-Ireland club medals, five Sigerson Cup finals and an iron-clad conviction that McGee was one of the finest football coaches in the history of the association. McGee had an intuitive understanding of what each of his players needed, and before those big Sigerson matches, he quietly told Kean that he was worth his weight in gold, because he knew the Mayo man was not the most naturally ebullient.

By the late '70s, Kean was becoming disillusioned with Mayo football. After he was honoured with the Mayo Footballer of the Year award following the triumph of 1974, an unsigned letter was posted to his parents' house claiming that the decision to select their son was a joke and a disgrace. It did not help that the football lives of so many of that team turned so sour so fast. Rushed through to the senior ranks, many of them played quite well in the first six league games of the 1974–75 season before they met Meath in the semi-final and were crushed in Croke Park. The final score was 4–06 to 0–08, and in his match report Terry Reilly's opening paragraph captured the sense of panic and disillusionment at this abrupt conclusion:

> Well, it happened and the moment we dreaded most struck with such impact at Croke Park on Sunday that Mayo's youngsters were turned inside out in unbelievable fashion by forceful Meath in the semi-final of the National Football League. For the first time in the competition, Mayo were really tested and found alarmingly wanting in so many quarters: so much so in fact that spectators were leaving their seats and heading for the exits ten minutes before the final whistle.

The demoralisation was made complete by Sligo later that summer. The following winter, Ted Webb was killed. 'Ted Webb was supposed to be a key figure,' says Kean. 'He was a fantastic athlete. He could turn himself to anything, he was a fielder and a scorer. He had it. And he was a charismatic, confident, warm kind of guy. There were a lot of games that Mayo lost by a point or two in the 1970s that Ted Webb would have turned around for us. I am convinced of that.'

Some of Kean's Under-21 friends, most notably Connie Moynihan and O'Mahony, were, as the euphemism goes, 'retired early' during the increasing desperation of those years. Kean played senior for the county until 1983, but by the late '70s, the joy had gone out of it. The sense of anticipation he had known as a youngster had just vanished, and with the gloom of defeat came the caustic throwaway remarks. Kean often bore the brunt of those.

'Because I had been a high-profile young fella and – I know a lot of people will disagree with this – because I was a professional in a professional job,' he says bluntly when asked why he was singled out. 'I guess I was the Liam McHale of my squad. I remember in 1983 when Liam O'Neill contacted me about playing for another few seasons, he said, "I have only one question for you: will you be able to cope with the vilification you are going to hear from Mayo supporters?" So I don't think I was imagining it.'

A few years after he had finished up playing, Kean invited the Meath forward Colm O'Rourke down to Claremorris for a presentation evening. The pair had played together at UCD and remained friends. O'Rourke had known several downtrodden seasons with Meath but had then enjoyed a spectacular autumn to his career, and by the late 1980s his reputation was gold-plated. After the medals were handed out, the college friends went to a bar to catch up and reminisce over old times. During the evening, football people came over to shake O'Rourke's hand, and eventually one man began noisily to destroy the reputation of a young Mayo player of the era who was beginning to show promise. 'He'll go nowhere,' the man told the bemused O'Rourke. 'F***en yellow.' Kean had heard enough and began to argue on behalf of the footballer in question. 'Sure, what would you know, Kean?' came the spat reply. 'You were f***en yellow yourself.'

'How many All-Ireland medals do you have?' Kean asked the man. 'Because I have four.'

O'Rourke smiled uncomfortably and tried to make light of the situation; he was probably thinking that they did not know how good they had it in Meath.

Martin Carney could not have picked a stonier decade to decide to convert to playing for Mayo. For many years now, the Castlebar teacher has been one of the voices of summer, providing television analysis and commentary throughout the championship months. He is so strongly affiliated with Mayo that the long and superb career he had with his native Donegal is often forgotten. In a sense, Carney has always been spiritually divided between those counties, and, wearing both jerseys, he kicked county ball for almost twenty years. That thought seems phenomenal now.

Carney was raised in Ballyshannon, the sloping fort town in the extreme south of Donegal. His father, Owen, was something of a wanderer, his trade as an electrician allowing him to work in Limerick, then in the Harland and Wolff shipyards in Belfast and then on RAF runways in County Fermanagh, which were used during the night flights over the North Atlantic at the start of the Second World War. He headed west to Ballyshannon in the early 1940s, when the state was undertaking a hugely ambitious project to transform the town, building a hydroelectric power station and dam on the sprawling River Erne. Owen Carney had been born in Lahardane, outside Ballina, and although he found time to play football with both Limerick (with whom he won a Munster junior medal in 1939) and Donegal, County Mayo was the sole possessor of his emotions. His brother Jackie – Martin's uncle – had played on the original Mayo championship team of 1936 and was a trainer with the 1950 team. Dermot, another brother, took the boat to England, signed up for service during the Second World War and was shot dead in a skirmish at El Alamein in February of 1943. Owen won a Railway Cup medal with Ulster the same year. As Martin Carney learned of those stories growing up, he was struck by the random ways in which the lives of his father and his brothers split. 'Different times,' he muses on the afternoon when we met.

And they were. Although Ballyshannon would have the stuffing knocked out of it economically in later decades, it had a veneer of grandeur when Carney was young, and he remembers it as a blissful town in which to grow up. His parents eventually settled on the Rock, a long residential street overlooking the Erne, in an imposing townhouse that once belonged to the local landlord and dated back to 1837. Even as a kid, Carney was astonished by the simple fact of standing before a lit fireplace that ancient. He went to school in De La Salle College – 'the Brothers' – an echoing hardwood building that had been a fever hospital before becoming a place of unsentimental schooling with a strong emphasis on Gaelic football. The Brothers was a few minutes' walk from Carney's house at the top of the Rock. From his front door he could see the Green, a grassy rectangle above the Erne, and the Allingham Bridge, which divided the town, with the commercial diamond of shops and hotels located on the far side. The Carneys reared their children to pay attention in school and to better themselves, but there was always time for football. Sometimes, Martin used to look at his father's medals; he still reckons the craftsmanship of that 1939 junior medal was as fine as he has seen. As a teenager, he was acutely conscious of having a Mayo heritage, and he had a vivid knowledge of the characters who starred in Mayo football in the 1930s.

His emergence as a young footballer, light and fast and exciting, coincided with a vibrant period for the game in the locality. In the 1950s and '60s, there was an exceptional group of football men in Ballyshannon and Bundoran, and although the rivalry between the towns was keen, they amalgamated to form a club called St Joseph's. Brian McEniff, ever ambitious for Donegal football, was at the heart of the union. Pauric McShea, Michael McLoone, Seamie Granaghan and Brendan McHugh would all go on to represent the county with distinction. Carney was still a schoolboy when he caught their eye and was eighteen years old when he began playing for

Donegal. In 1967, St Joseph's won a county championship. A year later, they won what was an unofficial club All-Ireland title, beating the celebrated Dunmore McHales, which featured the Donnellan dynasty.

'St Joseph's was strange,' Carney says now. 'It was a team rather than a club. We won six county championships while I was playing with them, and we never really celebrated any of them. I suppose not a lot of fellas were drinking then to begin with. But it was a marriage of convenience. We were never friends. Now, I believe there was a good night after we beat Dunmore, but I have no idea where because I had school the next morning. That would have been an exception. St Joseph's met up, won games and then everyone went their separate ways. But it lifted the boat in Donegal football. Before St Joseph's, we never had any idea where we stood in the wider hierarchy. I think it was the experience of St Joseph's that gave Donegal the ambition to go on and win our first Ulster title in 1972.'

Carney played for Donegal from 1970 until 1979. He led the nomadic student lifestyle for the first half of that decade, wintering in Galway and reappearing in Ballyshannon in early May, when the football was beginning to get serious. He spent a couple of summers in New York and was eager for more travel. In 1975, his head was filled with exciting talk of boys from up the county earning a fortune by laying pipes out in Alaska. They would work for three weeks and then fly down to Hawaii for a week of luxury. Then, that summer, his father had a heart attack, and that was that. As the eldest, he needed to be responsible. Martin went searching for a teaching post and applied for a vacancy in Castlebar. After Martin in the Carney family came Conor, Dermot, Michael and Mary. In later years, the children were told that there had been another sibling, Barry, the first child, who had passed away at birth.

'One of the saddest things we ever did was going around

the graveyard in Bundoran trying to find out where Barry was buried. And we couldn't. And for a man and woman whose entire lives revolved around church and prayer and devotion to faith, that was an awful blow to them. I suppose Daddy was more questioning than Mammy was. It wasn't something he spoke about much, but we knew it was something that was always there. And when Dad got sick, that was the end of any thoughts of my gallivanting. That was just the way we were brought up. My working in Mayo was only ever meant to be a temporary thing. But I suppose a lot of people say that about the way their lives go. And when it became clear that I was going to be staying here and was thinking about playing for Mayo, Dad gave me his blessing.'

It was not a decision that he made lightly. Carney was probably fortunate that Brian McEniff was in the midst of one of his blue periods, having been sacked as Donegal manager by the county board, and too distracted and busy and morose to pay close attention to Carney's movements. 'I think it was only when Brian became manager again that he realised I had gone. And he haunted me then. I remember around 1983 I was almost afraid to answer the phone, because I knew it would be Brian.' Others had tried to dissuade him. Pauric McShea met him and advised him to stay with Donegal. McShea felt that the county needed him. The move to Mayo was by no means an uncontroversial decision. Carney had won two Ulster medals with his native county and toured with the All-Stars in 1976. He was a classy, clever forward and, crucially, a free-taker. His departure would be a big blow. Had he heard more dissenting voices, Carney might have abandoned the idea of following in the path of his uncle. Then again, he liked Mayo; he felt like he knew and understood the county. And it wasn't as if he was bolting to a better football team.

'It was difficult. I felt very self-conscious when I made the decision. I felt I had forsaken the county of my birth. But the likelihood was that I would be living in Mayo for a long time, and my instincts were right. I felt in a way that I was betraying Donegal for a while. But this was where my future was, and I had that tangible link through my father's people, so that eased the burden. We were in the doldrums when I started, and I was just as bad as everyone else.'

But his arrival worked like a charm. Carney played championship for Mayo in 1979, and two years later he was captain when the county won the Connacht title for the first time in eleven seasons. By then, Mayo people were so relieved to have something to shout about that they wouldn't have cared if Carney had come from Mars, or even Roscommon.

You would not have wanted to buy a lottery ticket from Billy Fitzpatrick in those times. Fitzpatrick missed out on the 1981 triumph, on a provincial medal that was cherished by the men lucky enough to be wearing the green and red that day. Few footballers have received such cavalier treatment within their county as he did. He was a dashing young forward from Garrymore, with a devastating sprint and natural scoring confidence. He came from one of those devout Mayo football households. The Fitzpatricks lived in a big cottage with a thatched roof, and the stone fireplace was painted both red and green, bearing the legend '1950' on one side and '1951' on the other. When Seán Flanagan visited the town as TD, he held his clinics in the Fitzpatrick home. Billy would pray for a flicker of interest from the great Ballaghaderreen man, a casual enquiry about his football.

Fitzpatrick's ability was obvious, and there was no great surprise when he began featuring on the senior team in 1965. He played a match against Galway that October, and as the GAA season wound down that year he hoped, even presumed, that he would be called back into the panel the following spring. But it was just as well that Fitzpatrick didn't sit by the telephone, because he did not get another crack at Mayo football until 1976. Garrymore played in eight county finals between 1970 and 1982, winning six. Fitzpatrick was the top scorer in the county for plenty of those years. The Farragher boys, Ger and T.J., were playing regularly for Mayo. Danny Dolan was on the team. Pat Dixon made a fair few appearances and Johnny Monaghan had a good run with Mayo, so Fitzpatrick knew his exclusion was not based on any antipathy towards the club. Beyond that, he was mystified.

The bones of his story are that he was twenty-one years of age when he got his first taste of Mayo football and thirty-two when he got his second. Nobody ever offered an explanation for that lost decade. 'Everybody in Mayo would say it to me at the time. It was remarked upon. But I never asked anyone involved. I was content with Garrymore. I can never figure it. It does go through my mind from time to time still. To be honest, though, I was delighted to be asked back. I looked upon it as a second chance. I was always very serious about training. I took the occasional drink but never after training or anything. And I was well able to outrun fellas when I got back in. So there was no bitterness on my part.'

Fitzpatrick had the temperament of a saint. Far from receiving royal treatment in atonement for the disdainful handling of the previous decade, Fitzpatrick found himself bounced in and out of the team over the following years. In 1977, he had played corner-forward throughout the league and was the most accomplished free-taker on the team. On the Tuesday night before Mayo were due to play Roscommon in the championship, he stayed on after training and practised frees for three-quarters of an hour, as usual. Then the team was announced and his name was not called out. Fitzpatrick was completely dumbfounded, but, again, he was too respectful and too proud to start complaining. That Sunday, Roscommon beat Mayo in Castlebar.

A week later, the Mayo team flew to London to participate in a tournament in Wembley. Fitzpatrick scored 2–05 against Cork. Johnny Carey took Fitzpatrick aside and apologised for what had happened the previous week. Fitzpatrick had admired Carey as a player and liked him as a person. Carey had persisted with Mayo football, training teams when it would have been easier to walk away, and he seemed troubled as he tried to explain the reasons why Fitzpatrick had been overlooked – again. 'You could spend a lifetime trying to find out what was going on,' Fitzpatrick says, 'and still be no wiser.'

The only season in which he had the opportunity to showcase his ability on the national stage was 1978. Mayo had a decent team and qualified for the league final against Dublin. They lost by five points, but Fitzpatrick was purring, scoring 1–06 and feeling, after twelve years, as if he finally belonged. A month later, they lost to a terrific and rising Roscommon team by a single point in the championship. It was a stinging and abrupt end to what had seemed like a promising season. But at least Fitzpatrick felt he had proven himself. Despite Mayo's exit, he was listed in joint third place in scoring at the end of the year, with Mike Sheehy of Kerry. It was no bad return. Still, when Mayo opened their league campaign in Ballinrobe the following October, six new forwards were selected. Billy Fitz was back in the wilderness.

In that year, 1978, the Mayo minors won another All-Ireland under the stewardship of Austin Garvin. It was probably the most audacious victory achieved by any of the Mayo teenage championship teams, earned against the cream of Dublin at the height of Heffernan mania. Mayo trailed by six points at one stage in the second half, and just as the Hill began to sing home another coronation, a big leggy substitute, Tom Byrne from Kiltimagh, caused pandemonium when he crashed home

Kevin McStay on the move (© Sportsfile/Ray McManus).

Paddy Prendergast (© *Mayo News*).

John O'Mahony minutes after the finish of the 1989
All-Ireland final (© *Western People*/Henry Wills).

'I ate sand.' Anthony Finnerty bursts through against Cork (© INPHO/James Meehan).

Pauric Carney (centre) with (from left) Paddy Muldoon, Mayo Supporters Club, and Seán Feeney, Mayo County Board. (© *Mayo News*)

Ted Webb clams the ball in the 1975 Connacht final against Sligo (© *Western People*/Henry Wills).

John Maughan celebrates with his son, John junior, after Mayo defeat
All-Ireland champions Tyrone in 2004 (© *Irish Times*/Matt Kavanagh).

John Casey in his first football life as a Mayo forward
(© Sportsfile/Ray McManus).

John Morley.

The electorate supports John O'Mahony (© *Mayo News*).

The long walk: Liam McHale leaves the field minutes into the 1996 All-Ireland-final replay (© *Irish Times*/Eric Luke).

Noel Connolly consoles James Nallen and John Casey after Mayo lose to Meath in the 1996 All-Ireland-final replay. David Brady is on his knees (© Sportsfile/David Maher).

Irresistible force meets immovable object: David Brady addresses Croke Park
(© INPHO/Morgan Treacy).

Liam McHale in action for Mayo.

The natural: Ciaran McDonald practising frees on the 2005 All-Star tour of Hong Kong (© INPHO/Morgan Treacy).

two goals in succession. Kieran O'Malley from Achill scored another goal ten minutes from time and the momentum was irretrievably with Mayo. The final score was 4–09 to 3–08; it had been a genuine, heart-warming minor classic, the perfect beginning to a damp, grey September Sunday, and afterwards the pale-blue wall of city supporters applauded the country team warmly on their victory lap.

Jimmy Maughan scored the other Mayo goal that afternoon. The Ballinrobe teenager was unusual in that he was a basketball star and he was from the travelling community. Jimmy lived in a house in Ballinrobe town for all of his life, but his parents were born and raised 'on the roadside'. After his father started working with Mayo County Council, they moved into a house in Ballinrobe. 'That was nearly fifty years ago,' Jimmy smiles when we meet on a blazing April day at that same house. 'But I have to say, from the point of view of the traveller aspect of my background and football or basketball, I was always treated the exact same as anyone else. Both at school and with Mayo. Whether that was because I could play sport or whether they just took me at face value, I cannot say. But at trials, I always felt I had the same opportunity as anybody else.'

Maughan regarded himself as a basketball player who liked to play football. He played point guard, and, in the west of Ireland in the 1970s, there was a touch of Harlem soul about his game. Even now, sallow and silver-haired and wearing a crisp short-sleeved white shirt, he moves his hands as though palming an imaginary basketball as he talks about long forgotten games in the Goods Store, the old railway building in Ballinrobe that was converted into a makeshift basketball arena. The architecture was simple: Noel Ansborough, the local coach, put up a basket at either end of the hall and drafted a court using insulating tape. Standing in slacks and leather shoes, Maughan has the panther's lightness of step, the long hands and the alertness of a natural point guard.

The Goods Store had a tarmac floor and the dimensions of the court were so tight that players regularly crashed against the concrete walls. In winter, it got so cold they felt as though they were playing in a huge, hollowed-out ice cube, even though the schools team often drew good crowds. The place was incredibly dusty and you had to spit on your hands to stop the ball from slipping. But for Jimmy Maughan, the place was Madison Square Garden. He shot like a demon and loved the trickery he could work with a basketball. Ballinrobe had a fine schools team. Peter Ford, about six months younger than Maughan, played on it. They won seven Connacht A titles, habitually stuffing it to the big Galway city schools like the Jes and the Bish and Summerhill in Sligo. A Bish teacher, Serge Beruzzi, organised a tournament featuring the best three teams in each province. Tuam was the host town in 1979. Maughan and a local kid named John Moran were called to Dublin for Irish trials and made the national team. A month later, Maughan found himself flying to Belgium for a fortnight to compete in the European Under-19 championships. He will never forget the town, Arlon. Ireland lost six games on the spin, destroyed by the height of the Continental players more than by any deficit in skill.

During the same period, Maughan had begun to excite Mayo football people. In 1977, he got a call out of the blue for the inaugural Ted Webb competition. Prior to that, he could take or leave Gaelic football, finding the game somewhat slow and ponderous. From the beginning, he tried to leave his signature on any match he played. Maughan had pace and knew how to score, but it was the subtle flicks, the no-look hand passes, the feints and the shimmies that kept him interested and earned him his reputation. He was just sixteen when he played on that 1978 minor team, returning the following year when Dublin beat Mayo in the All-Ireland semi-final. Immediately afterwards, Johnny Carey called him up to the senior panel.

For the next two years, he hardly set foot in the Goods Store. Ballinrobe had a fine minor team in 1978 and won that year's A championship. A year later, they took intermediate and league trophies, and in 1980 they reached the senior semi-final against Knockmore. Ballinrobe were trailing by a point with a couple of minutes to go when Tommy O'Malley came jinking towards the Knockmore goal and spied Maughan lurking on the edge of the square. 'The hand pass was rampant at that time. I knew what Tommy was going to do, so immediately I started running out from the goal. I made sure I was outside the square, and sure enough Tommy flicked it in. But it was disallowed. That disappointed me for years, because I felt we would have beaten Castlebar in the final that year.'

But it hardly mattered. He was young. One Friday evening in July of 1981, Mayo and Galway met in Tuam Stadium in the Under-21 Connacht final. The match is just a footnote in the thick, dusty archives of football encounters between the big counties of the west, but it shimmers in the memory of those who witnessed it. This was a fancied Galway team, with future senior men like Tomás Tierney, Val Daly, Brian O'Donnell, Richie Lee and Pauric Coyne all appearing.

However, Mayo clicked and Maughan wove magic in a slick forward line featuring Gabriel Cuddy from Claremorris, his minor teammate Jimmy Lyons and Eugene Mackin from Hollymount. Tierney lasted fifteen minutes before the Galway sideline sent Ollie Burke from Corofin over to try his luck on Maughan. Twenty minutes later, they tried someone else. Maughan seemed to be conducting every Mayo attack.

'I was very aware and I was cocky. I knew I could do it. I wouldn't go talking about it, but I had confidence. We had a great understanding in that team, and that Mayo forward unit were the guys I loved playing with, because they were so unselfish. If I gave a pass to Jimmy Lyons, I was gone, because I knew straight away it was coming back to me. I didn't score a hell of a lot that day, maybe 1–02, but I think I created four goals of the 5–11 we scored. I felt sorry for Pauric Coyne that day, because he was a fantastic goalkeeper but he got so frustrated that evening, he was sent off.'

These were fast, exciting times. In 1980, Maughan played in the Connacht senior final defeat against a dashing Roscommon team that featured the Earleys and Tony McManus on a last burst of glory. The following summer, Mayo were young and fearless and beat Galway in the semi-final. Maughan was marked by Richie Lee. They won the final against Sligo easily. Kerry awaited them in the All-Ireland semi-final. Maughan was no stranger to Croke Park and Kerry held no fear for him, even though he was besotted with the way that team moved the ball. In the weeks before the game, however, he was the victim of a strange occurrence. Paddy Collins, the highly regarded Westmeath referee, was dispatched to both camps to clarify the legitimate use of the hand pass, an art that both Dublin and Kerry had perfected. Maughan had made it an embellishment of his game, sometimes flicking it without bothering to catch it first. Then, a week before the match, Jimmy was walking down the street in Ballinrobe when a shopkeeper came out and called, 'Are you injured, Jimmy?' Maughan looked puzzled. 'Well, it's in the paper that you've been dropped.'

A rumour went around that he had attended a rock concert in Castlebar the previous weekend. It was untrue. Then the word was that Collins had warned the Mayo management that he would pull Jimmy Maughan every time for the hand pass. He accepted the demotion and continued to train, looking over at Seamie Daly and Father Leo and Johnny Carey in confusion. 'I hadn't the balls to confront anyone. But in Croke Park, we got off to a marvellous start. It was 1–04 to 1–05 at half-time and I think we were a bit stunned to be in that position. And then, ten minutes into the restart, Kerry just went up a gear and left us behind. We didn't know how to stop that machine.'

Kerry were remorseless. Martin Carney remembers playing at wing forward and trying to stay with Páidí Ó Sé. Carney had trained so ferociously that his weight had plummeted to ten and a half stone and he felt like a ghost. Ó Sé just barrelled through him with impunity. Carney retired early, wrecked, and watched as Kerry inflicted a ferocious beating. Maughan came in – for Carney – ten minutes after half-time. By then, the rout was irreversible, but Maughan was still preoccupied with the hand pass, and as he flicked his first ball, he waited to hear the whistle. But Paddy Collins wasn't even looking at him. The whole thing had been one of those daft rumours. Kerry won by sixteen points anyway.

Maughan never knew if other teams were aware of his cultural background. He presumed people knew. It was only against teams from within the boundary of Connacht that he was ever taunted. He made a pact with himself when he was fifteen that he would ignore all provocation. When he heard the old slurs – nacker, tinker – he would just smile back. 'But to say it didn't hurt me would be a lie. The thing was, I knew nothing about the travelling culture, but I never denied that I came from it. There was a stigma there, but it was a stigma created by settled people. Of course it hurt me. And the other Mayo guys on the field would never have heard it. There might be 30,000 people in the stadium and this lad would be standing close to you. It was like being on a dance floor and you would be whispering into a girl's ear. That is how close it was. Nobody would even notice it.'

Only once did he reach flashpoint. It was a championship game against Roscommon, and Maughan was showing irresistible form, nonchalantly collecting 1–04 in what was a one-sided match. His opponent was making cheap remarks all the way through yet nothing was ruffling Maughan's composure. 'Then he mentioned my mother to me, and he went deeper than skin. I looked at him and went to hit him there and then, but, whatever change came in me, I walked. A few minutes later, though, we went for a fifty–fifty ball, and I hung back and let him have it. I didn't even get booked. I wasn't proud of it, because I was never a dirty player. But I couldn't leave that be. It was like that situation with Zinedine Zidane in the World Cup. You do what you have to do.'

In an ideal world, Maughan would have been an automatic Mayo selection for the next ten years. But life had different plans for him. A cold chill ran through Mayo football the following year. Liam Duffy, who had played on Mayo's 1980 Under-21 Connacht-winning side, became ill late in the summer of 1982. In the shower room after a match, someone noticed a lump near his neck. 'Must have got a wallop,' he joked, but he was absent from senior training the following Tuesday evening. Jimmy Lyons, who was from Duffy's club in Aughamore, told Maughan that Liam had gone to Dublin and that he was worried. A grave illness was confirmed, and just a few months later, in October of 1982, their teammate passed away. He was twenty-two. 'This was a fantastic young man and a great footballer. He would have been about Mayo teams for many years. It was the saddest thing.'

Early that summer, Mayo went to Tuam to defend their Connacht title against Galway. They had suffered a dreadful run of injuries: John Maughan and T.J. Kilgallon were confirmed absentees and Dermot Flanagan was stricken with shingles. At least three other players were scarcely fit to train. It was a broiling afternoon and the country was in the middle of a tense general election. Charles Haughey was visiting the Galway East constituency and attended the match. Mayo were destroyed by 3–17 to 0–10, and afterwards they sat in the dressing-room listening while some of their fans aimed kicks at the door in disgust. In the next edition of the *Connaught*

*Telegraph*, sports editor John Melvin left a blank space in place of the team photograph. The caption explained that 'To save any further embarrassment all round, we decided not to publish it'. The headline read: 'Mayo – God Help Us'. The general mood was seething, and it was Jimmy Maughan's first taste of the dark side of the Mayo game.

And then his father died. Pat Maughan was strong and young and he was always present. The sudden and complete absence, that vacuum, sent Jimmy into a tailspin. He quit his job in the ESB and hit the pubs. Word got around that he wasn't coping so well, and Joe Langan, who had always acted like a second father to him, rang him and tried to help out. He got Jimmy a job working in O'Donoghue's pub in Dublin, a great family-run establishment off Baggot Street. He found peace there. Six months later, he met his wife, and within the year they had gone to England and started a family. They moved to Galway city when they returned, and Jimmy took up with the St Michael's club, quickly rediscovering the old flair and speed as he became one of the chief architects of the county's intermediate win.

In 1986, Liam O'Neill invited him into his Mayo squad. Jimmy jumped at the chance. Four years had vanished, and Mayo had become the darling team of the nation after starring in a gripping All-Ireland semi-final series against Dublin the previous year. He found himself gasping for breath in his first league match against Cork, and so he hit the roads at night. Mayo qualified for a league semi-final against Monaghan that year, and Maughan tapped into the old form against a smart, strong defender, Gerry McArdle. That match made him feel like a teenager; it was a rerun of all the shimmies and fakes and instinctive passes that had made Maughan seem so promising.

That was as good as it got. Roscommon beat Mayo by a point in the 1986 Connacht championship. That autumn, there was a disorganised and truculent feel about the squad in early challenge games, and Maughan quit. He walked away. He was twenty-seven. John O'Mahony was appointed manager the following year, and he took Mayo in a different direction. Maughan continued to play impressive club football in Galway city and was covertly approached about training with the maroon squad. He declined. 'You only fly under one flag,' he says. He was hopeful that John O'Mahony would call him in, but that never happened. It saddened him, because he knew the Mayo players who went to the 1989 All-Ireland final; he could read their game like a palmist can read a hand. He believes he could have helped. But he watched the match from the stands, waving his flag, and afterwards they said, 'Pity we didn't have you out there, Jimmy.'

Martin Carney was still there then, labouring throughout the 1980s and finishing his career as a defender. Twenty years after his exile from Mayo, Billy Fitzpatrick, too, was still on the squad. His career was a testimony to the worth of loyalty. All the jewels came late. In 1985, he finally got the precious Connacht senior medal. He had been injured for the semi-final against Leitrim, but Liam O'Neill, conscious of how much of his soul Fitzpatrick had invested in this thing, made a point of introducing him with fifteen minutes of the final remaining. Mayo had prised the game away from a fading Roscommon team. It was a poignant afternoon, because Dermot Earley, whose brilliance had been a torment to Mayo people for the previous ten years, had made it known that he would retire after this championship. So after winning just their second Connacht title in sixteen years, some of the Mayo players sought Earley out. Fitzpatrick was among them. They chaired the man in primrose and blue around the field.

# SEVEN

# JOHN MORLEY

John Morley was killed on the week of the 1980 Connacht senior football final between Mayo and Roscommon. He was fatally wounded while giving chase to bank raiders across a field in Loughglynn. Morley was a plain-clothes detective and the designated carrier of the Uzi sub-machine gun that was kept at Castlerea Garda station for incidents of extreme violence. Patrolling the borderlands of Mayo and Roscommon was not regarded as a hazardous occupation then. None of the men who responded to the radio calls that crackled through the cars and stations on a humdrum Monday afternoon in July could have anticipated that they would be plunged into such a surreal and life-threatening episode. Up in Ulster, the towns and cities frequently resounded to the piercing crack of gunfire followed by the slumping on pavements of men in uniform. But violent crime was alien to Mayo. The consequences of the bank robbery in Ballaghaderreen were so terrible that it caused the temperature to chill across the country. Complaining about the Garda is a national pastime in Ireland. But we do not expect our lawmen to be killed.

Reading back on the newspaper reports of that day, it is clear that none of the four Mayo men who responded to the emergency call had any time to react or adapt to what unfolded in the seconds after their patrol car rammed into the raiders' white Cortina at Shannon Cross. Garda Henry Byrne, who was sitting in the back seat with Morley, died almost instantly when the raiders directed a volley of shots at the car as they fled on foot. Garda Derek O'Kelly from Kiltimagh was driving. Sergeant Michael O'Malley from Louisburgh was in the passenger seat. Both were unarmed. These men were trained to deal with robberies and extreme threats upon their lives, but no reconstruction or theoretical exercise they might have gone through in Templemore could have prepared them for the adrenalin and terrifying clarity of those few minutes. They did not flinch. After firing the bullets that hit Henry Byrne, the pursued men were no longer mere robbers but killers. They hurried in madcap fashion across the scrub fields, trying to get back to the main road towards Frenchpark. Morley followed them. He knew by then that these men were recklessly dangerous. But he ran anyway. He was still young and naturally fit. He could have paced them all afternoon. It is known that he opened fire on the criminals. And shortly afterwards, one of the men he pursued turned and shot John Morley. He was hit in the chest – a wound later considered not fatal – and went down when a second bullet entered his leg. It struck an artery near his femur, and although he was rushed to the county hospital in Roscommon, it was too late. By then, the grimmest news had already begun to eclipse the afternoon light in the west.

'It was what you would expect him to do. There was just no point in wishing that John would behave differently,' reflects his widow, Frances, one afternoon in the summer of 2007. 'He would always go in head first.'

Sometimes, bad and inexplicable turns visit decent and ordinary people. Time may have allowed Frances Morley to stop searching for the reasons why her husband and friend was killed. But although it would be wrong to say she has not enjoyed her family and her life in the subsequent years, that date – 7 July 1980 – has been burnt into her soul and, of course, she cannot but be aware, even in the moments of brightest laughter, of all that he has missed. Frances lives in Galway city now, and framed in the hallway is the medal for bravery that John Morley was honoured with after his death. Below it hangs a photograph of her husband in uniform, wearing the blazer and brass emblems and heavy navy tie of the day. It appeared in all the newspapers on the day after the shooting.

John Morley was known across Ireland as a Gaelic football player, having worn the green and red of Mayo for over a decade. The country halted to mourn Henry Byrne and John Morley in a way that probably would not occur today. Gathered around the gravesides in Knock were politicians who were tasked with steering the state towards modernity: Charles Haughey was Taoiseach. Jack Lynch was there, Liam Cosgrave was there; Albert Reynolds and Brian Lenihan and Máire Geoghegan-Quinn, all cabinet ministers of the day, were in the crowd. Seán Doherty, the political charmer from Castlerea, was present, along with Mark Killilea and Pádraig Flynn and Gerry L'Estrange. Enda Kenny paid his respects. And all through the crowd were the finest Gaelic football players of the previous twenty years, broad-shouldered men from Cork, Kerry, Dublin, Galway and Roscommon. School friends and former teammates from St Jarlath's, where Morley had starred on the Hogan Cup teams of 1960 and '61 attended. Men from the Mayo teams of the '60s and '70s paid their respects. They all bowed their heads, quietly sickened. They were state funerals, with the trinity of the Church, the Garda and the GAA in full ceremonial mode. The occasion was at once epic and terribly local. Seán Flanagan was among the Mayo football players who formed a guard of honour when the hearses arrived at the basilica in Knock. Monsignor James Horan read the gospel. The Garda Band sounded trumpets at the consecration. The *Western People* reported that 15,000 people paid their last respects, and its front-page headline was 'Red Roses for Dead Heroes'. The funerals of the two gardaí stilled the country.

Although it must have been a comfort, Frances Morley can remember little of it. Those few days were too quick and dreamlike to comprehend. 'The sensation was that everything was taken out of our hands. The state took over. I have spoken to other widows of gardaí, and they said the same thing. John's brother-in-law, J.J., was stationed in Castlerea, and I suppose he felt he had to pander to the whims or whatever. Things were being done in a certain way. We were in no position to argue. What I remember most about those few days is the faces of the lads that John knew – the Mayo football players and the lads in the station. They all looked shattered. All I remember is a neighbour saying to me that we had to decide where we wanted John to be buried. And young and all as Shane was then, I asked him. Shane was only ten years old. And he said Knock. It was the perfect choice. What nicer place? John and Henry grew up close to there, and it is nice that they were laid to rest so close.'

John Morley was pure Mayo. He grew up near Kiltimagh, the youngest of eight children. He observed the time-honoured tradition of boarding in St Jarlath's College, the football and academic nursery in the heart of Tuam town. He formed with Pat Donnellan probably the most splendid midfield partnership ever to line out for the college and won consecutive Hogan Cup titles in 1960 and 1961. He made his senior county debut for Mayo at the age of nineteen and, after leaving St Jarlath's, went to work in Collooney in Sligo for Gowna Wood Industries, travelling as a sales representative. He joined the club side and won a Sligo championship medal with Collooney Harps. It was through that local connection that he met Frances. He had applied to join the Garda, and after training in Templemore he got the anticipated posting to Dublin, working in the Kilmainham station and kicking football with Civil Service. After several unsuccessful transfer requests, he was moved to Ballaghaderreen, the home town of Seán Flanagan, who was then Minister for Lands. That was 1967, and a year later he and Frances married.

Although they would move to Roscommon and Castlerea and come to be fond of both towns, Ballaghaderreen always held magical associations. It was a pleasant, solid town, and the football club was active, with talented young players coming through. Acquiring Morley gave the side a powerful personality in the dressing-room and what is often referred to as 'an auld winner' on the field. Ballagh won the 1971 intermediate championship and were senior champions a year later.

'Morley was a big figure in every way,' says John O'Mahony, who was then an up-and-coming corner-back. 'He was popular, and he had an opinion on how things should be done. I would have had plenty of rows with him. He was terrific on the field, and he was great in the dressing-room. John would have managed the Mayo football team one day. I have no doubt about that.'

Frances was a camogie player, and it suited her fine that the social scene in Ballaghaderreen revolved around the club. They had nights out after the big matches or went to dinner-dances in the Railway Hotel or Cryan's, and the pace of life in the place was leisurely. Castlerea was close by for the cinema and shopping. She loved it in Ballaghaderreen. They had no phone in the house, nor was John particularly keen on acquiring one. Being unavailable had its advantages when you were in the force. He was conscientious about his job without being a stickler for paperwork or timekeeping.

He was the resident motorcycle garda and was in the habit of stealing a five-minute snooze on afternoons when he came home for dinner. 'I used to think it was insanity,' Frances laughs. 'But he would put the head down, out like a light for five minutes, throw cold water on his face and be off. One time, though, he was after a late shift from the night before, and he felt he needed to sleep for an hour. My mother was visiting, and I went up the town for a few groceries and noticed the super's car was there. So I came home and told John, and sure I never saw him move as fast. Then my mother says, "Well, actually, John, a man did call looking for you."

'"What did you say? What did you say?" he yelled.

'My mother said, "I told him you were up the stairs having a good sleep."

'Sure, poor John was horrified. My mother said she couldn't tell a lie. John went racing out the door shouting that he'd be lucky if he had a job to go back to. We would tease him about it for years. He believed in the Garda as a force. But I think it was a different job back then.'

There was really no crime in Ballaghaderreen, just trifling indiscretions and misdemeanours and occasional domestic disturbances. John Morley was known as being good for a lift home on bad nights when the pubs were closing, firing the bicycles into the trunk of the squad car and taxiing bachelors back out to their home places. One morning, Frances left the house for eight o'clock Mass and was reversing out in the car when she heard snoring in the back. It was one of John's regular passengers, who had spotted the Morley car after a tiring and emotional evening in the pub and decided it would do no harm to rest up. The car was rarely locked.

Morley was talkative and funny and optimistic. The football was important to him without governing his existence. He had friends from within the dressing-room and friends from outside Gaelic football. His career coincided with a frustrating time for Mayo football, when the promising team of the mid-'60s had to languish in relative anonymity as Galway completed the dynastic 1964–66 triple All-Ireland success. 'John and Pat Donnellan would fight like two devils on the field,' Frances says. 'They could be hard to look at. Then afterwards they would be old school friends again. When he lost, the old head would be down for a few days. It bothered him all right. Then he would just snap out of it and everything would have been all right again.'

He got ample rewards from the game, winning two Connacht medals, in 1967 and 1969, and a league title in 1970. He quit in 1974, just when a fresh wave of young Mayo players had won the All-Ireland Under-21 title. 'I was just delighted I got to play with him,' says J.P. Kean, whose precocious talent gave him an early elevation to the Mayo senior ranks. 'He was kind of a god to me. And one of my first nights in the dressing-room at training, he came over and put the big arm around me and told me I would be grand. He was confident and forthright in his views, a big statuesque man. John was the man in the dressing-room. That first championship game that I played, he nearly turned the game around on his own. He just had huge presence. It was a pity he didn't play for a few seasons longer.'

That first match was the 1973 Connacht final, an obscure gem played on a hot July afternoon. All games were eighty minutes long that year, and with just half an hour to play Mayo trailed Galway by 1–14 to 1–04, and a slow fade-out seemed inevitable. Although Morley's natural position was number six, he was selected at midfield that day, and over the last thirty minutes he performed as though the match had become a personal crusade, claiming ball after ball as Mayo began a comeback that engaged and finally thrilled the crowd. Morley broke forward and scored a goal in the midst of their renaissance, but time – as always – proved the ultimate conqueror. The final score was 1–17 to 2–12. That day was in sympathy with a lost decade that had started so promisingly.

Although an automatic selection in the 1960s, it is apparent from archive reports that Morley was at his most authoritative in the 1970s. He marked Mayo's league title in the first year of that decade in memorable circumstances, as Paddy Downey recorded in the *Irish Times*:

> The imminent Down breakthrough at this time is crystallised in a quip by a member of the press corps when the Mayo centre half-back, John Morley, had his knicks torn off and, finding the proffered replacements too small, played on in the brief blue trunks that had saved embarrassment all round when the rent outer garment fell away. 'Now,' said the wit, 'Mayo will really be caught with their pants down.'
>
> As it happened, they weren't.

That league success deepened the disillusionment when Sligo knocked Mayo out of the championship on 22 June by 2–10 to 0–09. Exactly a year later, Morley and Johnny Carey were the outstanding turns in the Mayo defence, but with the team desperate for scores they were switched to full-forward and midfield. Galway won by 1–07 to 0–07. In 1972, Roscommon had their way, winning their first provincial title in a decade in a final against Mayo that ended 5–08 to 3–10. That litany of defeats was bound to take its toll on Morley, and the following winter, he decided to finish up.

For years after the 1975 defeat against Sligo, there was a rumour that county-board emissaries had tried to persuade Morley to lace up for the replay. But it is unlikely that he would have entertained any such grandiose or presumptuous action. When he finished, he didn't really look back.

'I don't know why he called it a day,' says Frances. 'I don't think there was any particular reason. He just felt that he had had enough. I suppose the whole travelling to training was getting tiring. I know he was getting heavily involved with the Community Games, and he loved working with youngsters.

'I suppose many of his teammates were leaving. They had their frustrations over the years. But my memory of that team is that they were a fine group of men. They were friends, they had this camaraderie. In 1970, after we won the league, the team went out to America. John had had a good few trips, and I decided I was going this time. We had a brilliant time. John was great friends with Séamus O'Dowd and Joe Langan and Joe Corcoran. Jim Fleming, another guard, would have been a friend of his. So I suppose he stopped playing for Mayo with that whole gang.'

Shane Morley never bothered much with football in his childhood. His father never pushed him either way. Shane is the only one of the Morley children with vivid memories of his father. He can still place himself on the couch in Ballaghaderreen when his parents told him that they were moving to Roscommon, which might as well have been in India as far as the eight year old was concerned. His father was fascinated with Muhammad Ali, then an implausibly glamorous and compelling figure, and got his son hooked in the build-up to the Leon Spinks fight. They followed Manchester United and went to the cinema in Castlerea for the blockbuster openings like *Star Wars*. Shane's passion, above anything, was trains. When the family moved to Castlerea after John was rewarded with a promotion to the rank of detective, the big thrill was the level-crossing. A television advert at the time featured the iconic GAA commentator Michael O'Hehir talking about the safe procedures for negotiating a level-crossing, illustrating the uses of the yellow box and giving tips about using the courtesy telephone. It caught the boy's imagination, and the most exciting part was that the Castlerea crossing had been used in the filming. John Morley and another guard had happened upon the scene that day and watched O'Hehir's brief cameo as a small-screen frontman. After the camera stopped, they wandered up for a chat. Shane knew by heart the times that the trains were scheduled to pass, and he frequently persuaded his father to drive out with him just so the two of them could wait in the car as the locomotive thundered past. They would idle in the slipstream of its power and then pass through the barrier as the carriages rattled down the long straight track and disappeared across the flat fields. These are, of course, all commonplace childhood memories. What makes them so poignant is the fact that they are all rooted in such a brief period, with reference points that belong to a time now remembered in nostalgia hits and old news clips – and then they just stop. That, of course, was the true robbery committed that day, not the sorry haul of 35,000 punt found abandoned in the rear seat of the smashed-up Cortina on the quiet junction at Shannon Cross.

The Morleys moved to Castlerea in September of 1979, just as Ireland had taken a broom to the floor and filled the vases with fresh flowers in anticipation of the visit of Pope John Paul II. John Morley was assigned to work down in Limerick for the duration of the visit, and Frances decided to bring the children to Knock along with her parents. The shrine at Knock was, after all, the most celebrated symbol of the Catholic faith in Ireland. (Strangely, one of the witnesses to the apparition of Our Lady in August 1879 was Dominic Byrne, a grandfather of Henry Byrne.)

'As it turned out, it was bedlam. We were up at some unearthly hour and headed to Knock. Gordon, our youngest boy, was just gone three. We waited for the helicopter for hours and hours, and eventually we heard that the Pope was delayed in Ballybrit. Then when the helicopter arrived, Gordon needed to run to the loo. And it was a much shorter visit. He'd stayed so long in Galway that poor old Mayo was short-changed. And Knock people would say it was to us he was coming. The problem was, he couldn't fly after dark; there was some kind of law. So the popemobile never came around at all. Our daughter Gillian was in bits. We never saw the Pope, really.'

The papal visit was the great national drama of 1979. The Morleys were dealing with the more intimate theatre of moving to another new house. Frances had dreaded going to Castlerea, but she told herself that if she could leave Ballaghaderreen, she could leave anywhere if she had to in the future, and they spent a nice Christmas in the new place. It seemed like there were a hundred jobs to be done in the house. John was friendly with countless handymen and liked to use one particular fellow for plastering walls. He was brilliant, though somewhat erratic in his working hours, often falling victim to the pleasures of a long weekend. John's solution was to acquire an old caravan and park it in the front drive. He persuaded his man to lodge there until the job was finished. That way, he could keep half an eye on his hours. It was unconventional, but that was the way he worked. John laid the lawn sometime in late June, and it began to green in the weeks after he had been killed.

There had been nothing even remotely out of the ordinary about that last day. John had finished his dinner and wandered out the door calling, 'See ye later.'

'That was at two o'clock, and by quarter to three John was, I'd say, dead probably. That was the hardest thing to get my head around. I do remember one night, about a year before that, he left for work and was gone well into the early hours. It was three in the morning and they had to drive to hospital with a patient or something, and I had no way of finding out if he was all right. Whenever he did get back, I was on the attack straight away, because you are just so glad to see that person back in one piece. And that night, if someone had told me that something had happened, I might have been a small bit prepared for it. But not that afternoon; it was all so normal.

I met a lady in town just a few weeks ago who used to work in the telephone exchange in Castlerea. She told me, "Imagine. I will always remember that July day." She had left the phone to get a packet of biscuits, and Henry Byrne was standing on the footpath. His wife, Ann, was pregnant and this lady enquired after her. "She's big as a house," Henry said and told her he was finished at four o'clock. Henry just happened to be standing at the door of the Garda station when John and those came through in the squad car and shouted at him to hop in. Word had come through. Sure, they probably thought the excitement of a robbery in a small town like Ballaghaderreen wasn't worth missing.'

By late afternoon, the house was full of friends and even some strangers. Information was sketchy. Someone told Ann that John had shot one of the criminals, and she presumed they meant fatally. That was the worst blow. 'I kept asking why, if he had to go, he had to take someone with him.' The mere notion of John using a gun seemed preposterous. He did carry a small firearm and kept it in the top shelf in the kitchen. The sight of it used to alarm Frances. It always reminded Shane of Steve McQueen in *Bullitt*, with its fancy leather shoulder holster.

Burial arrangements were made as overwhelming Garda and army resources were employed to sweep through the woodlands of Mayo and Galway to search for the third man involved in the raid and shooting, who had evaded capture. Meanwhile, almost unbelievably, the Mayo football team had to prepare for a Connacht football final against this backdrop. On the evening of the shooting, the Ballaghaderreen football team met at the local pitch. Training had been scheduled, and there was no way to cancel it. But nobody had the heart to go running.

John O'Mahony had become aware of the tragedy when he returned home from school. He did the local notes for the provincial newspapers in those times, so national and international newspapers soon got hold of his number and the phone did not stop ringing. He left the house and walked down the street. 'It was the most eerie feeling. There was absolute quiet. That night at the pitch, we gathered around and my brother Dan said the prayers. We didn't know what else to do. It had a stunning effect on the nation, really. Then, of course, Mayo had the Connacht final, and there would have been some kind of lift if we could have won that.'

Mayo were hammered by 3–13 to 0–08 by a fine Roscommon team that would push for All-Ireland honours later that summer. Eleven championships had now passed since Mayo had won the Connacht title, but this one did not seem to matter very much.

Frances Morley had young children to raise and care for. Through the bleakness of the following winter, they got by. Curiously, less than a year after straining in the vast crowd at Knock, she found herself kneeling alongside Ann Byrne at the altar in the Vatican in front of the Pope. The women were chosen to bring the gifts during a Vatican Mass attended by a Garda pilgrimage. At the time, she was still too dazed to fully appreciate the sacredness of the moment, but somebody took a photograph, which she later framed, and as the years went on and the smiling Pope became more aged and frail, she came to value that brief meeting enormously.

Shane went to boarding school in St Nathy's in Ballaghaderreen. 'It was very odd going back there,' he recalls, 'and kind of a comfort as well. Like, I will never forget walking into the classroom and seeing John O'Mahony there. These were all faces that I would have known as a child, and to see them again was strange.' In the bluntly inquisitive way of the schoolyard, he was regularly asked about his dad. He never made an issue of his father's death but didn't downplay it either. If people asked, he told them. He began to kick football during those years, played some basketball and joined the legions of Mayo football supporters.

Frances grew fond of Castlerea, and it became home until the children grew up and started to move away. Gordon did not have his father's colossal strength, but he had speed and football instinct to burn, and it was clear by his early teenage years that he was a promising footballer. Donie Shine picked him for the Roscommon minor team. When he went to college in Galway, Frances decided it would make sense for her to move as well, and she relocated to the city in 1996. Around that time, Gordon was invited to train with the Galway Under-21 team.

Word of his potential was spreading. John Maughan phoned and asked him, 'Which way will you go?' Gordon had been born in Castlebar, and playing for the same county as his father had a powerful emotional appeal. Frances kept out of it. 'I think it was a hard act to follow, though. Now, I am talking as a mother here. We are biased. But I felt and feel now that it was difficult because people did see Gordon as the son of his father. He might have had a better crack at it here in Galway.'

One evening, the phone rang and a newsman from RTÉ television asked Frances how she felt about the release of one of the men imprisoned after the death of her husband. None of the authorities had had the courtesy to let the family know of his impending release in advance. She was shocked and even a little frightened. Gillian Morley was preparing to go to London to study nursing at the time. Frances and Shane accompanied her to Dublin airport. Mayo were playing in the league semi-final against Cork, so they decided to make a weekend of it. Shane was coming out of Eason's, scanning the sports pages of a newspaper as he walked, and he knocked against another person. The slight collision caught Frances's eye, and she knew immediately that the person her son had bumped into was the man. He had only been released a matter of days. A few years later, she was standing in line at an automated banking machine when she realised that the same man was waiting in the same queue. She could have reached out and touched him. He was that close. It gave her the shivers and does still. The Morley family never received any word of remorse or acknowledgement from the men who ended John's life that afternoon and nor would they wish to. 'We have never wanted nor asked for anything from those people. To them, we were just a number. But thank God we have done well since. We are fine.'

Gordon played for Mayo, a fast and sticky corner-back, winning a Connacht championship medal in 1999. He played in the All-Ireland semi-final against Cork that year. The following autumn, he got injured. Pat Holmes had come in as manager. He told him to nurse the injury and said they would talk after Christmas. Gordon never heard from any Mayo management after that. His career was bewilderingly and hurtfully brief.

In one of his last matches, against Sligo, he was taken off early. 'That evening, you never saw such a broken young man. My God, he was inconsolable. And I just thought: "I never want to see you like this again." I mean, I wouldn't be the most confident of people myself, so my children were never raised with me telling them they were the best, when I should have been saying, "Ye are the bloody best." And so they are, like. See, I came up through an era where we were never told that you were good at this or that. There was no real praise given. And I say it to them now all right, but then Gordon didn't have the confidence. I felt it was a massive handicap for Gordon to have John Morley as his dad in that situation. Some people can handle it – I suppose Dermot Flanagan did it. But Seán had come to prominence as a TD and was the last man to lift the Sam Maguire. What happened to John was different. I would say it was because of John that Gordon threw his hat in with Mayo. And my feeling is he never got a fair crack of the whip. But we supported Mayo through hell and high water. We would miss very few games. Gordon and myself would still follow them everywhere. I would think that John would be very proud of what Gordon has done on the football field and probably annoyed at the way it worked out.'

Shane empathised with his brother, but he also pointed out that other promising players had suffered the same fate. 'A lot of players involved with Mayo have been discarded without any real explanation. About ten or eleven lads come to mind straight away. And that whole experience helped Gordon, in that afterwards he was able to make up his mind about things straight away.'

Gordon continued to play, winning strong reviews for his performance with the Salthill team that won the All-Ireland club championship in 2006. Frances had been one of their most loyal supporters and would often lament their poorer matches. 'Some years they played like a crowd of latchikos. I would tell them that, too. A few years ago, you would never have imagined they would end up in Croke Park.'

It was a gilded team, though, containing half a dozen inter-county players and a modern genius of the game, Michael Donnellan, a nephew of the man whom John Morley had partnered at midfield some forty years earlier. They had a perfect season, and that blowsy March afternoon in Croke Park was weighted with happy significance for the Morley family.

For many years, the Ballaghaderreen club held a memorial tournament in honour of their fallen teammate. Clubs from Roscommon and Sligo and the Civil Service would enter, and it was a reunion of sorts. Gradually, though, the day came when all of John Morley's comrades had stopped playing.

After the final tournament, the cup was presented to Durkin's Hotel, where it is on display today. 'It was time,' Frances says. 'There were young lads coming on stream who would never have even heard of John.'

But he will be remembered. John Morley holds a rare and permanent place in the affections of Mayo football. Not so long ago, John O'Mahony stopped to pay his respects to his old friend, and as he stood in the graveyard in Knock he noticed the birth date on the headstone. When they won a county championship together back in the more innocent days of 1972, O'Mahony was little more than a schoolkid and regarded Morley as a patriarch, a seasoned man with years of good living behind him. 'It only hit me that day that he was thirty-seven years of age when he died. And I am fifty-three now, standing there realising, Jesus, he was awful young. He had done so much. He was cut off in the prime of his life.'

# Eight

# The Beaten Path

On a rainy afternoon this winter, David Brady was halted at traffic lights in Castlebar and, daydreaming, he followed the progress of a big old-fashioned Mercedes car. He caught only a glimpse of the driver through the fogged windows and spray and the glare of other headlights. But he knew immediately who it was. Brady said under his breath, 'God, there's another one.'

The man passing through town was Pádraig Brogan. For many Mayo football people who remember the 1980s, Brogan seems like the incarnation of all the possibilities and vexations that characterise football in the county. He had sensational talent, and over twenty years on the superb electric bolt of a goal he scored in the doomed 1985 All-Ireland semi-final replay against Dublin shines like starlight from the murkier passages of that decade. The son of a Knockmore publican, Brogan was literally a child star in Gaelic football, tall and athletic with a graceful running stride and a kicking style that was both languorous and immensely powerful. He scored a goal to turn the 1982 Hogan Cup final irreversibly in St Jarlath's favour and played minor, Under-21 and senior for Mayo a year later, kicking three points in the All-Ireland Under-21 replay win against Derry in Irvinestown. At his best, Brogan played the game with such ease that he might have been contemptuous of it. And yet he was ultimately a flickering presence in his Mayo years, with occasional bursts of brilliance suggestive of an unimaginably potent career. He played the game into his thirties. After losing a championship match against Crossmolina one weekend in the late '90s, he decided that was enough and has not so much as attended a match since. Brogan disappeared off the football radar.

When I phoned him before the 2006 All-Ireland semi-final between Mayo and Dublin to suggest we talk about that goal for a feature in the *Irish Times*, he was guarded and uneasy and explained that he preferred to leave his football days where they were: in the past. But after some persuasion, he consented, on the understanding that the conversation would not deviate from that 1985 football match. We met at the Welcome Inn in Castlebar, and although Brogan was slightly broader than in his playing days and had his black hair tied back, he still had the light, sauntering walk of a born athlete. When we walked through the hotel foyer, Brogan grinned nostalgically and said, 'We had some nights in this place,' and when we opened a copy of the *Mayo News* featuring the 1985 team photographed on the wooden bench in Croke Park, his eyes glinted in recognition. Brogan was being halfway mischievous when he said he had no interest in football any more. He spoke knowledgeably and generously about today's players and had very definite opinions about the future of the game. It was clear he possessed a great empathy for the sport and that he would probably make an excellent trainer.

About his own sporting life, though, he was much more hesitant and wary of how he would sound, having made the transition from being one of the most high profile and provocatively gifted Mayo footballers of his era to the courteous and private man he is today. Still, when we started talking about those days, he was comfortable enough to admit that the goal still represents something important to him, and I will never forget the way he spoke of it. 'That goal, 'twas sacred. To me, football was something I did. To bring happiness because you can express a bit of talent, well, that made me happy. Some people ask if its like will ever be scored again. If I was to brag about it, then no, I don't think so. It hasn't happened in my lifetime. And I could probably say before I die, "Well, I did something: I might have scored the greatest goal ever seen at Croke Park." I am not bragging. But that's the reality!' And he threw back his head and laughed loudly, because he knew that he sounded preposterously vain; his delivery was light-hearted and shot through with devilment.

But behind the braggadocio, Brogan was actually giving thanks, and, if anything, his admission was one of humility. To apply the word 'sacred' to the memory of a score from a half-forgotten football match was strange, but it also seemed apt because of what that goal represented. The '80s were not a prosperous time, and plenty of Mayo kids had already fled for America and England. Places like the remote and beautiful Tourmakeady, on the edge of Lough Mask, were in stasis because of emigration. That match in 1985 was important not only because Mayo won the Connacht championship; it mattered because they got to parade and play against Dublin, whose magnetism had defined the previous decade of Gaelic football.

'It felt as if Dublin and Kerry had proprietor's rights to the championship,' Martin Carney says of that period. 'In my time playing football, they were the only teams winning All-Irelands. And after eleven years of playing football, you begin to think that winning All-Irelands is not for you. That is why Liam O'Neill and then John O'Mahony were such huge figures in the 1980s. We felt we could beat Dublin in 1985. And people sensed that. There was real excitement in Mayo about football for the first time probably since the 1950s.

There were 50,000 people at the replay. I was 34 years old then and had never played in front of any crowd like that. It gave guys a flavour of big-time football for the first time in a generation.'

Mayo looked so promising in that mid-August draw, clawing their way back from a seven-point deficit early in the second half and holding Dublin to just a single score over the last thirty-one minutes of the match. Brogan was brought in and scored a huge long-range free, T.J. Kilgallon clipped a point and Tom Byrne, another substitute, fired over another to leave just one point between the sides, before Barney Rock managed to land that solitary point for Dublin. By then, Billy Fitzpatrick had been introduced and, to indicate that there may be a divinity, he was rewarded with perhaps his most famous minute in a Mayo shirt. Billy was forty-two but he was fit and energised and a natural scorer. 'Maughan drove it downfield. It was one of those skyscraper kicks of John's, and it broke off a few players and fell to me. I was out by the Cusack Stand and I hit it on the run.' The decades of practice paid off, and he curled the ball over with his right foot. Mick Holden, his Dublin marker, said to him, 'I hope the ref blows it up because we are f***ed.' Then T.J. Kilgallon broke free and struck an immortal equaliser thirty seconds from full time.

Mayo were rampant at this stage, and there was a late, glimmering opportunity that still haunts them all. 'We won possession again and a ball broke lovely for big Tom [Byrne],' Kevin McStay recalls. 'He did the right thing and hit the pass straight away, but it was just half a yard behind me and a Dublin guy intercepted it and the game was whistled. Your memory gets fuddled over the years, but that is how I saw it. We had them. Jesus, there is no doubt. We were not cute enough at first, but we were boring holes in them in the second half.' Martin Carney had been sprinting through on the other side, but nobody had seen him. 'I had run the overlap, and though my legs were giving out, I had a good wind at my shoulder and space had just opened up before me. And I always fancied it. Of course, it is an easy thing to say now.'

It didn't matter. Mayo fans were thrilled at the prospect of another such day. Driving back to the Ashling Hotel with Kevin McStay that night, selector P.J. McGrath said, 'No matter what happens now, Mayo football is back.'

In the chaotic way of the day, no replay date had been fixed that Sunday evening. Several of the players were reluctant to leave the Ashling, and once they got back to Mayo, there was no question but they were paying a visit to The Beaten Path near Balla. Gay Nevin's sprawling fantasy emporium on the dark country road had become the natural gathering point on championship Sunday nights. 'Gay and the staff treated us brilliantly,' Liam McHale says. 'It was a nice place. You could stay late and if you were stuck, they would always find you a bed.'

Peter Ford remembers hearing stories as a minor in the late '70s about the senior players heading to Mick Byrne's pub in Castlebar after training, that the wives and girlfriends would often meet them and that it was a great social club. O'Neill brought ambition and was a stern trainer, but he made sure the squad was treated well and didn't frown on fun. It is odd now, scrolling through the microfilms of the old Mayo newspapers, to observe how crammed the social pages were with nightclubs and visiting bands during a period of economic stagnation. The Beaten Path offered escapism. 'Everyone went there,' says Peter Ford. 'At the time, the idea of driving home after drinks was no big deal, so it was the place.'

Although he was one of the younger players on the team, Kevin McStay knew in his soul that sinking pints and dancing to 'Careless Whisper' was probably not the most sensible way for the team to conclude what had felt like an epic day. 'It sent out the wrong message. But this was all new to us. The excitement or the sense of having done something positive for the county did affect us. God, when you look back on it . . . I think there was even a bit of a row getting back on the team bus because we were confused about where we wanted to go. We didn't know when we would be playing again. And we felt we could have won it. We had those late chances. Maloney, the referee, was definitely going to give us another shot. I think even the likes of referees wanted us to f***ing win something at that stage. We had come from nowhere, and Dublin had this allure. We could hardly believe it ourselves.'

A long, strange fortnight passed between the draw and the replay. That period gave Mayo an opportunity to assess its standing as a football county and to glory in being at the epicentre of Gaelic culture again. Much of the energy and idle talk revolved around the fate of John Finn, the Mayo half-back who had his jaw broken when he shipped what he said was a deliberate off-the-ball blow in the first half. Finn actually played through to the finish despite the severity of the injury. He did not make it to The Beaten Path that night, instead being detained in Dr Steven's Hospital in the city for two operations over a ten-day period. His father, Martin Finn, a former deputy in the Dáil, denounced what had happened as 'an act of sheer gangsterism'. Although there were several calls emanating from the Mayo county board for the Dublin player to be named, a terse stand-off developed. The incident generated national attention and there was unusually strong interest in the replay.

This was a time when the GAA instinctively distrusted television, and it was decided not to show the replay. Dr Mick Loftus, then president, was forced to tell his county men in Mayo that the reason behind the decision was that broadcasting the match would either interrupt or cause the postponement of several county championship games scheduled throughout the country.

Dublin overpowered Mayo anyhow, winning by 2–12 to 1–07. Pride prevailed over the sense of disappointment. Ivan Neill caught the mood of wistfulness and optimism in the opening of his match report in the *Western People.*

> Visions of Mayo appearing in the '85 All-Ireland senior final in two weeks' time were as clear as moving statues were to some people over the past couple of weeks. However, if those visions became blurred late in the second half of this tense, physical and terribly exciting semi-final replay at Croke Park on Sunday, so what? The road to long overdue success for Mayo has been considerably shortened and don't fret: Sam will land at Knock, possibly next year if concentration is given on adding extra punch in the attack.

Mayo were strong in defence and played attractive football. Willie Joe Padden had given an authentic display of virtuoso midfield catching. Brogan appeared on the scene and delivered that audacious goal. Nobody has forgotten it, but when Kevin McStay revisits that score now, he shakes his head somewhat sceptically. In recent years, McStay has been introduced as a particularly sharp analyst on RTÉ's summer championship programmes and it is with a combination of the critic's mind and the player's heart that he remembers Brogan's extravagant ode to his sport, almost debating the truth of the goal aloud. 'In my opinion, Brogan was going for a point. It got goal of the year, and it was one of those that you shoot for a point and it dips. Maybe I am being harsh. I was running alongside him looking for the pass. It was outrageous ambition to think you could shoot from there. But then he had a very strong shot. I will grant that. Maybe he did! Good luck to him! How far out was he? Twenty-five, thirty yards? What do you see from thirty yards? Come on. You're joking me. Now, if you have the ability to kick the ball very hard, it will dip. And he had a ferocious shot. So maybe he did go for the goal and I am being harsh. But I don't think so!'

Like virtually anyone who played for Mayo alongside Brogan, McStay has ambivalent feelings – in thrall to the man's unquestionable ability and frustrated that he has not left behind a more substantial body of work. 'Pauric had a magnificent stride. If he broke away from you, he was like [Cuba's Olympic 400-metres sprinter Alberto] Juantorena. You wouldn't catch him. He could kick frees from sixty yards no problem. And he had this gorgeous, soft contact with the ball. It went on forever. He wasn't my style of guy. Nor I his. Pauric . . . there was a lot made of him. He was a guy of huge talents, a national champion tin whistler, he was very bright, all the rest. He had this artistic temperament. I think he came on the senior team back in 1983 and did all right. It was all too much too soon. I think by 1986 the game was going away from him. The Knockmore crowd would come in socialising to Ballina, and there were altercations and whatnot. Then he went and played for Donegal for a season before coming back to us, and we brought him on against Donegal in the 1992 All-Ireland semi-final. That was typical of us in Mayo. Making a mess of it. It was an awful pity he didn't realise his full potential. Because players like Pádraig Brogan, they don't come often. He nearly had the full package.'

Billy Fitzpatrick was astonished by the velocity and boldness of Brogan's goal but he can't say he was surprised. 'I saw Pádraig in underage games just take the ball at one end of the field and waltz up and put it in the net. He didn't need a team with him at all. At senior level, it was different, but he thought he should still be able to do it on his own. And there were times he did. That goal in Croke Park was one. I often saw him kick ten or twelve points. But he couldn't combine with the other players as he should have been able to. Ah, he was immensely talented.'

And in 1985, Brogan was just a kid on a strong team. Liam McHale, another terrifically athletic young man, was waiting in the wings. McStay wasn't much older but he always had a mature sensibility to match the innate confidence. McStay was a Ballina 'townie' whose parents had left Tuam when Kevin senior was stationed as overseer in the post office in Ballina. Kevin senior had played on the feted Tuam Stars team featuring Seán Purcell and Frank Stockwell, and although he quit the sport after he married, he immersed himself in the Stephenites club in Ballina. Kevin junior was keen on the game, but not obsessively so. 'I went to St Muredach's College in Ballina and I got a couple of hammerings from the teachers there and I hated the place. My father took me out of it. I went to St Jarlath's and stayed with my aunt in Tuam – which was the best of both worlds and it halved the fees. In a big family like ours, that counted. But I was only eligible to play one year with St Jarlath's and I was also overage for the Mayo minors, so I kind of drifted away from the game for a while.'

He had bigger dreams. McStay was a skilled soccer player and a scout for Nottingham Forest based in Derry had noticed him in a tournament he had played for Connacht. A letter arrived, complete with the Forest insignia. This was 1980. Forest had become the darling team in England and Ireland. Many teenagers, including McStay, revered Brian Clough. The trials were to be held at Easter, less than two months before the leaving certificate. The Mayo newspapers ran a few stories about the local lad on his way to Nottingham. His father sat him down one evening and said, 'You are going over there one of hundreds. It would be like one of them coming over here to try and beat you at Gaelic football.' Ole Big 'Ead never did get to run the gimlet eye over McStay. 'It all seemed very romantic,' he smiles now, 'and my friends were aghast that I didn't go. I never regretted it.'

The irony was that he figured he would be going to England

a year or two later anyway. A lot of his friends in Ballina had begun to leave. He headed to the Regional Technical College in Galway but kicked no football and felt as though he was just drifting when he got a call, at his second attempt, to join the Cadets. In The Curragh, he fell into an extreme fitness regime, and although he felt he was invisible as a football player, John O'Mahony chose him for the Under-21 panel on instinct. Liam O'Neill then drafted him into the senior panel, and his first competitive match was the 1983 Connacht final. He felt both weird and fearless.

McStay's reference points for Mayo football were fairly hazy. He remembered being at the 1975 Connacht-final defeat against Sligo because of the heavy silence on the way home in the car. Hanging around the Stephenites clubhouse, he became accustomed to meeting men like Willie Casey and John Forde. He watched the 1981 All-Ireland football semi-final with some pals and chuckled when Eugene McHale did 'a kind of mental celebration' after scoring his goal. He had performed scoreboard duties for a few league matches in Ballina. 'Listen, I knew nothing. I came down on a Friday to meet the team, and I knew Martin Carney. That was it. Anthony Egan was captain, and he was very welcoming. When I look back, O'Neill picking me probably caused some consternation, but it was desperation really. I played all right and got a good reception, but I had no sense of what a Connacht final was about or what it meant to Mayo until that day.'

That experience, along with winning the Under-21 All-Ireland in the autumn, fused McStay to the Mayo football cause. But the senior team developed slowly. On a frosty January day in 1984, they were trounced by ten points playing Limerick in a Centenary Cup match and heard plenty booing in Castlebar at the beginning of the league a week later. In the 1984 championship, McStay contributed 1–06 against Galway, and still Mayo lost. By 1985, Liam O'Neill was desperate to deliver a Connacht championship. He persuaded Seán Lowry, the great Offaly player who had won two All-Ireland medals with his county, to come out of retirement and wear the Mayo colours. Lowry was charismatic and ostensibly gruff, but only because he had an acute sense of what his adopted county men needed.

'Seán was working at the power station outside Ballina, and he was perhaps thirty-five years of age then. When you are young, that seems old,' says McStay. 'And here was a guy who would stand up and not take shite from anyone. And Seán was huge, monstrous. You could not mark him. He was just brilliant. He would do the spadework and feed you this great ball. Lowry put his reputation on the line for Mayo. He gave these talks that made me not care about anyone else. He didn't give a shite who was marking him. That was it. It was simple: "You don't realise how good you are." And we had some seriously good guys. He said, "We are what we are." Against Roscommon in the Connacht final, he sensed something was holding us back, and he said, "When I get the first goal, I will put the hand up and you'll know we are on our way." And it seemed daft, because, in fairness, Seán wouldn't kick a lot of goals. But sure enough, he did that day. We were motoring then anyway, but he caught this great feckin' drop kick from Jimmy Browne, nailed it and strode out. He was marvellous.'

Lowry started at full-forward in the drawn game against Dublin. Of all the tactical errors and mistakes made in Mayo football down the years, McStay believes the decision to demote Lowry for the replay was borderline criminal. In the long fortnight between the draw and the replay, Lowry's performance had come under scrutiny, and the fact that he hadn't scored became an issue. When it came around to the Thursday evening, when the team selection was to be made, there was heavy pressure on Liam O'Neill and the backroom team to make a change. Tom Byrne had come on as a substitute for Eugene McHale in the drawn match and had played well. He had a knack for getting big scores and got the call at full-forward. As it happened, he would get little change out of Gerry Hargan, the formidable Dublin number three, in the replay.

Regardless of whom Mayo picked, McStay felt that Lowry was treated terribly. 'That is something that always screwed me. Maybe it comes down to a lack of success, but Mayo people get a bit iffy about talent. Lowry might not have scored against Dublin, but he tapped ball down all day for Eugene and me. His paws were all over it. But people didn't see that. Seán didn't feature in the hotel that night. It was a bad scene. I knew his wife, and she was hugely supportive of what he was doing for Mayo. You know, they had young kids, and he went out and gave this huge commitment, and now here was Mayo, with a sniff of the big time, dropping him. And it went down badly.'

But overall, these were far from sour times. The team were rewarded with a holiday for their endeavours, an unprecedented luxury then. The following year, 1986, was to be the year of Mayo's coronation. But then the championship rolled around, and Dermot Flanagan was cancelled out with shingles, John Maughan was injured, Mark Butler had a broken hand and T.J. Kilgallon had to cry off. Roscommon, as ever, had no sympathy and beat Mayo convincingly. Kerry won the All-Ireland that year, too. And Billy Fitzpatrick retired for good.

One morning in May 2007, Anthony Finnerty was checking an order of beer barrels at the cellar of Ward's Hotel in Salthill, Galway, when one of the delivery men realised who he was and shouted cheerfully, 'We would be bowing down before this man now if he had scored the goal!' Finnerty did not know the man, but he heard the broad Mayo chords in his voice and knew instantly which goal was being referred to.

When most people think of the year 1989, they think of the Velvet Revolution, of Tiananmen Square and the fall of the Berlin Wall, totemic images of the late twentieth century. In Mayo football, however, 1989 has become a code for 'Larry' Finnerty's goal chance against Cork in the All-Ireland final. The Moygownagh man has lived the counterpoint experience of Offaly's Séamus Derby. Instead of firing the goal that delivered salvation and Sam Maguire and the rest of it, Finnerty sent a reasonable – if tightly angled, instinctive and much trickier than fading memory allows for – chance flashing past the Cork post early in the second half. Mayo were performing smoothly in their first All-Ireland final since 1951, and had that shot been goaled, it would surely have irreparably damaged the morale of a Cork team that had previously lost two bruising finals to Meath.

'It didn't go in,' Finnerty smiles some seventeen years later, beaming broadly as he sits in an alcove in Ward's. He still has the curls and plump cheeks that made him look cherubic in his days playing senior with Mayo, when he was a seemingly happy-go-lucky forward with deceptive speed and strength and a cold eye for goal. It is easily overlooked that Finnerty had also scored a brilliant goal ten minutes before the chance to put Mayo in such a strong position. 'What happened was that I had to make a split-second decision, and I kicked the ball similarly to the first goal. I hit it straight on rather than side-foot it. And I felt I had to go for power, because John Kearns [the late Cork goalkeeper] had come out and I felt he would expect me to go high again. And it just flashed by him. John was a good goalkeeper and he had his angles. I was in a similar position to where I'd been when I'd scored the first goal. That time, though, I'd been aiming at an open goal. When you're in that situation, it feels like a massive area, but with John there, I was trying to kick it low under his feet, and it felt as though I had a really small window to aim at. Maybe I should have rolled it. But it happened in a flash, and I went low and hard. I still can't understand how it stayed out. I hit it too well.'

It is as good an explanation as any, and although it is convenient to say that events in the 1989 final began to conspire against Mayo after that chance, the truth is less simple. The final score was 0–17 to 1–11. Cork had put up all their scores from play, and Mayo had wasted many opportunities to reverse the fortunes of that afternoon. All summer, they had been defying expectations. John O'Mahony had replaced Liam O'Neill as manager in 1988 and had had an immediate impact. Mayo reclaimed the Nestor Cup and in the All-Ireland semi-final performed credibly against a Meath team that had class and experience and an aura of invincibility. But the following season, Mayo looked ordinary in the league and might well have been caught in the Connacht championship. Their semi-final against Galway ended in a draw, a match that was overshadowed by the death of Liam McHale's father, Tony.

'He had been ill with cancer, and on the morning of the match I was talking with him up in his bedroom and put a radio beside the bed so he could listen to the commentary, but he was very weak,' McHale says. 'All I remember is leaving the stadium in Tuam as soon as I could get off the field.'

The replay was controversial and rancorous. Willie Joe Padden ended up with cracked ribs, Noel Durkin was replaced when he sustained an ankle injury and Seán Maher, who had landed two points, was sent off with Galway's Michael Brennan after one of those shambolic sketches of gamesmanship that feature in Gaelic matches. McHale was named at full-forward, seemed to play everywhere and scored a goal which prefaced a succession of Mayo scores. The final score was 2–13 to 1–08, and the Galway goal was a formality, an injury-time penalty struck by Tomás Tierney. In the final, Mayo faced Roscommon in Hyde Park in what was arguably the outstanding match of the championship. It hinged on a Finnerty goal, conjured from a chink of light he spied through three Roscommon defenders five minutes from the end of extra time.

It was the first time in thirty-eight years – since the 1950–51 epoch – that Mayo had managed to retain the Nestor Cup. O'Mahony was young and bright and had brilliant managerial instincts. He had almost instantly created a championship-quality team out of the remnants of the 1985 bunch and the next generation, like McHale, the Mahers and Michael Fitzmaurice, who had captained the Mayo minor All-Ireland-winning side of 1985.

After the Roscommon game, McHale said simply, 'I did it for Dad.' The season was a vindication for the Ballina player. He had endured some fierce public criticism and barbs during his first couple of seasons as a Mayo senior. In the corresponding fixture of 1988, a section of the crowd had been calling to O'Mahony to get him off the field. McHale was regarded then as a basketball player who moonlighted as a midfielder. He moved differently, with the easy grace of a panther, he had a tan and he put his hands on his hips when the play was at the other end of the field. Traditionalists were suspicious of him. It probably took a while before O'Mahony was able to read him properly as well. 'I suppose I found Liam a strange enough guy when I came along at first. One of the big problems I had with him at that time was just getting in touch to finalise training arrangements. His sister would often call for him. There was a sense of "make it happen for me" then. He was into the image and whatnot. But Liam was the main reason that Mayo got to the All-Ireland final in 1989. Against Tyrone, he was a colossus.'

McHale was carefree about football during that period. Basketball was his passion; he was simply good at football. But although O'Mahony may not have known it, the younger man took notice of what was said to him. 'I remember I was acting the maggot for a while under John. I was partying hard like any young fella. And John pulled me aside one night and said, "I know well what is going on down there in Ballina. You have to shape up or you are gone off the panel." Like, I would never bitch or give out and I would show up at training. But, yeah, I found it difficult. You take Ballina in the summer, the heat is on and you maybe have a club match and then there is ten days of a festival on, you are twenty-two years of age and it seems like the whole town is going out on the tear – it is hard to go home. When I reached the age of twenty-eight, I had a different mindset. But look, we enjoyed ourselves then. After league games with Mayo, we would have a few brews. I remember John said one time, "Listen, Liam, you have ten years at this. Maximum. Get your timing right. You have from thirty on to party." He was right.'

But in the summer of 1989 it dawned on even the naysayers that McHale was not only indispensable, he had become Mayo's chief weapon. Tyrone were the Ulster champions that year. On the weekend of the semi-final, McHale drove to Dublin with John Maughan and McStay, and when they stopped for a bowl of soup, there was a clip on *Saturday Sport* showing some of the Tyrone squad wearing T-shirts that read 'Unfinished Business'. They clearly felt it was their year. 'I was surprised. And I just thought, "Well, we will see."'

Mayo scored just 0–12 in that semi-final, but they held a seasoned Tyrone attack containing Eugene McKenna, Kevin McCabe and Damian O'Hagan to just a single point from play. McKenna fisted a second-half goal when the ball came back off the upright to keep the contest interesting, but it was Mayo's day. McHale was omnipotent, running Plunkett

Donaghy and Harry McClure from one parallelogram to the other, spectacular in the air and so easy on the ball. Padden went off with a head wound and returned to the field with a bloody jersey and a bandage, a rousing sight for the faithful. The moment was preserved in a *Western People* photograph bearing the caption 'The Vikings are Coming'.

The final whistle provoked a pitch invasion. It was 16 August 1989, and the county had a full month to come to terms with the reality of an All-Ireland final. O'Mahony was determined to do everything properly. In addition to his skills as a football tactician, he was scrupulous about attention to detail and seemed to have a clairvoyant knowledge of anyone and anything related to Mayo football. He had pieced his team together in the face of considerable odds. Noel Durkin was one of many young Mayo people working abroad in those years. Durkin was from Ballaghaderreen, and O'Mahony was a huge fan of his game. He was a big, rangy, confident attacking forward. But Durkin was an electrician, and in the mid-1980s London was in the throes of the Thatcherite boom. It was the logical place to go. Durkin essentially commuted for the 1988 season, with O'Mahony often making the drive to Dublin airport himself. They agreed that he would stay in Mayo from May through the duration of the 1989 All-Ireland season.

On the morning that Durkin was due to fly home, O'Mahony received a phone call in his house. Durkin was on the line, sounding awkward and apologetic. He had just accepted a job in America that was too good to turn down. His flight was already booked. O'Mahony stood in the stillness of his hallway, and he realised he could hear in the background the honeycomb sounds of the Underground.

'He was heading out to Heathrow. It was that close. So I said, "Jesus, Noel, look it. Come home and sit down. If you want to go afterwards, I will pay your flight." Noel was in two minds, and I understood that. Like, times were the opposite to now. As a football manager, you would be going around begging businessmen to try to find jobs for players so they could stay. And someone like Noel Durkin would have taken a serious pay cut by coming home that year. Electricians could earn three times in London what they could in Ireland then. So we sat down in Gurteen and had a couple of drinks and a chat, and he stayed. After we won the All-Ireland semi-final against Tyrone, he told me he knelt down and kissed the field in Croke Park. I suppose that was part of it. Getting to an All-Ireland was a real dramatic lift to all that gloom and worry about jobs. And it was unknown.'

Ger Geraghty was the other absentee whom O'Mahony tried to lure home. He had played at centre half-forward for O'Mahony on the 1983 All-Ireland Under-21 team. Geraghty was a dazzling player from Ballintubber, but he went to Chicago sometime in 1984. Nobody could blame him. That was the reality.

'Ger Geraghty was the best Mayo player I ever played with,' reckons Kevin McStay. 'Why? Because he could do anything. He was a better catcher than Padden for his age. He had a magnificent left foot. He could be as subtle as Liam Brady or have the power of Peter Lorimer. He could put a bullet on it or he could give you the most beautiful pass, a bit of curl on it wing-side. He could do everything and was the nicest lad you could hope to meet. He was just good fun to be around. Maybe it didn't matter all that much to him. He went away very young. Like, he played in 1983 in that Connacht final. I always thought he was just heading off for a year or two, but he never came back. He had this most beautiful, graceful catch. It wasn't power à la Brian Mullins. He just soared. He had great composure. Pound for pound, he looked like he was going to be a huge, huge player. Liam McHale was the best on that team that I played on. Ger was a good bit better than Liam.'

In January 1989, Mayo had played Donegal in a challenge match, and just as O'Mahony came in the door after the game, the phone rang. It was Geraghty, calling with the news that he was coming home to play ball. O'Mahony had sounded him out the previous year, having heard that his former vice captain was still playing scintillating football on the Gaelic fields around Lake Michigan. Peter Ford had summered out there and was stunned at the ease and quality of his game, given that he was just playing for fun. O'Mahony was thrilled at the news. With Jimmy Browne and McStay and Durkin, Geraghty would bring an entirely new dimension. The manager secured a job for him, driving an oil truck, and over the phone they agreed a date for his return.

'And what happened,' remembers O'Mahony with a rueful grin, 'was that he met a girl who turned out to be his future wife. And that put the kibosh on it. Caroline – I remember the name. God. Ger was such a nice lad that he wouldn't just tell me straight out what was going on, but I knew he was dragging his feet. Like, they would be heading out to work at six in the morning, so I would be ringing at five Chicago time to speak with Ger. After Galway won the 1998 All-Ireland, I was invited out to this thing in Chicago, and I was introduced to this guy who used to be a flatmate of Geraghty's. 'Do you remember me?' he asked me. 'Well, I f***in' remember you. You're the f***er who used to be wakening me at five o'clock every morning looking for Ger.'

Geraghty's return never happened. For years afterwards, O'Mahony wondered about the difference it would have made. His one consolation was that at least Geraghty had had a good reason for staying in America. 'He was the missing link. I believe that if Ger had been living in Ireland in the 1980s, Mayo would have won an All-Ireland.'

A passage from the editorial in the souvenir supplement that appeared in the *Western People* the week before the All-

Ireland final reflects the fierce sense of pride and manifest destiny that took hold of the county during those weeks:

> On the football field, Mayo have won over thirty national titles at all levels, including three All-Ireland senior championships. And the exploits of the county team at national level has gone into the history book, indelibly imprinted by the men of the thirties who were acclaimed as unbeatable in that competition. To all occasions, Mayo have brought a sense of grace and respect with the accent always on playing football of the highest calibre. Mayo teams have thrilled by the sheer exuberance and inventiveness of their play, notably the solo run patented by 'Baller' Lavin.
>
> Win, lose or draw – and let it be recorded that the players will not hear of defeat – the team has done the county proud. They have restored the faith in the old county, they have given the young heroes to emulate, they have generated new confidence, a confidence which has transcended sport into business and other sectors, they have shown that despite massive emigration fuelled by a constant and wilful neglect of the West by successive governments, the heart pounds with a pride that cannot be quelled.
>
> On behalf of our readers throughout the world and on our own behalf, we wish the players, the team management and the backroom personnel and the officials fortitude and success. You enjoy the wholehearted support of all as you set out to bridge a gap of 38 years. And we extend heartfelt wishes to our colleague, Jimmy Browne, who leads the team on this great occasion. Go neiri an bother leat agus le do chairde. Mayo forever! Mayo abu.

It remains a marvellous salute, reading more like an inspired piece of political oration than something from the traditionally sober confines of the editorial space, capturing the delicious sense of a county standing on that high ground between the past and present, with the lovely unselfconscious reference to 'our readers throughout the world' making clear that for those few weeks Mayo was, as T.S. Eliot had it, 'the still point of the turning world'.

Many hundreds came home for the All-Ireland final, and it seemed as if most of those were determined to visit the team in the dressing-rooms at McHale Park after training. There were bigger attendances at training than had been the case at many league games down the years. O'Mahony did everything he could to make the preparations seem ordinary, but he knew in his heart that the players were coping with a very intense and localised type of fame. The squad used both dressing-rooms, and the long corridor would be impassable with people looking for autographs and photographs and simply to be part of it. Saying no was difficult.

'I used to escape back to Galway after training,' says Finnerty. 'It seemed like half of America was landing on us. Midwest Radio was new, and this was manna from heaven for them. There seemed to be a new Mayo song out every day of the week. It was a month of a bloody carnival. The lads living in the county had their heads soaked with the stuff.'

Finnerty had been injured in a challenge game in Longford and still hadn't fully recovered on the week before the final. The selectors decided against starting him. He was acutely disappointed, thinking about the pageantry of the parade and meeting the president and the fact that he would not be in the official team photograph. 'All that kind of stuff goes through your head. You think it won't be the same. But I said, "John, look, if you need me, I am ready." And he said, "I know."'

Ryanair paid for the team to fly to Dublin. It would have seemed daft to refuse. O'Mahony tried to keep control of the situation by refusing to allow journalists on the flight. But there was a desperate clamour for some sort of concession, as though nobody could bear the notion of the team being in the skies and literally untouchable for an hour. It was agreed that two photographers could travel on the flight and take photographs for posterity. 'It was crazy. I cringe when I think about it,' admits O'Mahony. 'But we felt as long as they weren't writing about it, there wouldn't be much harm. As it was, a photographer from the *Sunday Independent* gave a journalist his pass or something, and there was an article about it. It wasn't the right way to travel.'

Peter Ford couldn't have cared less if they had travelled by bicycle. He was completely nonplussed by the excitement of those weeks. The fact of the All-Ireland final didn't hit him until he ran out with the team through the old tunnel at the Canal End. That side of Croke Park was predominantly filled with Mayo fans and the roar seemed to cause a tremor in the ground beneath his feet. 'Never had I felt anything like it. I was just thinking to myself, "God, this is different."'

Within half a second, his adrenalin was pumping. The Mayo defence was regarded as strong. Ford played full-back. In thinking out his strategy for the final, O'Mahony remembered a coaching seminar he attended in which Eugene McGee said that in the 1982 final Offaly did not concede any free within the fifty-yard line against Kerry apart from a penalty. He had forced the Kerry machine to score from play. O'Mahony decided to do the same with Cork. The problem was that it did not translate properly on the field. The game became too free-flowing, with the Mayo cover loose and inviting the Cork players to run at them.

'We had emphasised not fouling, and it took the edge off us,' says Ford. 'Like, John Finn was aggressive, Dermot Flanagan was aggressive. I was aggressive. Even in training, selectors were marking our fouls down – stuff we knew we would get away with. I distinctly remember a few times when Cork guys came through, and in any other game you would have taken them out. F*** the free! I was thinking, "How the hell am I letting this guy in so easily?" We were afraid of the foul.

But John would be wrong to blame himself on that. I should have addressed it before the match. We should have left it to the referee to call our fouls, not ourselves. If anything, we played too much football. Because up to that match, we were aggressive. Tyrone only took seven scores off us. We didn't concede much, like.'

It was an odd game. Cork were understandably haunted by what had happened to them the previous two Septembers and were inhibited for long periods, as though waiting for Mayo to go ahead and win the thing. Mayo looked relaxed to the point of being casual at times. At midfield, McHale and Seán Maher got involved in a bruising struggle with Shea Fahy and Danny Culloty. But there were a few passages of play when McHale appeared capable of overshadowing the other competitors. Late in the first half, he claimed a ball and embarked on one of those sauntering, unstoppable runs, taking a return pass from McStay and then firing his shot wide.

When he turned to run back outfield, he was smiling. Few players smile in All-Ireland finals. 'I laughed,' he remembers. 'Yeah, I was laughing. I got a slip pass from Kevin and booted it wide, and I was thinking, "I don't f***ing believe that." But I am against this thing of putting your hands on your head. I didn't want anyone to see I was struggling. I was trying too hard in the first half. I had been going well and was an unknown quantity, and I had such huge respect for T.J. and Peter Ford and Kevin and these guys that I wanted to make sure we won. But I relaxed in the second half and played better.'

McStay had an almost serene conviction that they would win the match. Finnerty's goal was more than they had planned on, and he can still hear Niall Cahalane screaming something at Colman Corrigan. The Cork sense of fear, of another September crashing down on them, was strong enough to smell. Then Mayo had three easy chances for points and failed to make one. That was when the first shadow of doubt crossed McStay's mind.

At the other end of the field, Ford felt that the Cork full-forward and captain Denis Allen was also beginning to feel dejected. 'There was this sense of "that's another one gone". But they really came back at us. They got a run and they hit the scores. If we'd been a bit more experienced, we probably would have started hitting the ground with injuries to break the thing up.'

Cork came at Mayo in waves and hit four unanswered points in the last ten minutes, from Paul McGrath and their classy wing forward Dave Barry, who had turned in a dream of an All-Ireland performance. For Cork, losing would have been unthinkable; for Mayo, winning was all but unimaginable.

As John O'Mahony walked across the field to console his players, a Mayo woman appeared behind him carrying a huge banner that read 'John Says Keep the Faith'. Henry Wills from the *Western People* snapped the famous photograph. The beaten team stood bereft in front of the Hogan Stand as Allen raised the cup and then launched into a peculiar and passionate speech that included a broadside against the fickleness of the Cork supporters. Ford was in tears. Finnerty stood near McStay and Flanagan, both of whom were too dejected to speak. It wasn't the goal chance that bothered Larry but that series of wonderful scoring opportunities the team created afterwards. After that, there was nothing for it but to leave Croke Park and meet family at the hotel and drink together.

On Monday evening, the team flew back to Knock. As the aeroplane began to descend towards the tiny rural airport, the passengers looked out the window and began to see the long illumination of a procession of car lights across the dark countryside, and as they sped towards the runway it was apparent that thousands of people were waiting there. It was an unforgettable sight, at once fabulous and lonely. Ford was sitting beside a man named Toby McWalter. When he caught his first sight of the crowd, Ford was instantly choked up. He was a no-nonsense full-back and a champion boxer, not given to extravagant displays of emotion. But the tears came rolling down his cheeks, and he was powerless to prevent them. 'It just cut me in two. I suppose I was just thinking, "Ah, f\*\*\* it, how did we blow that?" Afterwards, it was said that there shouldn't have been a homecoming of that magnitude, that people treated us as if we had won. But the thing was, it was spontaneous. People drove out there because they wanted to. For years afterwards, I would meet Toby at different things and he would say, "Christ, Peter, do ya remember that night on the plane?" I was getting pissed off. I eventually had to take him aside and tell him to quit telling people about it. But that night was extremely emotional.'

When the aeroplane began to slow down, they could see the hundreds of faces pressed against the wire. 'The crowd got us all. There was something very sad and very rural about it,' says McStay. 'It almost had the look of a massive country funeral.' The forward had had his fill of drink and managed to escape the crowd. He was drinking a cup of tea with his mother long after midnight on the Monday evening when McHale landed at the door. 'I was jarred up and I couldn't get a grip on the whole thing. But we stuck together.'

The beaten team did a barnstorming tour of the county. They were received as heroes. Finnerty labelled the tour 'the homecoming without the cup'. When they arrived in Moygownagh on the Tuesday, they started and finished the day in Mitchell's pub. Finnerty stood up and gave a long, theatrical speech about missing the goal, which had his audience in convulsions of laughter. 'If I got it, ye'd be talking about me for years to come,' he bellowed. 'Because I missed it, ye'll never f\*\*\*ing stop talking about me.'

In snatched moments between the fatigue and the speeches, the players began remembering sequences of the match. Cork had been brave enough to win the final, but it was clear the Mayo men had enjoyed no luck. Mayo had hit the post twice and the ball came back into play. Cork hit the post twice and it went over the crossbar. 'They got two points in the second half after double hops from Dave Barry and Paul McGrath,' McHale remembers. 'And Paddy Collins was the best referee in Ireland then. He would rarely miss that. These things happen.'

The homecoming seemed eternal, like some kind of messed-up electioneering campaign. 'We completely forgot that we had lost the bloody All-Ireland,' admits Finnerty. 'You are good and jarred, and you stand up on the stage and the crowd roars and you wave. Brilliant! There was hell to pay. Like, when we went to Moygownagh, some of us went on the beer in the Downhill Hotel in Ballina and the bus headed on to Belmullet half empty. And the county board and Midwest Radio were going crazy, like. "Where is the team? Where is the team?"'

In Ballaghaderreen, the St John's National School Band walked ahead of the team bus as it pulled into the big square. O'Mahony stood in front of the microphone and gave a tremendous speech that invoked Seán Flanagan and the spirit of 1951 and the efforts that Noel Durkin had made to be part of this adventure, and he concluded by promising, "We are thinking of next year already."

Every night it was a different venue. The *Western People* carried the homecoming schedule, which 'includes a tour of West Mayo, Westport and concludes in Castlebar'. The beautifully formal closing line read: 'The festivities will conclude with a reception in The Beaten Path.'

By the Wednesday evening, John O'Mahony was nursing serious reservations about the nature of the homecoming, fearing that it had been pitched into another dimension. Martin Carney, who had returned for O'Mahony in 1988 to kick frees and was a substitute in 1989, accompanied the tour until the Wednesday. 'I was old then, and I suppose because I wasn't swept up in it all I could see the absurdity of the thing.'

O'Mahony could not back out. It wouldn't have been fair to people in the towns that were still waiting to show their appreciation. So he did his turn, standing in front of the microphone and delivering a speech that had ceased to have any meaning. 'All you had to do was stand up there and promise you were going to win the thing the following year. Just shite, like. But of course, people would hold you to it later on.'

All through that winter, O'Mahony felt like a teenager trying to control a party in his parents' house. There were interminable fundraisers and dinner parties and GAA club galas, and the presence of a Mayo football player was considered compulsory. There were dozens of distractions from the business of football. When O'Mahony heard on the grapevine that the Mayo Men's Association intended giving the Mayo Man of the Year award to Willie Joe Padden, he met privately with some of the committee members to try to dissuade them. Like everyone else, O'Mahony was immensely fond of Padden. The flair and honesty that the Belmullet man displayed on the pitch had made him a cult figure in the county, and after the All-Ireland final he was in as much demand as any of the ballroom entertainers of the day. O'Mahony wanted it to end. He asked the Mayo Men's Association to honour somebody else.

'Anybody else. And, of course, Irish country people have this complex human nature. Some of the boys thought I wanted the thing for myself. Nothing could have been further from the truth. But I could see their point. The place was packed for that dinner. We were at training the Tuesday night afterwards, and Willie Joe came up and told me he had to go to London for another function. There was good money on offer, too. Like, it was hard for lads to turn down. But it wasn't helping us in terms of next season. I said, "F*** it, Willie Joe, you'll get twice as much if we win the All-Ireland next year." But it was hard for everyone to come back down to earth.'

Galway helped them. Mayo lost to their great rivals in the first round of the 1990 Connacht championship by 2–11 to 1–12. All the speeches and euphoria of the previous September suddenly seemed like echoes from another lifetime. A week later, Kevin McStay collided with Henry Gavin while playing for Ballina against Castlebar in the club championship. He broke his leg in eight places and it ended his football career. 'I think I had lost interest by then anyway. That 1989 final didn't screw up my life, but it is a place I never want to be again.'

He stayed involved, managing the Roscommon minor football team and later guiding the Mayo Under-21 team to the All-Ireland final. John Maughan asked him to consider returning to Mayo football in 1996, and although he was only thirty-four then, he dismissed the idea with haste that he later regretted. Like Martin Carney, he has managed to combine tremendous underage work in Mayo football with a weekend role as a match analyst for RTÉ. Now both men are familiar television faces during the championship. In the beginning, McStay was anxious about the whole television game, questioning how people could accept his point of view given that he had never won an All-Ireland senior medal. Carney, always so moderate and polite, repeatedly told McStay with some steel in his voice that his opinions were just as worthwhile as those of the rest. Gradually, McStay came to believe him.

There have been nights, though, particularly after Mayo's

most recent crushing All-Ireland defeats, when he has sat on that couch in the studio in Montrose and felt acutely conscious of the fact that Mayo is different. Dara Ó Cinnéide, the former Kerry captain, might be there or Tony Davis, who played wing-back for Cork in 1989, splendid men both. 'I sometimes think they look at the naivety of me and Mayo people like me and just think, "God help ye." We go up with big happy heads on us on the trains to All-Ireland finals thinking this will be the year, and so and so will flash over a couple, and sure we will be grand. But winning an All-Ireland is not that simple. And I can't fathom it now. Just the pain – it gets more difficult every year. And I suppose I fear at some level that it has to be getting inside the heads of the players that are there now.'

Maybe that is the reason that Pádraig Brogan dropped the game stone-cold dead once he had finished playing. When I called him to request another meeting, he was polite and awkward but firmly repeated that he had nothing more to say. 'I don't mind what you write about me, but that part of my life is gone. It doesn't matter to me now.' Perhaps he is right. But still. The Brogan goal was sacred. And those September nights in 1989, when they lost the match and still somehow felt like champions, were sacred. Losing would never feel as good again.

# NINE

# IN THE PALM OF HIS HAND

On the Friday night before the 1996 All-Ireland final, John Maughan was visiting his mother, Kathleen, in Crossmolina when the telephone rang. Waiting on the line was a man who had approached Maughan earlier in the week. He'd said he was putting £40,000 sterling on Mayo to land the Sam Maguire. Maughan had looked at him with that amused, charming smile of his and told him he was laying a good bet. Now the man had tracked him down at the home place with less than forty-eight hours to go until the match. All of Mayo was aflame with nervous, jubilant expectation. All-Ireland finals are about nothing if not homecomings. The county was packed with sons and daughters returned from the roaring American cities and from across the Irish Sea for a weekend that promised completion. Maughan could hear the faint lilt of years toiling in Britain when the voice came down the receiver.

'John, are you sure?' the expatriate pressed. 'I'm putting another forty grand on.'

'Go right ahead,' Maughan replied, as though he were assuring the man that the sun would come up tomorrow.

John Maughan's football world will ever spin on the axis of that fortnight. Ten years on, he can admit that phantom details from the tough, drama-choked All-Ireland series against Meath will still suddenly jump from the well of his soul, startling in their keen immediacy and in their pain. Maughan has lost two All-Ireland finals since with Mayo, but now, when making a humdrum phone call or lifting iron in the gym or just lying awake at night, it is back to those furious hours against Meath that his mind transports him. He can still hear and smell 1996, the blood and the sweat of it. The freakish turns, the malevolent fist fight that overshadowed the replay and the final truth that Mayo, on the cusp of a perfect season, were somehow foiled by the brutally obdurate and resilient spirit that distinguished Seán Boylan's championship-winning Meath teams.

All this has been pored over before. It was an All-Ireland series that left a bitter aftertaste, with the Meath players unrepentant and resentful at being painted as the archetypal bad guys in the affair. Whatever unrest the Meath players felt, however, was cushioned by the fact that they had won. The Meath men moved on. They would win an All-Ireland title again just three years later in less acrimonious circumstances. But Mayo football has never quite recovered from what happened in 1996, and because John Maughan was the evangelist behind that adventure, it has become his final.

'I'll probably think about it at some stage today,' he muses, sitting behind his desk one fine spring afternoon in Castlebar. 'Look, it haunts me. It will just go through my mind. And it did change me. It still hangs over me. I would love to have won an All-Ireland title with Mayo, and that match was there for me. It was. And I know for a fact that there are plenty of people in this county who feel that I have blown All-Irelands for Mayo. That's the way it is here.'

John Maughan's great skill has always been to hide that pain. Strangely, Tom Carr, his great friend from their army days, has a face that often betrayed his concerns and doubts when he managed football teams, a giveaway flicker across those solemn, intelligent features. Maughan, though, learned to present himself as a man who never doubted, and even in his darkest football hours, no ripples of fretfulness crossed his face. Through army life and his seriousness about football, he became fantastically fit, and, with the sallow features, the sculpted frame and the cobalt certainty of his eyes, he commanded a following. Maughan dresses immaculately and he speaks with the easy, self-assured loquaciousness of the Irish officer class. He is a fastidious man – when we sit down for lunch in a hotel in town, he automatically examines the silverware and water glass before he uses either. Maughan walks tall, and even though he is greying at the temples now, he maintains the athletic demeanour of his youth. He has a vague movie-star quality, that surfeit of energy which catches eyes when he comes into a room. That is particularly true in Mayo, where literally everyone seems to know him by his Christian name.

In 1996, Maughan had the audacity and the charisma to behave in a fashion that made people believe he could bring Mayo football from chronic disorganisation to an All-Ireland title. From the muddy beginnings of third-division football to the sure ascent through Connacht and the devastating victory over Kerry in the All-Ireland semi-final, Maughan dazzled Mayo folk. He had them in the palm of his hand, and they believed him. But it wasn't smoke-and-mirror stuff. They believed it because Maughan was telling the truth. He radiated self-belief. 'I had no fear,' he remembers wonderingly. 'I was convinced we would win.'

Mayo would be an emptier and lesser place without John Maughan. Nothing in his early life pointed towards county football becoming his chief obsession. His uncles, Frank and Paddy Maughan, had both represented Mayo at junior level, and his father was interested in the game, but the family had a shop in Crossmolina and a farm. 'We were workers.

We worked hard. My father drove a hackney car to Dublin every single Friday and then in holiday periods to take people to the boat. We milked cows before school, and the shop was always there. We were expected home ten minutes after school. And it was grand. I was never afraid of hard work because of it.'

John 'Goo' Maughan died suddenly when the children were still young. It is not an episode in his life that John Maughan likes to talk about, other than to say it left him with 'responsibilities'. Because he was big and had a full-hearted athleticism, Maughan's potential had already been noticed by John Cosgrove, his national school teacher. Maughan used to wear his football boots going home at lunchtime so he would not waste any time tying them up when he got back to the school for a kick-about before the bell rang.

'Football was difficult in the summer. There was hay to be cut. I would always be racing about on a bike. Those are my memories, of tearing from the farm to play a game. I rarely saw Mayo play, although I would hear about Joe Corcoran on the wireless. My mother had lived on the Jones's Road, and so she often spoke of having seen the Rackards of Wexford and the Murrays of Roscommon. Gaelic games was in the background in our house. But my father never went to matches. I was twelve or thirteen when I saw my first real championship match, the 1975 Connacht final. I had my face glued to the wire. I was disappointed, I suppose. But there was no great tradition if you were a teenager then. I played with Crossmolina, and anytime we togged out it seemed to be so Ballina Stephenites could hammer us. The 1951 thing and all that Mayo tradition had no meaning for me then.'

Had it not been for the decision to send him to boarding school, it is possible that Maughan would not have pursued football. As a teenager, he had a falling-out with his teacher in the local school, 'some little thing, and I was sticking to my guns that I was right. So we decided I wouldn't go back.'

There was a strong tradition between Crossmolina and the Carmelite College in Moate. Several local families had sent children there. During the boisterous, darkening shopping afternoons at Christmas-time, Kathleen Maughan would meet those parents down the town and hear glowing reports about the Carmelite. She decided it would do John good. 'It did, too,' he grins. 'It hardened me. I won't forget seeing this big intimidating building the day I was dropped off, and certainly when that big Ford turned for home, there were tears in my eyes, yeah. But it set me on a path. It meant that by the time I joined the Cadets, I was used to that way of life. It made the army easier.'

At Carmelite, Maughan's football career bloomed, nurtured by Father Michael Cremin, the phenomenal Cork teacher and football man who had transformed the school's football from mediocre 'B' level to an elite 'A' standard by the late 1970s. Maughan played on the 1980 team that won the Hogan Cup in a 0–12 to 1–08 victory over St Patrick's, Maghera, played in Croke Park. He was the biggest player on the team, a well-nourished midfielder with a mop of a brown hair. Val Daly, the classy Galway player who would also go on to manage his native county, had an immense game that afternoon, winning the late free that was dispatched by the captain and local boy Jimmy Bradley.

By that time, Maughan had his heart set on the Cadets. The idea of teaching or the civil service frightened him then. One afternoon, he met Dermot Earley, the great Roscommon man. Earley looked splendid in full uniform and seized Maughan's hand in a ferocious grip when they shook hands. It made an impression. And Earley, of course, was the supreme footballer in the west of Ireland at that time. Army life meant plenty of football. Maughan was a well-established Mayo minor, having been called down for trials at the age of fifteen by

Austin Garvin. Although he missed out on that All-Ireland-championship vintage of 1978, he was an automatic selection for the following two years.

He summered at home and inherited his value system from his mother, but it was boarding school and the military that shaped him. The organisation and the drills, the sense of ceremony, the pride in appearance all made sense to him. His one flirtation with trouble in The Curragh occurred because of football. Carmelite made it back to the Hogan Cup final in 1981, and the 1980 team were to return for their official medal presentation on the same weekend. Maughan outlined in writing three reasons why he should be given a day pass and received three flat refusals from his superior officers. It seemed unfair and unreasonable to him, and on the Saturday night he made a call to Father Cremin from the public phone in the hallway of the barracks. His old teacher got hold of a friend from Monasterevin and the arrangement was that Maughan would wait at the side of the church in the town to be picked up at one o'clock the following day. He attended the game in Hyde Park, in which Carmelite beat St Colman's College, Claremorris, by 2–02 to 1–04 and sneaked back into The Curragh at around eleven, assured by his classmates that he hadn't been missed.

At the eight o'clock foot drill the following morning, he was told to fall out. 'I was sat down in the office and told, "We know your movements between 0800 hours and 2300 hours yesterday. If you tell the truth, you have a chance to stay in Cadet School. If you lie, you are finished here. Pack your apparel and report back in two hours." AWOL was the worst crime. I wasn't allowed talk to anyone. I felt they were bluffing, and to this day I suspect that. They knew I was keen to go to the match and probably figured I would take a chance. But it was a great bluff, because I sweated for those two hours and was thinking of how scandalised everyone would be if I was booted out of the army. I had nowhere to turn. So they wheeled me in and I told them everything. It was apparent after ten minutes that they weren't going to expel me, but I was stripped of all privileges and grounded for a full month. That was it for me with stepping out of line.'

Maughan became firm friends with Tom Carr, and the pair went to study in UCG. The only time Maughan becomes in any way sentimental in conversation is when he mentions his college days. Galway was a big liberal village in those years, a bastion for hippies and bar hounds and musicians, a kind of Greenwich Village in the rain-soaked west. Army students stood out. They had an income; several had cars. But within the football fraternity, that didn't matter. Maughan fell under the stewardship of another strong, patriarchal figure in Tony 'the Horse' Regan. It so happened that they had a fine team, and they won two Sigerson Cups, in 1983 and 1984. But what Maughan constantly refers to are the nights of training by the Corrib. They used to make a big pot of stew for afterwards, and when Regan set them to a task, the army boys prided themselves on going just beyond the realms of absolute commitment.

'Look, I knew John Maughan when he was a big soft eighteen year old,' recalls Anthony Finnerty, who studied and played in UCG during the same period. 'He was about three stone heavier than he is now. He was a big soft ladeen. And he was great fun. In the army, he came under the influence of Tom Carr, who is a pure animal for training. And whatever the Horse demanded, they wanted to give back more. They were mad into getting fit. And I remember thinking then that if ever John went about managing a team, he would demand something similar.'

Maughan was impressed by the steely intellect with which Carr approached football. The Dublin man was sinewy and thoughtful, had a black-edged humour and was unflinchingly ambitious about the game. Maughan sat with Carr one night when he wrote a letter to Kevin Heffernan pleading for the opportunity of a trial. When the godfather of Dublin football assented, Carr headed east across the midlands the following Tuesday night. It was during exam time. He made it back to the dormitories after two o'clock in the morning and was in an exam hall seven hours later.

By 1985, Carr was playing on the Dublin team that met Mayo in that year's All-Ireland semi-final. Maughan was centre-back. Carr was centre-forward. They joked and clattered into one another. Although Mayo lost after a replay, 1985 had triggered a kind of rebirth within the county. People reclaimed the championship heritage from the early 1950s. Maughan belonged to a rich vintage. John O'Mahony had chosen him as centre-back on his gilded 1983 Under-21 team. Maughan liked the Ballaghaderreen man, admiring his quiet efficiency and the formidable authority he carried for a man still in his twenties. The final against Derry ended in a draw and the replay was set in the strange location of Irvinestown, the first GAA All-Ireland final to be played in the North. Maughan had a holiday booked in Cyprus, a rare exoticism in the early '80s. He approached O'Mahony about it, and he wasn't forbidden from going. Instead, compromises were made. The holiday was shortened by a week, and O'Mahony asked him to take a pair of football boots and to look after himself for the seven days. When he returned to training with full tan and in high humour, O'Mahony didn't so much as blink but murmured something to his defender about staying behind afterwards. Maughan was glistening and happy that he had come through the session fairly comfortably. He presumed they were going to have a private chat. Instead, O'Mahony explained that he needed to be sure the reserve of fitness was still there. 'And for forty minutes, he murdered me. He ran me into the ground that night.'

The period of time when Maughan was permitted to play elite football without the spectre of injury was brief. Sometime in 1988, Mayo played Longford in a challenge game in Pearse Park and Maughan had a good tussle with Frank McNamee. In the dressing-room afterwards, he mentioned to John O'Mahony that he felt something vaguely bothersome in his knee. O'Mahony took the opportunity to encourage a break. By then, Maughan was voracious about his physical fitness. He was the embodiment of how O'Mahony imagined Mayo should be, and even when the army took Maughan on tours of the Middle East, he trusted his player would never cut corners. In fact, sometimes O'Mahony probably feared that Maughan would push himself too far in the arid heat of Lebanon. 'I was in the form of my life around that time. But the knee got more troublesome. And it just didn't work out.'

Although he is a rationalist, Maughan tried everything. He met an Israeli doctor who was famous in Scandinavia for successfully patching up every Olympic skier with a dodgy knee. He worked on Maughan out in Lebanon in the spring of 1989, and after that Maughan spent a couple of months just jogging, being careful of the knee. When he came back, he trained for four nights perfectly untroubled by the injury, and he can still recall the sense of invincibility that comes with taking the field feeling absolutely strong. 'I was like an iron man then. I said to John O'Mahony that I felt great, that I could have a real crack at this.'

O'Mahony was delighted. He knew how desperate Maughan was to be part of what they all sensed could be a defining season. Mayo were the reigning Connacht champions and had learned a lot in a bruising semi-final defeat against – who else? – Meath in 1988. Then, while training with Castlebar Mitchels, Maughan felt his knee collapse, and that was that. It was blown up like a balloon. That summer, he stalked eminent surgeons and he went tracking down faith healers. His wife,

Audrey, ended up trying to humour him out of his fixation. He did manage to play again eventually, starring in Castlebar Mitchels All-Ireland run in 1994. But in order to do that, he was injecting himself with painkillers towards the end.

We forget. John Maughan has become so completely defined as a manager now that it is easily forgotten how badly he simply wanted to remain a player. He gladly accepted John O'Mahony's invitation to remain with the squad throughout the 1989 All-Ireland championship, and although he maintained the veneer of easy good humour, privately he was distraught.

In hindsight, he recognises that he was always learning about the management game, from Father Cremin and from O'Mahony. In those years, he was living in Galway and working in the army barracks in Athlone, and when he arrived home one evening in 1991, someone from the Clare county board had called wondering if he would consider training the senior football team. For the first time in years, he felt excited. He met a delegation in Gort. The Clare football team did not present a promising portfolio. They had played in the All-Ireland B championship in Sligo and had barely been able to field fifteen players. After listening to friends advising him of the folly of the task, he accepted.

From the beginning, Maughan blended what he had observed from his own managers with his instinctive edge for physical fitness. He was empathetic and ruthless. After two sessions, he concluded that an able group of footballers had become content with mediocrity. They were casual about training and sloppy about timekeeping, standards that were unacceptable to him. In the 1991 Munster championship, they competed with Kerry for about fifty minutes and then settled for the honourable fade. Maughan vowed to himself that he would not permit that to happen again. Early the following season, he took Audrey down to training in Lahinch. She was a good athlete and in a series of running drills left several of Clare's elite footballers trailing in her wake. Maughan began training with them himself and eclipsed a few of them in the runs. That was his yardstick. He chided them for not being able to outpace a crocked man. Praise was dished out sparingly, but by the following spring training was going like clockwork. Players abided by the first rule of being on the field by 7.30 p.m. or staying at home. When they trooped off at dusk, they were spent and satisfied. When the day of reckoning inevitably rolled around in 1992, Maughan knew they would beat Kerry in the Munster final.

'We talked through the eventualities of it. Ambrose O'Donovan had been dropped and that had caused a bit of a stir down in Kerry. We knew he would be coming in and spoke about how we would deal with that. We painted a picture of the game. And see, there was a lot of untapped talent in that team. I just gave them organisation. There were some heroic performances in that match. I can still see Séamus Clancy bulling out of defence with the ball. It was Clare's day, and I was happy for them. But I think I underestimated the magnitude of it. It seemed reasonable to me that a group of players like that should be able to win a Munster championship.'

It was a time of dire straits for Mayo football. They had underperformed dreadfully in a woeful All-Ireland semi-final against Donegal in 1992. Because it was a parched time in Connacht football, they emerged from the province again a summer later, only to receive a terrible and embarrassing hammering at the hands of Cork. Mayo football was struggling. Maughan looked like the solution. In 1995, he was at home on furlough from a tour of Cyprus when the official offer was made. Maughan was adamant the only way he would take the position was if he was allowed to bring in his own selectors, Peter Ford and Tommy O'Malley. That was a luxury rarely afforded Mayo managers, but he was invited to address the board at a meeting and was appointed that night. Then he returned to Cyprus until his tour had concluded and showed up in the Mayo dressing-room one cold evening in the autumn.

After three years of turmoil, the senior panel members were back in a place that they understood. In social situations, Maughan was one of the boys. But at training, it was boot-camp stuff. Training started out extremely tough, and by the following summer it had a psychotic edge to it. The team had somehow played their way through to a league semi-final during a training programme that meant that the Sunday matches were more of a reprieve from Maughan than an event in their own right. 'No matter how hard it got,' remembers David Brady, 'fellas never minded, because we could all see the benefits of it. We were all in it together.'

The trip to London at the outset of the 1996 championship is the one they will carry with them into old age. Maughan had decided that the result was a foregone conclusion. He had drawn up a programme that involved a rigorous running session on the Saturday before they flew across to Heathrow and then a get-together on the Sunday morning before they took the bus to Ruislip for the match. 'It was a fierce hot morning, and John kind of lost the run of himself a bit, because before we knew it, we were in a hard session,' explains Anthony Finnerty. 'He found some kind of a park, and I'll always remember these Indian lads playing cricket and stopping to look at this bunch of Irish lunatics going hell for leather.'

Finnerty was Maughan's favourite whipping boy. He was fondly known as 'Fat Larry' throughout Mayo after heading out for a summer in New York as a student in 1982 and availing himself of the cheap pizza and quarter-pounders with copious mayonnaise. He returned in September cheerful and chunky. One of the huge pop songs of that year was 'Zoom' by Fat Larry's Band. Someone took a look at Finnerty and coined a classic. Maughan and Finnerty were friends. The manager knew that Finnerty had the temperament to cope with the blunter truths of his training philosophy. And it helped to curb Finnerty's enthusiasm for the social side of county football. In 1991, John O'Mahony had gently dropped Finnerty from the panel, frustrated by his lack of fitness. He nudged him in the direction of Maughan, who was then just beginning his purges in Clare. So Finnerty trained in Lahinch. Worse for him, he was living in Galway and grew to dread and expect the knock on the door at seven in the morning. This was long before the commuter frenzy afflicted Ireland, and the pair of them could cycle the leafy road to Oughterard and back in solitude. When Finnerty rejoined the Mayo panel later that summer, he was superbly fit. But by 1996, he was thirty-five years old, and on that weekend in London, he was suffering.

'We almost lost that match!' he insists. 'Only for Maurice Sheridan was on song, we were in trouble. I had damaged my back in a car accident and then I aggravated it in a challenge against Dublin, so I was unfit, but John had a bit of a crisis getting a full-forward. John Casey ended up there and had a brilliant year, but I think he had yet to try him. So Maughan had written London off and we were flat. I was the worst of the lot, got taken off early and shouldn't have lasted as long as I did.'

The final score was 1–11 to 1–05. The team were scheduled to fly back to Dublin that evening for a final session on Monday morning. In the dressing-room, Maughan hinted that a few pints would be acceptable, but he warned his players that if they went to town, they would regret it. So they went to both towns, starting in London, tippling on the plane, cruising the country bars in Dublin and paying the inevitable social call to CopperFace Jacks nightclub before finishing up late in their hotel. David Brady's last distinct memory is of Finnerty, a champion Irish dancer, entertaining the gathering with a jig performed on the top of a grand piano. Nobody is sure how late the night went. 'But I'll put it like this,' Finnerty says, 'most fellas would have had the breakfast before they went to bed.'

Maughan hadn't been joking. At ten o'clock, he stormed the rooms and more or less marched his team out to the field at Westmanstown, and he ran them until they literally began to drop. Finnerty felt the strain more seriously than others. Brady remembers not knowing whether to laugh or intervene as Maughan stood above the senior player, who was on his knees. 'You're a disgrace, Anthony. You haven't got the heart.' And then the immortal groan: 'I have the heart all right, John. I just haven't got the lungs.'

That morning was the closest Finnerty came to quitting. He never felt as low. 'Look it, we ran for two hours straight with a few gallons of beer inside us. I was on my knees. I crawled! I could have died. The worse I got, the harder he got. At one point, I said, "F*** it, I am going home." Noel Connelly was beside me, and he wouldn't let me, he kept saying, "Don't quit on it now. You are through the worst of it." But was I f***.'

The personal tutorials that Maughan gave Finnerty became one of the motifs of that summer in Mayo. Somewhere along the way, Maughan grew tired of 'Fat Larry' and took to addressing Finnerty as 'Meatball'. The message was serious but never vindictive. Finnerty never felt bullied or threatened. The Tuesday after they regained the Connacht championship, beating Galway by 3–09 to 1–11, Maughan organised a treat on the beach at Enniscrone. They ran an acceptable five miles, and then Maughan chanced upon a stretch of soft sand. He almost passed out at the sheer bliss of it. 'Sure, he thought this was heaven,' Finnerty says. 'It felt like quicksand. Look, I was thirty-five years old then, I had played a Connacht final and ran five miles. And in fairness, we had a fair crack at it in the pub after winning. I was bunched. I ate sand that evening; I tasted sand. Like, it was no problem to the younger lads. Guys like James Nallen and David Heaney, these were different athletic specimens to the likes of me. These were super-athletes. Sure, I would beg Maughan for a bit of leniency. And he would just grin back at me and say, "Look it, Meatball, I'll knock that belly off ya yet." I vowed I would never have more than three beers after a match for the rest of the championship. And the hoor must have guessed, because he never ran us as hard again.'

There was always a purpose behind the attention that Maughan paid his players. He regarded it as his moral obligation to convert those players with motivational issues. When Martin Carney told him that a kid from Balla named Ronan Golding was one of the best minor players he had ever coached, Maughan was obsessed with guiding him towards the path of righteousness. Golding was hugely gifted, immensely laid back and wasn't sure if the path of righteousness was one he wanted to travel. Nor was he certain if he was physically mature enough for the rigours of senior football.

'There was a period in my life,' smiles Maughan now, 'when I spent more time with Ronan Golding than everyone else. What Martin said was good enough for me. I met Ronan in the morning, at lunchtime, in the evening. We met all over the county. We biked. We went rowing. We ran together. I challenged guys in the gym, me being the benchmark – see if you could beat me type of thing. But I didn't go out to kill guys. I have often heard about this Maughan 'regimental' tag, and I don't know. My teams were disciplined. I just wanted them to reach their own potential.'

Those sessions had healing qualities. After the 1996 All-Ireland senior final, nobody was in a more pitiful state than Liam McHale. The big Ballina man has a sensitive temperament to begin with, and the savagely dark turn that the series took for him gnawed at him through the winter. He consoled himself on the basketball courts and by sinking pints with the brothers, Seán and Anthony. Although he had shown himself to be among the best footballers in Ireland the previous September, he wasn't sure that he could stomach playing for Mayo again. Maughan rang him constantly and wanted no big commitments or promises. He just persuaded him to show up for the first few training sessions before Christmas. McHale obliged. It was a practice of Maughan's to produce a big weighing scale to determine what sort of shape his charges were in at the beginning of any football season. They used to strip down to their briefs like prizefighters and hop up on the scales so one of the selectors could take notes. McHale knew he was carrying a nice winter coat and was almost fearful of Maughan's reaction. As he waited in line, John Casey was muffling guffaws behind him, because they all knew the big man was hefty. McHale made a show of daintily hopping onto the iron platform, bending his legs and flexing his arms in a parody of the Mr Universe contests. Then he skipped away like an ingénue from a screen test. 'Get back up there,' yelled Maughan. 'Eighteen stone. Holy Christ!'

'That yoke must be broken,' McHale shouted as he scuttled back into the pack. But he knew. Maughan had the glint in his eye. Liam McHale was the latest project.

'John and I are friends, but we had rows too. As a senior player, I would often let my feelings be known in private,' McHale admits. 'But there was no way he was going to let me off the hook on this one. So we decided that evening that he would hammer me for three months. In addition to training, he met me at the gym every Wednesday and Friday for forty-five minutes' lifting and forty-five minutes' running. I had to shed two stone before he stopped. And it was three months of a nightmare. He never let up. Even then, I was conscious that the time and energy he was putting into just getting me back to fitness was amazing. But I was too knackered to appreciate it. Not a lot of managers would do it. By Christmas, I was back on form.'

Maughan was like a circus master of old, a flamboyant figure shouting and coaxing and cajoling the very most out of the material around him. He was a desperately young manager, just twenty-nine years old when he led Clare to that Munster senior championship and in his mid-thirties when he led Mayo to the brink of an All-Ireland title. And he looked modern. In an era when many GAA managers were wearing their shirtsleeves rolled and Farah slacks, Maughan wore shorts on the sideline.

It was the players, of course, who made the runs and blocks and saves and scored the points and goals. But it was Maughan's phenomenal energy that made the season so special. It would be wrong to state that the relationship between Maughan and the Mayo public soured after the failure to clinch the Sam Maguire that autumn. However, it definitely grew more complicated. Even though Mayo returned to the All-Ireland final in September 1997, when they lost to Kerry in a final salvaged from mediocrity by the nonchalant brilliance of Maurice Fitzgerald, there was plenty of criticism of his managerial style. His decision to play Dermot Flanagan in that match even though he was labouring with a hamstring problem (and was replaced early) was the chief stick used to beat him with in a critical backlash over his handling of that game. But the plain fact was that Flanagan, one of Mayo's most consistent defenders, had passed a fitness test that weekend. Maughan's tactical instinct was often held against him. Musing on the issue on one dank February afternoon when we met in 2004 to discuss his return to the Mayo post, Maughan thought for a while and replied, 'Well, people have said Maughan should have done this or should have done that on the sideline. Hey, you can only dance with the girls in the dancehall.'

In 1998, after two years of ferocious effort, Mayo were beaten by Galway in the Connacht championship. The county sat idle as John O'Mahony led a scintillating Galway team to a famous All-Ireland victory. Invariably, there were mutterings about how stupid Mayo had been to ever let the Ballaghaderreen man go. And yet the following July, when Mayo reclaimed the Connacht championship from Galway, John Maughan was chaired from the field by ballyhooing Mayo fans. It was the stuff of political fable, and it illuminated the notion that west of Ireland football had become a theatre of competition between O'Mahony and Maughan.

'How do you handle that?' Maughan asks of that occasion now. 'Do you physically throw yourself off a chair? I was well aware of the stupidity of me being in that position, given all that had gone on. I just wanted out of there quickly. I was hugely embarrassed. I was quite conscious of how it seemed. And sure a couple of weeks later we lost the All-Ireland semi-final, and the knives were being sharpened again.'

He agrees that in his playing days he had a close bond with O'Mahony but argues that the nature of football means that confidences are built around the purpose of the team and dissolve with those teams. 'We were close, yeah. But it is different now. I have a relationship with guys now that I know I will not have in ten years' time. When I got into management, it just didn't enter my mind to be ringing and asking around for advice or whatever. I did sit down in 1996 with an All-Ireland-winning manager, just to get a feel for it in my own mind. But when you start doing this, relationships fall to one side. John was off doing his thing in those years. When I came back to manage Mayo the second time, through the last year of my tenure, John was writing locally and was doing his radio show. And I felt as though I could have done without that. I never said anything. I just thought, well, this wheel will go around, you know. But John and I get on fine as people.'

He shares with O'Mahony the strange sensation of being known absolutely everywhere within the county. It is an odd, intense sort of fame that is never remarked upon. If there is a crucial difference between the men, it is that the Mayo public has always been more deferential towards O'Mahony than to Maughan. The years of absence and the reputation for greatness he achieved with Leitrim and Galway gave O'Mahony an almost untouchable status. For Maughan, the ride was always going to be rougher. There have been many days when he has heard the jibes from behind the wire. After high-profile disappointments, he has received letters the contents of which he declines to elaborate on other than to say they were unpleasant and, always, anonymous.

Over the years, he learned to steel himself to the point of indifference. In the frenzied melancholy that fell over the county following the 1996 loss, he hid away for a few days, almost catatonic with exhaustion when he drank three pints at the homecoming. A few nights later, some friends insisted that he come over to Newmarket for a few days of racing and peace. In later years, the disappointments didn't take as much out of him.

Although he left the army, the stubborn streak and sense of absolute certainty it had bred in him stayed with him. Maughan knows how bad David Brady felt throughout the last month of the 2004 All-Ireland campaign, when Maughan decided to relegate him to the substitutes. It was a controversial issue. 'It was hard to know how to manage that,' he sighs. 'Look, if I meet David Brady socially, we will have a drink. People think we would take the eyes out of each other. He was annoyed, I know that. But I made a decision. The last thing I wanted to do was to bring grief to the team. And, look it, when David came in against Kerry last year, he was great. He brought presence to a terrible day for Mayo. I heard he turned in his best-ever performance against Donegal in the league last month. And that defies logic, given his age.'

If dropping Brady was a mistake, Maughan will live with it. He has had his failures. His time with Fermanagh did not end happily. After the 2003 season, he arrived for an emergency meeting with players to find some were late and others had cried off with dubious excuses. Maughan walked. He says he had lost the confidence of the players. He has no regrets. Yet even Fermanagh people felt a brief sprinkling of the Maughan magic, when he guided the county to a famous win over Donegal in a wretched match at the beginning of the 2003 championship. Afterwards, as he walked the length of Brewster Park towards the dressing-room, the home crowd rose in a standing ovation and the sun shone over Enniskillen as Maughan waved to acknowledge the acclaim. For that evening, anything seemed possible.

Maughan has managed Roscommon for the past two years. But regardless of whatever success he achieves there or with any other county, the distinction must be that with Mayo he always made it seem like a vocation. On a television show on the eve of 2006's All-Ireland football final, Maughan was asked if he would ever consider going back and managing Mayo. Looking tanned and relaxed, Maughan beamed and asked jokingly, 'Would they take me back?' It got a laugh but there was something poignant about the reply, a hint that, for all the strong and important guidance he had provided for Mayo football, he remains unsure of his place in the affections of the county. Not enough time has passed for the crystallisation of his legacy. But the more years that go by without Mayo regaining the Sam Maguire, the more fondly Mayo football people will recall the excitement and possibility of the John

Maughan years. However, if John O'Mahony can take it that one step further, the loose talk will be that Mayo would have won plenty more if they had had the cop on to stick with the Ballaghaderreen man all those years ago.

'Course they will,' acknowledges Maughan with a broad smile. 'But then there will be a lot of people who won't mind. They will forget about all that stuff for a while. All they want to do is win the thing. And I am the same. I will be delighted if they do it under Johnno. Hand on heart. And I will wish that it had been me in charge. I would tell a lie otherwise.'

It could be that in ten or one hundred years' time, the name of John Maughan will not feature on the gold-tipped scroll of football managers who got to experience those heavenly, perpetual seconds of standing at the edge of Croke Park and knowing that their team was about to win the All-Ireland. He came damn close.

That fact does not diminish his standing. Like all managers, like all people, Maughan made mistakes. But he was and is still an immense force of nature within Mayo football. In those melodramatic and emotional nights after the 1996 defeat, Maughan briefly crossed paths with the emigrant who had gambled big on his native county. For once, the manager was filled with trepidation and lost for words. The stranger gripped his hand and offered a reassuring smile. 'Don't be worrying about that, John. I had the draw covered at eight to one.'

It was the first time Maughan had laughed heartily in weeks. He understood. He was big enough to accept the hero worship and the jagged edges of dark talk as inevitable. Because there were days when Mayo loved John Maughan, there were days when they had to hate him. He had the grace and bravery to understand that the truth is somewhere in between. He pauses for a few moments when asked how he views his years with Mayo, poised and alert behind his desk.

'I know in my heart I made a contribution.'

# TEN

# BALLINA BRAVES

Liam McHale strolls up towards Caffolla's restaurant on Bridge Street, the mackerel glint of the River Moy at his back and a broad smile on his face. In Ballina, everybody knows Liam. During more than fifteen years of playing football with Mayo, he was both lionised and treated as a pantomime villain by the public. From the beginning, when John O'Mahony persuaded him to turn out for his Under-21 team in 1984, McHale was different: tall and languid and almost smooth in the way he played the game of football. His attributes were not as immediately obvious as those of the high-flying Willie Joe Padden or Peter Ford, with the shuddering intensity he brought to teams. McHale was first and foremost a basketball player of unusual ability, and he brought the sensibility of the American sport to the Mayo football teams with which he played. In the 1980s, McHale appeared loose-limbed and full of jive alongside the stiff, mechanical athletes of the day. He had a tan and was easily distinguishable, and he was no hatchet man. In the beginning, some people felt he was a dilettante. He heard plenty of insults. That had all changed by 1989, when McHale emerged as the most powerful young midfield player of the year. He would remain a target for a minority of disaffected Mayo fans, but by the '90s it was abundantly clear that despite his exploits on the basketball court, big

Liam could not really bear to leave Mayo football to its own devices. Famously, he lost six All-Irelands in a Mayo jersey and declared that the success he enjoyed for Ballina on the basketball courts staved off the bleaker repercussions of those defeats. 'I reckon I'd be a wino on the streets now if I didn't play basketball,' he mused three summers ago when he was a county selector under John Maughan.

These days, you will find McHale behind the counter in Mac's, the bar he owns with his brother-in-law Brian McStay. The night work and the sociability of the bar life suit his easy-going nature, although the late hours mean he can't shoot hoops as frequently as he would like. When McHale talks about his football life now, he is brutally straightforward about the legacy of his football career. 'If you were trying all your life and won nothing on a national level, you would regard yourself as a loser. I don't, because we had great success in the basketball with a small club. But I think I would trade all of that for one All-Ireland football medal at this stage, which is a very hard thing for me to say. See, I still get shudders thinking about the All-Irelands that we lost, and I will always carry that with me. You imagine that if you play in six, you would get one of them. But we never got that bit of a break in those games. And I tried my best, but we just couldn't win them.'

The supreme years of McHale's basketball life coincided with the most anarchic period for Mayo football, the early 1990s. Two disappointing championship defeats in Connacht after the heroics of 1989 presaged the abrupt removal of John O'Mahony as manager. The appointment of Brian McDonald, a proven football man with an All-Ireland pedigree from his Dublin days, seemed fundamentally sound. McDonald was probably more abrasive in his approach than O'Mahony, and his attempt to impose a new order on a panel of football men set in their ways was understandable. But it ended with a players' coup in the autumn of 1992 as a result of which reports of the senior panel pushing cars around a car park in the depths of the previous winter came to the attention of the media. The bare story made it sound as though a proud football county had lapsed into the realms of farce.

Peter Ford was captain that year and became the man most associated with the players' revolt that forced the resignation of the manager. 'I regretted it almost immediately,' Ford says now. 'It became apparent that Brian's family were being taunted and threatening phone calls were made to his house, and I had never imagined that could happen. I suppose the thing achieved its immediate aim, in the sense that Brian resigned. Ultimately, what we should have done was resign as players. The thing was, the evening in the car park was great fun. We pushed the selectors' cars. And we loved it. But what annoyed us was that we were in the car park because there was no field organised to play on. There was actually probably merit in that drill. It was bloody hard. The thing was, we hadn't such a bad side – we could have been in an All-Ireland final in 1992. But it took a while for Brian to get things going. Maybe there was fall-out from the way John O'Mahony was let go, but the first night we met only ten guys showed up. I was captain, so I was motivated to do as well as I could. It just didn't take off for us, and it was terrible the way it ended.'

It was during that turbulent winter that Anthony Finnerty delivered perhaps the best one-liner in the history of Gaelic games. The team were training one night, and a designated drill involved leaping in the air to catch an imaginary football. If anything, the exercise was ahead of standard thinking, designed to improve timing and focus, but the more traditional players were dubious about its usefulness. The squad of Mayo men moved across McHale Park under the floodlights, leaping every few yards for footballs that were not there. Near the halfway line, Finnerty suddenly broke away and began jogging towards the dressing-room on his own.

McDonald shouted after him, demanding to know where he thought he was heading. 'I'm goin' to get me gloves,' Finnerty called back. 'The ball is wet.'

All these years later, it remains a delicious, blackly comic episode. In his parting address to the county board, McDonald actually reported the story, in part to demonstrate how unruly his players were but also, perhaps, because he appreciated the simple, killer genius behind the retort. It was a smart-ass gesture, yes, but it was also a timeless observation on the ultimate vanity and folly of grown men chasing a football – and in this instance literally a fantasy football – around a field for a contest that, as history has repeatedly instructed, they will ultimately lose. It is hard to imagine such a wicked and surreal and self-deprecating story emanating from any county other than Mayo.

'The gloves? That was just a just a bit of banter,' Finnerty smiles, remembering the story. 'I felt sorry for Brian McDonald because the stand the players took ought to have happened as soon as O'Mahony got the axe. It was a hard one to call. Like, Brian was a good football guy, but the players were used to John's style. And McDonald was trying to improvise. His methods were different, and he probably wanted us to be a tougher team. He was always all right with me. I think he took me with a pinch of salt. Like, I don't know how hurt Brian was about all that happened, but I am sure it can't have felt too great. After the whole story about the cars broke, we felt like a laughing stock, but we had brought it on ourselves. The players' revolt was regarded as a success, but I am not sure that it was, because it led to the humiliation the following year.'

The image of Mayo's elite football men labouring to move a car with a perfectly good engine might have been a symbol for those years. In an appalling period for Connacht football, Mayo simply weren't poor enough to lose the provincial championship in 1993. Jack O'Shea had been the solution after McDonald's resignation. The Kerry man was an inexperienced manager, but he was one of the most prolific All-Ireland-winning football players of the century, and he regarded All-Ireland finals as no big deal. O'Shea was seen as the chemical needed to set Mayo alight. After winning a desultory provincial title against Roscommon (it finished 1–05 to 0–07), Mayo met Cork in the All-Ireland semi-final. It was the worst championship defeat that a Mayo side had suffered since O'Shea's rampant young Kerry team had destroyed them back in 1981. The *Western People* branded that day, 15 August 1993, Black Sunday.

Cork were the ascendant team, with a young and almost svelte Colin Corkery giving a fine exhibition at full-forward. The Mayo side was made up of a fragile group of veterans from the 1989 campaign. Dermot Flanagan had to leave the field after five minutes with a severe hamstring tear, and it was as though his departure destroyed their equilibrium. The final score would become the most infamous in Mayo football history: Cork 5–15, Mayo 0–10. Many thousands of people left Croke Park midway through the second half, and by the end of the match the broad steps of the Canal End were strewn with green-and-red flags.

A story was told about Josie Munnelly, one of the enduring heroes from the 1936 team, leaving the stadium early to return to Mayo buses parked on Dorset Street. The driver was listening to the commentary, and he shook his head gravely at Munnelly as he climbed the steps. Cork had added the rattlesnake sting of two goals in the seventieth minute. 'It's 5–15 now, Josie,' the driver sighed. And Munnelly snapped back, 'Did I ask you the bloody time?'

The most damning aspect of that miserable match was that after fifty minutes Ronan Golding had clipped a point from play to leave the score at 1–10 to 0–07. With twenty minutes of play remaining, the match was notionally alive as a contest. Then Cork went to town. They scored 3–02 in the last four minutes of the match. Mayo had disappeared, and if they were not quite complicit in their own downfall, they were compliant. There was no anger. Kevin O'Neill, the young Knockmore player who would finish the year with an All-Star, performed valiantly and left the field having kicked five points. It was reasonable to assume he had a long, bright future ahead of him.

One of the few other players to emerge with an enhanced reputation was McHale, but in the dressing-room afterwards he sounded genuinely sickened as he admitted that Mayo had quit on the field. 'It was terrible, disgraceful,' the Ballina man said that afternoon. 'It's that bad to be beaten when you've given it 100 per cent, but it's very hard to take when you've given up halfway through an All-Ireland semi-final.'

That night, McHale disappeared into Dublin's drinking caverns with Maurice Buckley, an old pal from his basketball life. Buckley listened to McHale's woes. The thought of returning to all the grief and antipathy in Mayo was genuinely bothering him. So they hatched a plan. In the morning, they nursed raging headaches on the SeaCat across to Anglesey. They headed up to visit a friend in Manchester and then took a train down to London. The Notting Hill Carnival was on. McHale was absolutely unknown and safe among the Rastafarians and Marley doppelgängers, and he liked that just fine. 'I think it must have been ten days after the match by the time I made it back to Ballina. I was so embarrassed and low after the whole thing that I just wanted to forget about it.'

It was odd that he bothered to put himself through it. In the world of Gaelic games, the television men often alluded to McHale's ghost life as a basketball player, but very few people understood just how good he was. When he was still a teenager, McHale had decided against taking up several offers of scholarships to American colleges. It might seem like a perverse decision given that hundreds of young Mayo people were flying to nothing but uncertainty in America. McHale would have had the advantages of the collegiate scene. He enjoyed receiving the visiting scouts and listened to their pitches, and in later years he spent summers in the east-coast cities. 'I loved America, but I could never live in a country like that. Too fast. Too hectic.'

Ballina was Manhattan enough. If McHale was small-town, then he was gloriously unapologetic about it. As a basketball town, Ballina always had ideas slightly above its station. And once the McHale boys grew up, they had the substance too. Seán was a fine, crafty player with a brilliant intuition for the game. Anthony was, in the parlance, 'a banger': a long-haired strongman who knew the darker arts of rebounding but who also possessed a sweet shooting touch. Liam was the youngest, and he could play anywhere. He was six foot six and could dribble like a point guard, he had swift hands, excellent vision, he could play the big-man role and he had the strength and speed to shadow the professional American players who began playing for Irish national league clubs in the early 1980s. Ballina used to play in the community centre in Killala, and for twenty years it was the most raucous and intimidating indoor sporting arena in the country. Ballina could go entire seasons without getting beaten there.

Tony McHale used to watch his sons play regularly. He was a Knockmore man and didn't know much about the game, but he became deeply interested, and in the years when Ballina were challenging for the league, he took to storming the dressing-room at half-time to give impromptu talks. Tony would come barging through the door, and Terry Kennedy, the team coach, would look up and, although he was vexed, give Tony the floor. The advice was always the same: 'Ye need to get the ball to Liam more. And, Anthony, you're shooting too much.'

When he was a teenager, McHale was obsessed with basketball. In the summers, he would spend four hours a day just shooting a ball at a battered ring on an outdoor court in Ballina. He regularly outscored opposing American players, knocking down 30 and 40 points a game at weekends. One Saturday night, he dropped a record 58 points against LaVerne Evans, one of the best Americans ever to play in Ireland. He shot 29 out of 39 free throws that night. Ballina won two national cups in the '90s. The most satisfying was against Neptune of Cork, when the last seconds were falling from the electronic clock and the western celebrations, distinguished by the hammered bodhrán that became the Ballina symbol, had already begun. Liam got his hand to a slack pass and spied his brother Seán belting up the court. Seán had quit playing at twenty-eight when Ballina needed a coach, but he had suited up for this cup run and even though his hamstring was destroyed by now, he was tearing up the court like a ten year old. Liam slipped his brother a pass, and watching him make a simple lay-up of no real consequence was probably the happiest moment of his sporting life. It was as close as he got to saying thanks.

The brothers always looked after Liam. There were squabbles in the basketball club but never anything poisonous. The club was like a family. In the worst days of Mayo football, it was like an escape. They had interminable road trips to Cork and Dublin and Belfast, big men crammed into economy minibuses to play in halls that were usually empty in comparison to Killala. He could call in to Deora Marsh, the smiling Ohioan who ended up in Ballina by accident and never left. Deora drank coffee and Guinness and smoked cigarettes and can still produce unbelievable, showboating dunks long after his fortieth birthday. McHale was great friends with the McStay brothers. Paul was an unorthodox left-handed guard. For several winters, Kevin used to drive down from Roscommon to take Ballina for training. Liam began going out with Sinéad McStay, and later they married.

In the worst days of football, McHale could disappear into this basketball family. On the night after Leitrim beat Mayo in the 1994 Connacht final, Liam and Sinéad were standing at a bar in town when a drunk man walked up and started barracking him. Liam tried to charm him away, promising they would talk about the match another time. 'You have to talk to me now, McHale,' he growled. 'I paid good money in to see that. I paid ten pound.' For once, the mellow giant snapped. 'You think I saw any of your money?' he yelled.

It was remarkable that McHale didn't quit, for by 1995 playing for Mayo appeared to offer nothing but disappointment and humiliation. But McHale turned up at training, and all he saw was kids glimmering with potential. He liked the Crossmolina gang. Jimmy Nallen was raw and gangly and had an astonishing athletic capacity. When he moved with the ball, he seemed to have the genetic hardwiring of a hare. Sometimes Liam watched a young blond-haired forward named Ciaran McDonald with something close to awe. In basketball, Liam had a keen enough eye to recognise the perfect, flawless jump shot when he saw it. McDonald kicked the football with the same hypnotic technique. He enjoyed this cocky Ballina kid, David Brady. They had tight young defenders like Kenneth Mortimer and David Heaney. They had a thoroughbred free-taker, Maurice Sheridan. He kept an eye on John Casey, an amusingly confident young lad from Charlestown who had the burst of speed of an Olympic sprinter. It was not as if the county had stopped rearing football players. Liam was there for the long haul.

The supporters had begun to sense that. In the 1993 championship, McHale had been racing for a ball with a player from Roscommon and because he was being dragged back, he struck out wildly with his elbow. The blow caught his opponent square on the face and McHale was mortified. It looked more dangerous than it was, and he was sent off. Leaving the ground that day, he received back slaps like never before. It confused him. He felt as if the fans needed him to do something provocative to show that he cared. 'I think Mayo people began to see that this thing mattered to me then, but, funnily, I was never as disappointed as I was that day.'

By 1996, it was abundantly clear that he cared. Under John Maughan, McHale had the experience and the edge to match the athleticism, and in the drawn All-Ireland final against Meath he was the outstanding performer on the field. Back in 1989, he was too light to absorb the joint attentions of the Cork big men, Shea Fahy and Danny Culloty. Now he was the senior man, pitting his wits and muscle against the superb Meath midfielder, John McDermott.

During the long build-up to the replay, letters of a vaguely unpleasant nature used to arrive at the McHale house. Annabelle McHale was desperately nervous about the sporting pursuits of her sons. She never went to see them playing football or basketball and refused to watch matches on video, even when they guaranteed her that they had won the match and had not been hurt. On championship Sundays, she would go for a walk or visit a friend, trying to avoid the radio and television commentaries, in a state of high anxiety until she heard that her boys were safe and well. She found the fortnight leading up to the Meath replay unbearable, particularly when Liam or his brothers opened envelopes bearing scrawled messages that contained nonsense threats. 'You are not going to finish this game.' 'You are going to be sent off or carried off.'

'Mum would be throwing holy water on me. She was freaking. I would be saying, "Mother, I am not going to be able to finish this thing if you don't leave me alone. This is driving me crazy, I'm going to have to move into a hotel." And then, of course, we went up for the replay and I did get sent off, and when I got back to the house, she would say, "I told you this would happen. Why did you get involved? Why didn't you stay up the other end of the field?" And sure what could I say?'

The photograph of McHale walking off the field, head bowed in dejection, just six minutes into the All-Ireland-final replay has become one of the most recognisable Mayo football images. He had been the most influential footballer on the field in the draw, but, more importantly, he had a decade-old reputation for being a supremely clean player. There was no question that he had come barrelling into the heart of the action when what might have been a minor incident involving Finnerty and Ray Dempsey of Mayo and Darren Fay of Meath quickly flared into what appeared to be a general riot.

'I got blamed for starting that row,' acknowledges Finnerty now. 'Darren Fay had the ball, and he was coming out. I saw the ball, and I did lift my elbow, but I was trying to swipe the ball so it would pop out. On television, it looked very much like I had thrown my elbow at his face. But my elbow was nowhere near his face. It was silly, because Ray Dempsey was coming in hard from behind. Between the two of us, it looked like an assault. My theory on the row situation is this. Before the final, Pat McEnaney [the referee] came to visit us in Ennis and he said, "Look, I saw ye guys coming in pushing in the semi-final, and it seemed to me ye had this preconceived notion that it was one in, all in." He said, "If this happens, two players will go." We said fine. So Maughan told us, "If something happens, let no Mayo man strike a fella. Go in and push, but you must not be sent off for striking." But in Meath, they interpreted [McEnaney's words] to mean if there was a shemozzle, they had a licence to flake. Because only the first two guys would get sent off and then fourteen guys could flake all round them. So there was my challenge and Ray Dempsey's, but then the blows came from Meath. I got a bad punch, and nobody really saw it. It came over my shoulder into my ear, and I had a sore ear for a good two months afterwards. I went down. McHale jumped over me, but all he was doing was pushing. The Mayo guys did not start punching until they had been hammered. Meath lads were picking guys off from behind. McHale got a fierce belt from behind when he was struggling with McDermott, and he had blood coming out of him. It was terrible that Liam was sent off. Funny, I met Trevor Giles since that, a lovely lad. And I had a good chat with Mark O'Reilly, and we spoke about a lot of things but not that match. See, I pushed myself really hard and wanted to play in that final, but, being honest about it now, I was past it. I started the replay instead of David Nestor, and now I feel it was a game too far for me. I cannot watch those matches to this day, and I don't think I ever will. I retired. That was the end of me. I never played a game for Mayo after that. And those few days after the final were different. Grainne was with me on the Monday, and I drank nothing. I was back home teaching on Tuesday. I just wanted back into life. That was that.'

For McHale, it was not so easy to draw the curtains. Always the peace-broker, he found it hard to accept that he had been singled out as the arch-culprit in a mass brawl. He had been deprived of the chance to pair up against McDermott in what would have been the defining game of his career. Instead, he watched as, for the second time in a month, Mayo came within touching distance of All-Ireland victory before Meath tracked them down like prey and then finished the contest with a brilliant, deathless point from Brendan Reilly. For all of Mayo, the disappointment was almost exquisite in its nature. For McHale, it was unbearable.

He had long stopped enjoying big-time football. The reason he continued under John Maughan was that he was genuinely scared that he might miss out on winning an All-Ireland medal. It had become a craving. He played for three more years but would never recapture the peerless form of that September. His instinct to stay on was almost right. A year later, McHale was back in an All-Ireland final. The match was wretched, memorable for the bizarre leg break inflicted on Kerry's Billy O'Shea in a race for possession with his teammate, Maurice Fitzgerald. After that, Fitzgerald went on something of a personal rampage, as though in atonement, finishing the match with nine points. That 1997 defeat to Kerry has become curiously opaque and insignificant in the consciousnesses of Mayo football people, as though the meaning of the game was eclipsed by the prevailing hurt of the previous September. It was as if John Maughan and the team had returned there on instinct but found the whole exercise meaningless when Meath were not there to face them.

The end came for McHale when his old teammate and friend Pat Holmes took over as manager and, in an empty dressing-room, gently suggested that the basketball and football were becoming an intolerable burden. McHale protested, but Pat was firm. New-millennium football was on the horizon. He couldn't make allowances. And Liam accepted that, but he couldn't forsake basketball. It would have seemed wrong. It would have seemed disloyal. 'Maybe Pat had a point. But I was convinced that the basketball was what was keeping me sharp. So, anyhow, that was it.'

When Maughan returned to manage Mayo for a second term in 2004, he invited McHale to become one of his selectors. All through that season, he found he was living vicariously through the younger generation of players. When Mayo made a surprising run to that year's All-Ireland final, McHale wanted to warn the younger guys like Alan

Dillon and Keith Higgins and Conor Mortimer to value the experience.

'You have to learn this. At twenty-two, defeat does not hurt as much as it does when you are thirty-one or thirty-two. When we lost in 1989, I felt there would be plenty of other days. I got the football bug then. When you are thirty and you have back pain and shoulder pain and you are not as mobile as you were, that is when the pressure comes. Those last few years, I did not enjoy. I was just trying to win something. And I suppose seeing the young lads go through it all again from the sidelines was strange. I remember I suggested to John and George [Golden, selector] that we go to Manchester or some place before the All-Ireland. In Mayo, people do go a bit crazy. The phone is going constantly, and you hate saying no to people, but if you lose focus at all, it is going to affect you. When we lost that final, it was like being back where we were in 1989 and 1996. I had always hated that homecoming thing. I always just wanted to hook up with the people I knew. Players are exhausted and depressed, and all they want to do is go to a corner of a bar with family and friends and be a bit selfish.'

At forty years of age, McHale remains an incredibly potent basketball player. Last winter, he came out of retirement to help the club on the way to a late charge for league glory. He is a natural football coach and may well manage Mayo some day.

It is hard to imagine McHale growing old. There has always been something of the eternal teenager about him. He laughs as he remembers a moment of humour from the 2004 All-Ireland final. In the weeks before the match, they had been running forward patterns at training, and McHale fancied there was a decent chance that Alan Dillon, the tireless half-forward, would find himself in and around the Kerry goalmouth. On the weekend of the match, he noticed the Ballintubber man was at great odds to score the first goal, and he called Sinéad to ask her to lay a fairly handsome wager.

At the beginning of the match, Dillon popped up in the precise place that McHale had envisaged he would, and he buried the goal. As a cheer detonated around Croke Park, McHale suddenly remembered the bet and began jumping up and down on the sidelines. There were only four minutes gone. George Golden was nearby, and he hissed, 'What the f*** is wrong with you, McHale? Would you calm down and get your act together?'

For a second, he had forgotten completely where he was and who he was. He was just a kid who had won a bet. Then reality came in green-and-gold waves. They stood there and watched as Kerry went to work. Afterwards, in the hospitality suite, Sinéad arrived and confessed that she had completely forgotten to place the bet. Liam just grinned and nodded and sipped on a bottle of Heineken. He had learned to expect nothing from Mayo All-Ireland-final days. 'When your luck is out, it is out.'

Maybe Liam McHale was unlucky on the football field. In comparison to most sportsmen, though, he experienced indescribable highs. But that he never did and now never will win an All-Ireland senior medal will stay with him like a dull ache. Walking from the field in 1996, denied the opportunity to compete, will be his lasting regret. One night last winter, a few Ballina friends came into the bar and told him excitedly that they had seen John McDermott, his old adversary from those mad September days, among a wedding party down the town. Liam just smiled. McHale can hold on to regrets, but he is unable to cherish grudges. 'Fair play to the man. That match is long over. I suppose I had no real wish to see him. What was I going to say?'

But it is not hard to guess what he would have said to the Meath man had they crossed paths. McHale might have fleetingly considered the temptation to bring up old hurts, but he would have banished it. And then, he would have extended that big arm, and he would have said, 'Welcome to Ballina.' For that is who Liam McHale is.

Ballina has shaped David Brady, too. Like most people who grew up in a provincial town, he has had his wars with the place, but at thirty-three he knows its streets and its brickwork so well that the town is in his soul. He still lives very close to his parents' home on the pier and is little more than a stone's throw from his old secondary school, St Muredach's, a forbidding, impressive building now a century old and standing on a height overlooking the River Moy.

When we meet on a bank-holiday Friday in March 2007, the heavens have opened and a line of saloon cars are parked in front of the school waiting for kids who sprint helter-skelter through the rain. Although it is only four o'clock, it is already darkening. Brady flashes the lights of his Volvo car, and we drive to his home. He makes us coffee, and when we sit down in the living room, he flicks the television onto mute. It is the last day of the Cheltenham racing festival, and, like virtually every other punter, Brady is bamboozled by the form, talking through the misery of his wagers while we watch a highlights show of Ruby Walsh races.

He is fascinated by the horses and joined a syndicate for fun, but with the football he rarely gets the opportunity to drive off for weekend race meetings. And any plans he had for this year are now on hold. Brady looks lean and fit and is very much unretired. Just three weeks before, he gave what John O'Mahony considered the performance of his career in a league defeat away to Donegal.

This was the second time Brady has come out of retirement. Despite all the promises he made himself, despite the lost weekend after the All-Ireland-final blowout, Brady was simply unable to walk away when it became clear that O'Mahony was going to accept the post of Mayo manager. As with his long-time Ballina and Mayo midfield partner Liam McHale, there might have been an element of pure fear behind the decision – the frightening thought that Mayo might go and win the thing the very season that he retired. And also, all through the winter, memories of the previous season troubled him. Although he had been a leading Mayo player for ten years, it was only in the 2006 season that Brady evolved into a kind of cult figure among Mayo people.

Like many Mayo football men, he had had his critics down the years, and he originally retired after the 2004 All-Ireland loss, following a strong disagreement with John Maughan. But as Brady entered his thirties, it was increasingly evident that the county team were reliant on his uncomplicated, positive aggression and his leadership. Mayo needed his presence. And when Mickey Moran and John Morrison were appointed by the Mayo county board, one of their first moves was to come knocking on Brady's door. He liked their sincerity, the lemony freshness of the Ulster accents. Moran was an exceptional coach with an almost evangelical faith in his own players, while Morrison was one of Gaelic football's great mavericks, a brilliant, unconventional coach who was as likely to turn up to training with a ghetto-blaster as a bag of footballs. He married sports psychology with American drills and his own originality to draw up training sessions that flew in the face of conservative GAA practice. Brady knew that whatever else happened, the season would not be boring. They shook hands.

Brady is both highly efficient and highly restless. In his work for Wyeth Pharmaceuticals, he is regularly in his car at half past six in the morning to be in Galway or Athlone for early-morning calls, always well presented and cheerful and optimistic. But he has a habit of getting into situations.

On Christmas Day 2005, just weeks after agreeing to the Ulstermen's overtures, he called around to visit a neighbour who had bought a horse. He was entreated to climb up on the saddle, given assurances that the animal was, as he puts it, 'quiet as a lamb'. He has since turned what happened next into a highly comical turn. 'Giddiest lamb I ever sat up on, anyhow. Maybe it was from Galway. But it left me on the concrete with a broken collarbone.'

Mayo had reached the league semi-final – ironically against Galway – by the time Brady had nursed the shoulder back to health. That match, played in McHale Park, was an unusually hard encounter, both teams anxious to yield nothing in advance of the meeting in the championship, and Brady was introduced in the last twenty minutes. He was on the field for about thirty seconds before he received a broken jaw leaping for a ball. He insisted afterwards there was no malice behind what happened, it was just pure bad luck, and he played the match out, reasoning that even though he couldn't talk so well, he could still jump and catch. That meant another visit to the operating theatre, to have his jaw lifted, a few weeks of milkshakes and another few weeks of recovery.

By the time the Mayo squad travelled to Portugal for pre-season training, he felt in robust form. Moran and Morrison had drafted seventeen training sessions. By the last day, Brady was getting blisters from the hard ground, so he opted to wear just a single pair of socks instead of the usual two. Halfway through the session, he twisted his foot and heard a snap; he said nothing. He headed home and even took a few injections to try to play in an 'A' versus 'B' game the following Tuesday evening in Castlebar, but it was torturous. He drove himself down to a clinic in Galway and emerged with a cast on his foot. For a full half-hour, he sat in the car park questioning his own sanity. The medical staff had been worried that a seemingly fit man could break three bones in as many months and were sceptical about his excuses of horses and footwear. They were dubious about the ability of his body to take much more punishment and arranged scans for osteoporosis. He was advised to keep the foot rested and in a cast for a few weeks. Instead, he drove home, cut the plaster of Paris away and went to the gym the next morning.

Those setbacks meant that by the summer Mickey Moran had decided to use him as a reserve. During the All-Ireland quarter-final against Laois, he was bursting with adrenalin and couldn't understand why he wasn't getting the call. 'I suppose they didn't know me. They hadn't enough faith in me.'

So by the semi-final against Dublin, it seemed as if Brady had become an intermediary between management and players. That was never more apparent than during the terse, anarchic minutes when the Mayo team broke an accepted tradition by taking the premeditated decision to warm up in front of the Hill 16 goal. When the Dublin team took the field, they were temporarily flummoxed and then gravitated to their traditional warm-up goal, with chaotic consequences. Through it all, Brady walked slowly and deliberately around the field, his tracksuit zipped up to his neck, solemnly whispering incantations to his teammates. At that moment, he looked less a Gaelic football player than a religious figure.

'It wasn't an accident but it wasn't fully premeditated either,' he grinned. 'It is like a bar-room brawl. You look a mate in the eye and you know what he is thinking and he knows what you are thinking. Mayo players and people feel like second-class citizens too often, and we just wanted to make a stand. But I thought there was going to be trouble. I saw Paul Clarke come out and he had the chest out, and I could see by his stance there could be problems. I went over to him and said, 'Keep it cool here, like a good man, because there could be people hurt.' I remember [Dublin selector] Brian Talty walked by and pushed against Ger [Brady, David's brother]. There

225

were some hairy moments. Dublin were definitely psyched up. And there was no talking going on. I was conscious of what happened in 1996 against Meath. It could have been the same thing, except it would have been thirty against thirty because we would not have backed down. And I had the benefit of knowing I wasn't starting the game so I could concentrate on keeping this thing calm.'

For those few moments, he was boss. Moran and Morrison directed the Mayo squad over to the Cusack Stand so there was some little space between the teams. John Morrison seemed taken by the spirit and adventure of the gesture, but Mickey Moran, whose nature goes against pyrotechnic displays of machismo or defiance, was inclined to leave well enough alone. He began gesturing his boys down towards the Canal End and through the bedlam – a low din of disapproval coming from the Hill End and howls of appreciation emanating from the Mayo sectors – came the sonorous Derry voice. 'We've made our point, boys, come on now.' And both Heaney and Brady, almost in chorus, said, 'No f***ing way are we backing down now.'

'It was meant as no disrespect to Mickey. But if we had retreated, we would have been a laughing stock. We might as well have handed a four-point lead to Dublin.'

After that startling cameo, Brady took his place among the substitutes, torn between impatience to be out there and a hope that the starting fifteen would excel. When Ronan McGarrity, who went into the match as one of the leading midfield players in the championship, was floored by a mercilessly late challenge by Ciaran Whelan, Brady could no longer contain himself. Barry Moran, the young Castlebar man, was sent in as a replacement. At half-time, Brady said to Moran that it was a mistake to leave him sitting there in that kind of a broiling match.

In the dressing-room, McGarrity was inconsolable, having

been told that he couldn't take the field for the second half. Although they had both grown up in Ballina, Brady and McGarrity had never crossed paths much. They were of a different generation. McGarrity was an exceptional basketball player and had headed off to America on a scholarship. He came home early, at Christmas-time in 2004, and Liam McHale, then a selector for John Maughan, spotted his potential as a football player. He was an instant success. Brady thought McGarrity a likeable young lad, a curious mixture of a competitive intensity like Brady's own and an introverted nature that was quite unlike his. At the Mayo press night before the All-Ireland final, McGarrity told an amusing story about his early days on the county squad. He was still reeling from his own decision to quit America and was readjusting to life back home in Ballina when he bumped into an old acquaintance from school on the street. 'Heard you're on the Mayo panel,' the old face grinned. McGarrity nodded. 'What the f*** are they doing picking you?' he laughed, and went about his business. But McGarrity knew he was home and went about proving just why. If he shared one thing with Brady, it was a deeply serious attitude to the game. They roomed together and talked sport and talked rubbish, and it worked, Brady full of noisy charm and McGarrity batting back wry comments.

When Brady saw the younger man floored in Croke Park, a kind of paternal instinct kicked in. In the dressing-room, he found himself making an impromptu speech, urging the others to think of McGarrity. Dublin began the second half in sensational fashion, and Brady's patience broke. He shouted down to Moran and Morrison on the touchline that he was going in. 'I knew I had to get in there. If you're watching a game, you can see where things are going wrong. I always felt I never let a team down coming on as a substitute. Of course, within thirty seconds of me being on the field, Dublin hit another point and we were seven down. I was thinking, "Jesus, D.B. Great impact."'

But after that, fortunes turned irreversibly. Shortly after entering the game, Brady became entangled with Ciaran Whelan and pushed the Dublin man, who stumbled backwards onto the turf. Brady leaned over him and shouted, 'You f***ed McGarrity around. You won't f*** me around.' Later, he felt bad for Whelan, a majestic, high-fielding player capable of taking over a football match with his power and grace, and consequently often vilified on big days when the metropolitans failed to deliver. But on the field, Dublin had become inexplicably nervous, and Brady was conscious of a rush of conviction and emotion flowing through his teammates. They were looking at each other and they knew. Goalkeeper David Clarke began clipping restarts out to the wings and Mayo won enough possession to begin to seriously trouble Dublin.

As ever, Brady can only recall flashes of detail. But he will always see the winning point clearly. He was trailing behind the play and felt like a spectator watching Kevin O'Neill in possession while being madly harried by two Dublin defenders. He was idly wondering where the score was going to come from when McDonald came sprinting into his line of vision, the blond mane drawn back and hands held out primly, like a communicant.

In that instant, Brady realised that he had almost forgotten about McDonald, who had been quiet in the last quarter. And it made sense, seeing him claim the ball at that instant, as everyone in the stadium breathed in sharply and waited for what seemed like an eternity for the defining kick. Even as he watched it, Brady knew he must have seen McDonald making this move a thousand times, jab-stepping off his right foot to buy himself that precious half-second of time and space and then leaning back into his shot, as if unburdened by gravity, judging the angle and distance perfectly with his left foot. Immediately, it felt like what it was: one of the great championship scores and one of those transcendent, thrilling Mayo football moments that are probably the most vivid explanations of why the county is so helplessly obsessed with the All-Ireland quest.

McDonald wheeled away towards the Hogan Stand. For probably the first time in his long Mayo career, the Crossmolina enigma looked fulfilled and happy, wagging a finger at nobody in particular. It was the most complete Brady had felt since St Patrick's Day in 2005, when he won his only All-Ireland senior medal with Ballina in the club final. 'I knew what Mac was going to do, just the little jink and then the chip with his left. And it was magic. It was beautiful.'

Mick McCormack took a unique photograph for the *Mayo News* that caught Brady in the raucous, jubilant aftermath. Although it seemed as if every Mayo man, woman and child in Croke Park was embracing someone, McCormack managed to find Brady standing completely alone, making six-shooter symbols with his hands and firing them at the sky. It would have been a comical image but for the expression of solemn rapture on his face. Although it might have looked like an exhibitionist gesture, it was clear that Brady was doing it for nobody other than himself.

Forty minutes after the final whistle, Brady was in a taxi with his brother Ger, McDonald, O'Neill and Aidan Higgins. They were still wearing their Mayo tracksuits and just wanted to escape and prolong the evening. A bus was scheduled to head west, but most of the players were busy making plans to stay on in the capital. They asked the driver to find them a bar that was likely to be halfway quiet, and he drove them way down the quays and pointed to a place across the Liffey from Heuston Station. It was a traditional city local on a championship Sunday: mahogany furnishing and grainy sunlight and hefty men in sky-blue Dublin shirts. There was a disbelieving silence when the Mayo boys walked in. *The Sunday Game* had just finished its live transmission, and after watching McDonald arc that point until they were sick of it, now the Dubliners saw him standing in their bar.

Brady loved the theatre of the moment. 'As the man says, it was like walking into a saloon. The door opened and there was silence, like a scene from a western. We walked in. Howya. And for thirty seconds, the whole place was just staring at us. And then boys just got up off their stools and shook hands with us, and they were using their phones to take photographs with us. They couldn't have been more sound.'

When they tried to buy a drink, the barman shook his head. 'The drinks are on the house,' he said. They settled into a corner, the five of them, and just savoured the ache in their bodies and the intense afterglow of winning. The strictly professional thing would have been to board the bus for home, but this felt like a seismic moment. Later, they crashed in a friend's apartment, got dolled up and hit the town. Two bouncers with Mayo connections accompanied them on their tour through the demi-monde. As is the tradition on epic championship Sundays, it seemed as if by two in the morning the entire population of Dublin had wedged itself into CopperFace Jacks, the popular country nightclub on Harcourt Street. Through the steam and flushed faces, Brady saw some of the Dublin players, and they exchanged brief, respectful nods, like people who had shared a dentist's waiting room earlier in the day. Anything more would have been gloating. The only reference the Mayo players had made to the All-Ireland final came minutes after the match, when the panel gathered in the bare warm-down room adjacent to the dressing-room in Croke Park. There, they agreed that the only thing they would focus on was the game itself. They promised they would not suffer the same distraction as the previous Mayo All-Ireland-final teams. 'And then,' Brady says, 'we went out and made the same mistakes again.'

The frenzy that overcomes Mayo as a county in the weeks before an All-Ireland final is strange to behold. All counties go in for the pageantry of bunting and flags and go through the obligatory shows of street bravado and cheering when the RTÉ cameras visit the towns for colour reports. But in most cases, the mood is fun-filled. In Mayo, since the fervent scenes that preceded the 1989 All-Ireland final, the atmosphere has become too high-pitched and shrill to be considered enjoyable. It is as though with just this one match between Mayo and a perfect football summer, one match between Mayo people and winning, there has been no option but to be outwardly confident and flippant about how the team will fare. And that kind of harmless boasting has never come easily to Mayo people. It is not in their nature. The last five All-Ireland-final appearances have had a blinding effect on the people of the county. The waiting and anticipation and the hoping have become drenched in superstition. For the Mayo public, the last five All-Ireland football finals have meant a fortnight of hope and fear, with the high optimism that glory – an end to the great hunger – may be imminent tempered by the unavoidable fear that another monumental disappointment is the more likely outcome. In general, Mayo people are warm and open, and sometimes during All-Ireland weeks, over shop counters or in pubs, they speak of the Mayo team's chances in the impending All-Ireland final with motherly concern, as though fretting over their child's first day at school and exposure to the harsher realities of the world.

Shielding the players from the intensity and complexity of the public mood has been paramount to the plans of successive managements, and perhaps because of that, there is always a focus on the movements of the Mayo squad before the finals. It was unfortunate for Mickey Moran and John Morrison that they had no first-hand experience of dealing with the Mayo All-Ireland experience. Rather than opt for seclusion, they decided to place the squad among the supporters, staying in the Bewley's Hotel on the outskirts of Dublin. The victory over Dublin had created such a force of public goodwill that the management was hoping that the squad would draw strength from it on the eve of the All-Ireland. The intention was probably sound, but the reality was that the players felt caged in all weekend. Brady remembers sneaking down in groups of six or seven to various team meetings, trying to avoid youngsters looking for autographs and people wanting to say their piece. At around ten o'clock on Saturday night, he was returning to his room when the door opened across the corridor and a couple stepped out, done up in glad rags and heading out for the night. They were Mayo to the bone and astounded to see that Brady was sharing their hotel. As they made their way to the lift, he could hear them on the phone telling friends that the Mayo squad were staying there. The next morning, the team ate breakfast amid the din of supporters, and a few former players wandered over to offer handshakes.

'None of these things have anything to do with the game itself,' says Brady, 'but they do contribute. Back in 1997, we headed to Maynooth College. John [Maughan]'s idea was to get away from everything. But that was just grim – the rooms were cold and there was no television and the showers were a bit wrecked back then, so it backfired a bit. It is hard to get a balance. But let's just say the preparation was not ideal in 2006. It was a circus.'

The other problem was that because Moran and Morrison had not been in charge in 2004, they didn't want to fixate on that defeat. They wanted to inculcate the belief that this was a new time and a new team. They didn't want to flood the team talks with ways of coping with the opposition, preferring to accentuate the near-miraculous journey which Mayo had taken. 'They didn't want to revisit the scene of the crime. They didn't want us to think about that match and to open up all the old doubts. It was madness, because Kerry annihilated us in the very same positions.

'But I have to admit that in Croke Park before the match, things were good. We were up for it. You do believe. No matter how pessimistic you might be, on that All-Ireland Sunday, you have to have a good feeling. If you show any sign of weakness or fear at all, it will be picked up on. But we lacked that edge. We thought it was going to happen for us again. We weren't ready to go and jump off the edge. If the Kerry team and the Mayo team were lined up on a cliff and you said, "The first thirty men to jump win the All-Ireland," they would be gone while we were still considering it. That's how it felt at the start. We had no structure. We knew what we wanted but hadn't fully worked out how to achieve it. We had more structure in the madness of the Hill against Dublin than we did against Kerry. I can see that now, but I could not see it at the time.'

Three weeks after the All-Ireland-final loss, Brady played for Ballina in the county championship semi-final against Crossmolina. What was to have been an attractive autumn contest between the contemporary giants of the Mayo game quickly turned into a fierce and bitter scrap. Three players were sent off over the course of the match, and many of the players who had sat numbly in the dressing-room a few weeks earlier were now competing with visceral intensity. At one point, Brady found himself squaring up to Peadar Gardiner, who would go on to score the winning goal during injury time. Ger Brady took a rap in the face and had teeth broken, and although David Brady implored Gardiner to tell him which Crossmolina player was the culprit, his county colleague refused. Ever the protector, Brady was incensed, and he kept badgering Gardiner during breaks of play, begging him to just tell him who it had been and promising not to retaliate.

Afterwards, he warned the guilty man never to walk down

the street in Ballina. 'I meant it at the time. You say these things in the heat of the moment,' he says, throwing his eyes to heaven. 'The thing was that Ger and this lad were friends. This was a decent lad. But when those teams met, we tore into one another. The passion and the sheer will to win was something else. I suppose it was this thing of getting it out of the system.'

Through the following winter months, the mood of fury with which the players conducted that match disturbed Brady. It was as though the rage that should have been directed at Kerry had had to spend itself internally. Players hit and tackled with the ferocity and meaning and borderline hatred that is possible only among athletes who know and like and respect one another. They met with the stark, unrelenting anger of brothers. And it bothered Brady. Where was that meanness when they had needed it in Croke Park? Maybe the problem was that they were just too nice, too decent to summon up hatred towards a bunch of strangers 'It's the oldest sporting cliché. Nice guys win f*** all. If you want to play with Kerry, you have to be mean. And dog mean. Maybe that's a demand we do not make of ourselves in Mayo.'

The more he dwelt on it, the more difficult it became to walk away. When John O'Mahony signed up for the job, he knew he wanted to come back. After Ballina won the club All-Ireland final on St Patrick's Day 2005, Brady shed tears and famously declared, 'I've been a loser all my life. Well. I'm not a loser today.' Among the visitors to the dressing-room that day was O'Mahony. Brady told him that he would consider it an honour to some day play under him. So, despite having vowed in the underworld of Croke Park that he was bowing out after that last All-Ireland crushing, Brady was prepared to give it one more shot under O'Mahony. He came back. They all came back. If there was one truly admirable thing to be taken from that pitiful All-Ireland-final loss, it was that every single Mayo man came back for more.

# ELEVEN

# HEALY COUNTRY

Four minutes of injury time had passed when the man in white abandoned his place between the goalposts and made an alarming dash outfield. John Casey had noticed something that the others had not. This was the last Sunday in August 2007, and Crossmolina, the gold standard in modern Mayo club football, were pressing hard for another county-final appearance. The scores were equal, and Crossmolina, champions of the county for the previous two years, had worked a free. From the hooded stand and the broad terraces came desperate instructions and pleas from the Charlestown supporters. But they could stop nothing now. Crossmolina had a free, and although it was a good distance out and the breeze was early-autumn tricky, the general assumption was that Ciaran McDonald would strike a point, as swift and clean as the thrust of a rapier. McDonald stood over the football, socks pulled high and the maroon jersey hanging loose, and he seemed oblivious to his teammate, Stephen Rochford, who was standing unmarked in front of the Charlestown goal. But Casey read McDonald's mind.

Once, in a different lifetime, they had operated together in the ranks of the Mayo forwards. Years ago, they had almost done it all together. Casey minded nets now, but his brain still responded to attacking instincts, and this was like a clairvoyant impulse. He began yelling for someone to cover Rochford, studying McDonald, who was reading the field like a book and was about to clip a nonchalant, deceiving pass. It had been a terrific match, and the Charlestown boys, who had stormed through the last fifteen minutes with just fourteen men, were almost completely spent; nobody heard Casey clearly. He was always yelling something, so they did not appreciate the urgency of his message. In desperation, the goalkeeper came charging out of nowhere, and the crowd in McHale Park watched him in puzzlement, the only figure in motion in a frieze of tired football players. Then McDonald, after studying the posts, delivered his quick, disguised pass and Rochford, as Casey had guessed, had possession of the football and the easiest chance to kick the winning score. Casey kept running. Once he had been fast. Once he could cover one hundred metres in less than eleven seconds. Now he moved at a more common rate, but he was closing hard on the Crossmolina player. Everybody else in the ground was at last tuned to his frequency, and many people recalled, watching this thirty-three-year-old man running at full tilt, that tantalising year when he had been the bright-burning and fearless hope of Mayo football. Casey dived as Rochford kicked, arriving a half a second too late. The point was good.

Casey trundled back into his goal and hurriedly sent the ball booming back into play. He felt certain that they had blown it. Tradition dictated that Crossmolina always won these hand-wringing semi-final classics. This was the worst part for him, standing there helplessly in the goalmouth watching the definitive action downfield, spotting all the right moves and feeling that his natural place was out there. He saw his brother Enda in the thick of things. Somehow, Charlestown scrambled possession, and as they charged with the desperation of Confederates across the open field, Anthony Mulligan was hauled to the ground.

Now Charlestown had a free, to be taken by Paul Mulligan. Back in the goals, Casey couldn't look. The ice-cold finisher of yesteryear turned his back to the field and rubbed his brow with his gloved hands. This was the frustration, the punishment of keeping goal. He was part of the game, but he wasn't. The true goalkeeper is a loner at heart, and that was never John Casey's form. 'I can't bloody watch it,' he shouted to the umpire. Seconds later, he heard the cheering, and he knew. The full-time whistle went. The match finished all square. Casey collected his glove case from the back of the goals and headed for the tunnel, glad to have another chance.

'It is strange,' he says of the goalkeeping life a few days later, sitting in his house. 'You feel like a bit of a dick, sometimes. Like, my jersey is a different colour to the rest, and you feel a bit stupid and conspicuous. I have often wondered what I must look like to people. Making that crazy run outfield probably comes from having been an outfield player. Like, when I started playing goals, I was twenty-eight, and I had no experience there. None. But I was cocky as f***, and I could catch. I felt I was smart enough on the ball, and I could take a kick-out. I would be confident under a dropping ball. I would have started studying goalkeepers. The way I looked at it, playing in goals was better than not playing at all.'

Casey's life as a Mayo footballer was like a lightning storm. He made his senior debut at nineteen during the infamous summer of 1994, coming on in the Connacht semi-final against Sligo, along with Ciaran McDonald. Eamonn O'Hara, who would become the talismanic figure for the Yeats County over the next ten years, also made his first senior appearance that afternoon.

Casey had gone to boarding school in St Nathy's and was a teenage contradiction of callow self-confidence and deeper self-doubts. His athleticism was boundless, and when he was nominated by his club to attend county minor trials as the obligatory Charlestown kid, he surprised even himself by how easily he played in that company. Martin Carney trained superb minor teams in those years, and the 1991 vintage, captained by Ronan Golding, was particularly rich. Casey played wing-back during a trials match. Afterwards, guys like Golding and Maurice Sheridan came up and patted him on the back for his performance. 'I was amazed that these lads knew who I was. That was the day I probably started thinking I could do something.'

He didn't make the cut, foolishly opting to go on a family holiday instead of to the final trial. Mayo made it all the way to the All-Ireland minor final. A year later, though, Casey was still eligible for the side and played at midfield on a glittering team that contained Kenneth Mortimer, Fergal Costello, David Brady, Ciaran McDonald, David Nestor and Diarmuid Byrne. They somehow contrived to lose to Roscommon while planning on winning the national silver.

Casey was in college in Letterkenny when he was summoned to a lecturer's office to take a phone call from Jack O'Shea inviting him into the senior squad. He managed to suppress his awe towards men like John Finn, Liam McHale and Dermot Flanagan when he attended training and presumed, as he sat on the team bus on the day of the 1994 Connacht final, that he was about to win his first senior provincial medal.

'It was meant to be a handy title,' he says now, glancing disparagingly at his ceiling. 'That was the feeling. We were deplorable. That had to have been Mayo at their lowest ebb. There was no talk about the team. I remember heading up to Tyrone in those years to play a league match and in the programme "A.N. Other" was printed fifteen times on our team sheet. That was like sticking a dagger through my heart. Because it didn't matter how low things were to me. I felt great about playing for Mayo. Against Leitrim, Golding and

McDonald and myself were thrown in. Three kids, really. But I think we made a bit of a difference. I was pulled down for a penalty. We had a lot of seasoned guys who didn't show up that afternoon. And a lot of guys were seriously nervous beforehand. I couldn't understand it. I suppose it was because of what had happened in the semi-final against Cork the previous year. Like, I watched that match in the Canal End, and I was up in Quinn's before it finished. That was as bad as it got.

'Losing to Leitrim was just weird. I wasn't really conscious of their long wait; none of that history meant much to me. My brother Enda was about fifteen then, and he came into the house with one of Leitrim's footballs. Some lad took a shot warming up and the ball nearly knocked him off this pillar he was sitting on, so he kept it. He was delighted with himself. I suppose the importance of that match didn't sink in until the All-Ireland semi-final, watching Leitrim in Croke Park. Then Séamus Quinn got an All-Star that Christmas. I used to slag Séamus for years afterwards that it was a sympathy All-Star because I had screwed him in the second half. He used to call into our shop and we had awful banter about it. I used to say to him, "Sure, they had to give it to one of you poor souls."'

By the time John Maughan was placed in charge of the team, Casey was seriously considering dropping out. He insists today that he cannot remember anything about 1995 because nothing positive happened. Kevin Cahill from Ballaghaderreen used to collect Casey at Charlestown on training evenings, and on the first day of the new season, Casey phoned Cahill and told him he had lost all interest. Cahill persuaded him to show up for the first evening at least. They had assumed that the first night would be an informal meeting filled with the usual fervent speeches, and it was nine o'clock when they reached McHale Park. After they parked their car, they stood in shock watching as Colm McManamon and Noel Connelly came trudging across the twilit field looking purged. Other Mayo players followed, drenched in sweat and silent. 'He is after crucifying us,' someone said.

That night, Maughan left the players to talk about their ambitions for the year, and Connelly, a youngster who had just been called into the squad, stood up and gave a sustained and passionate speech about what they had to do. Even Casey was taken aback by the chutzpah of the Hollymount man. 'Like, Noel wasn't even on the panel the year before, and here he was addressing the likes of Flanagan and McHale. I couldn't believe it. I was more entitled to speak than he was. But he had the balls to do it. Pete Ford and Tommy O'Malley and Maughan must have been listening outside, because he was made captain afterwards. And it was a great choice. Noel had it. And that first night set a standard.'

If Casey felt that his student life in Donegal might give him sanctuary, he was wrong. Maughan had recruited an army buddy named Michael McGeehan to take the exile for training exercises in Letterkenny. Casey finished the first session on his knees with exhaustion in the sand dunes. McGeehan grinned down at him and said, 'You better tell Maughan we did twice the work. That man told me to take you under my wing and screw you.'

Casey was impressed and intimidated by Maughan. He had considered himself to be deeply conscientious about training. The weekend of the 1994 Connacht final had coincided with the Charlestown Rose festival. The Caseys lived in a townhouse above their hardware business. It was a sunny evening and there was open-air music in the square, and Casey remembers looking through his bedroom window and seeing five of his school friends hanging out, sitting on the kerbstone and swilling tins of cheap lager. He felt like a recluse for a few seconds and then let the blinds fall and put in a set of earplugs to block out the drifting sounds of carnival. Casey was gregarious and had enjoyed social nights. Most Saturday nights as a teenager, he had been on the buses that rumbled from Charlestown over to the bright lights of Castlebar. His gang always went to Julian's of Midfield. But that all stopped once the football promised to take him places.

Occasionally, he would break out with Colm McManamon and David Brady. 'We hunted in packs, and when we drank, we drank. But that was not too often. Most of the time, I was a demon for training. That was why I looked so gaunt back then. Half the time, I was too sick after training to eat properly. But Maughan kept me guessing. If he said "jump", it was "how high?" He had this great saying if he was giving permission to go out for a few: "Drink as much as you feel you will be able to train with in the morning." What does that mean, like? You knew you were better off going home.'

Casey's rise to prominence mirrored the sudden elevation of the Mayo team from the depths of division-three football to Connacht champions. Their 1996 provincial-final victory of 3–09 to 1–11 was their first over Galway since 1969. Casey struck 1–02 with his first three touches of the ball. A few weeks later, Mayo beat Kerry by 2–13 to 1–10 in the All-Ireland semi-final. The match went down in folklore for James Nallen's euphoric goal. He started a move around his own forty-yard line and then ran like a Kenyan before taking a pass from Liam McHale and hammering a goal. Casey was unstoppable at full-forward. Páidí Ó Sé tried Mike Hassett and then Seán Burke against him, but Casey was supremely influential, scoring four points from play and earning another three frees in front of the posts. He had a strong, elegant style and played as though intuitively conscious that winning against Kerry in Croke Park had once been part of Mayo's football heritage.

It had been a remarkable turnaround. In early spring, Casey had ruptured an ankle ligament trying to clatter Maurice

Sheridan of Balla in a club league match. That injury sidelined him for thirteen weeks, and he would have opted out for the season but for the counsel of Peter Ford, who warned him that Mayo could do something special over the summer.

After that semi-final, his world spun off its axis. Mayo's sudden reappearance as All-Ireland contenders captured the imagination and all at once Casey was a poster boy. He was approachable and talkative and found it difficult to say no when the phone rang. Supporters called into the store looking for autographs and photographs. It was good for business, and Casey told himself that it was no sweat, that he was born for this kind of attention. He became a dab hand at posing for the newspaper photographers and facing the television cameras. One afternoon, a camera crew landed unannounced in the shop. They were from Eurosport.

A fortnight before the final, Casey contracted one of those inexplicable viruses and couldn't eat properly. He felt drained and lost a stone in weight. Still he told himself there was nothing wrong. But one afternoon on the week of the final, he went into the Broadway Café near the shop for a bowl of soup and made the mistake of leafing through a tabloid newspaper that had been left by a previous customer. Several established players, including Mickey Linden of Down, towards whom Casey was reverential, had listed their candidates for player of the year, and his name featured prominently. At that moment, the importance and the scale of what he was involved in came at him in a rush, and he felt light, as though he had inhaled surgical gas. And then he felt one hundred years old. 'My head was spinning,' he says now.

To understand why, it is important to remember that Casey was a Charlestown kid. This was supposed to be the town from which heroes fled. Of all the towns in east Mayo that had been soul-plundered by emigration, Charlestown was the most evocative. When, in the late 1960s, the Mayo journalist

John Healy began writing a series of articles in the *Irish Times* on the slow decline of his beloved home town entitled 'No One Shouted Stop', he presented a town so quiet it was as though you could hear the individual clocks ticking in every living room. The first paragraph of the first column, which was published in October 1967 managed, in a few simple and beautiful lines, to nail the elusive atmosphere of the Irish small town, with its ritual patterns and vague sense of boyhood restlessness and the power of the outside world to come crashing in at any moment.

> I was nine years old that morning. We were coming down from Mass. On the busy street, high-chimney-potted jackdaws clacked and gabbled self-importantly in the quiet grey morning. Then from the bottom of the street we heard the crackling of the radio in Jim Mulrooney's shop and it grew louder and louder until the voice seemed to fill the whole street. It was the voice of Neville Chamberlain, declaring war on Germany, and we all stopped where we were, listening to that sombre voice.

Healy was a force of nature, both as a journalist and as a Mayo man. He kept goal for the Charlestown football team some fifty years before John Casey. He too made the winter voyages to board at St Nathy's, but he abandoned formal education at fifteen, begging his parents to allow him to join the *Western People* newspaper, where his unerring nose for a story and his shrewdness quickly earned him a reputation. The legendary *People* editor Fred Devere, probably with a mischievous sense of humour, sent Healy to his home town to cover the Charlestown agricultural show for his first assignment, reminding the cub reporter to request the standard press facilities, including two catalogues and a lunch voucher. When Healy grandly presented himself, he was promptly told to buy the catalogues and trot off home for his lunch. Instead of writing his report, Healy typed up a brief paragraph regretting that the *Western People* could not carry the results of the show because the standard press facilities had been refused. Within a week, he had succeeded in provoking a set-to between Charlestown society and his newspaper. It foretold of the years ahead.

Healy remained in Mayo for just two years. He proved a resourceful stringer and enjoyed some notable scoops for the London dailies, but his passion was reporting on the county football team. In his memoir *Healy, Reporter*, he wrote of his maiden trip to Dublin to see Mayo play Cavan in the All-Ireland final.

> 'Where are you staying,' John Walsh asked me.
>
> 'Drop me at Barry's Hotel.'
>
> That was where the Mayo team was staying. Barry's was thronged with people all milling round the steps outside trying to get in. Half of Mayo, it seemed, was trying to push in the doors – the other half trying to get out. Among the Mayo people trying to force a way out as I was trying to get in was Tom Langan, whom I had described as 'the raw-boned man from Ballycastle'. He caught sight of me going towards him and let fly with a straight right hand. The fist crunched on the bridge of my nose. A priest beside him restrained him from anything further. 'Now who's raw-boned?' he shot back as he was bundled away. Someone asked me if he hurt me and I said no, not at all. The Charlestowners and Swinfords were all over the place.

Two years later, Healy recorded the homecoming of the 1950 champions in a long *Western People* piece entitled 'The March Triumphal', which appeared on Saturday, 30 September, after he had spent the previous five days touring with the team.

'And along the line a railway man waved a Mayo flag as the train sped by,' he wrote of the departure from Heuston Station in Dublin.

His flag was made of his red and green signal flags tacked together. The journey home had started. We sang and chatted and we played a modest game of Pontoon. Members of the team were enjoying a singsong and all along the line passengers were up and down the train meeting and congratulating the team. At Athlone autograph hunters swarmed over the train, and at Roscommon a few footballers came down to congratulate the team. It was eight o'clock before the train crossed the border into Mayo – a quiet, bright moonlit night. Our song, 'Moonlight in Mayo', was taking on a new meaning. And it was not long until we knew we were in Mayo. Along the line were cocks of hay that were saturated in paraffin. As the train sped by, the hay was set ablaze and proud farmers and supporters held their beacons aloft as the train sped on into the night. At Ballyhaunis, fog signals exploded and as the train came to a halt eager and frenzied supporters ran down the platform with blazing torches and hoisted the cup aloft.

At Castlebar, Healy found himself barred from the official dinner because local GAA officials had taken exception to columns he had written earlier in the year. The discrimination was reported with high tones of indignation by the nineteen year old, but before too long his mood of high humour had returned.

Healy moved to Dublin to take up a position with a Gaelic games magazine but was quickly employed by the Irish News Agency and then the *Irish Press*. He became the youngest editor of a national newspaper, the *Sunday Review*, and would also edit the *Evening Mail*. He joined the *Irish Times* in 1959, writing satirical columns on the shenanigans of the day in Leinster House, as well as a Dublin newsletter in which he was frequently the star turn. In one column, he took great delight in being the subject of a chastising article in *Comhar* magazine.

> You didn't read, my buttie, Michael Judge, last week? He was very good on 'Mr Healy's role in Irish society'. My mother loved it – a son of hers had a role in Irish society! There he was, above in Dublin, keeping up the Establishment and all the times she thought I was the bad rearing.

Back in Charlestown, however, Mrs Healy rarely read her son in the newspapers, particularly after he began his series of features on the town. Healy wrote the articles because of the prevailing sense of affection he had for the town of his youth and the obvious anger he felt at its slow and silent disappearance.

In an early column, he lamented:

> Jovial Jimmy Gallagher's is no more. Jack Donoghue's is closed and a nameplate on what was the shop reminds you that he still operates the town's bakery. And Tom McCarthy's place. And James Parson's place. And the saddler Vesey's is gone. You are still mentally reeling off the names when the brother says, matter-of-factly: 'Luke Mulligan has the cinema up for sale in this week's *Western* – did you see it?'

Gerry Healy was the youngest in the family. One evening in early September, we sit in the pleasant conservatory of the house in which he and John had spent their childhood while Gerry recalls the notoriety of those first articles. The Healy boys were born in a townhouse – John was actually birthed in the neighbouring village of Bellaghy, on the Sligo side of the railway tracks – but they moved to the solid house on the Galway road in the early 1930s. While John was causing a stir with the articles, Gerry had to get on with the trickier business of living in the town. Privately, many Charlestown people may have agreed with Healy's views, but it was no fun seeing them splashed across the pages of a national newspaper. It felt like being spoken down to from the pulpit by a young upstart who had gotten notions above his station up in Dublin.

'I can assure you that once those articles appeared in the *Irish Times* and in book form, I couldn't go down the town there,' Gerry tells me. 'It was regarded as a sell-out, and a lot of people didn't like it. It was very hard-hitting, and he was telling people to get up off their arses and do something. My mother never read those articles. She did not approve at all. She never read the Charlestown book nor did she read the *Nineteen Acres* book. He could never have written that when she was alive. I mean, he spoke about his views, and he used to write a column for the *Western People*, too, and that often annoyed her. Of course, John was a big critic of the Provos as well, and one particular weekend, a letter came here with his article inside it and across it was written: "We'll get you the next time you are down." And she found that very upsetting. He was right in a lot of what he wrote but that didn't make it any easier for people to accept. At one stage, there was forty-eight licensed premises in Charlestown. That is a lot of pubs for a small town! Today, there are eleven. John felt strongly about the emigration. He went to America for a few months and decided that Ireland was a better place to make a life. And he felt Charlestown needed an industry. He felt that about all of east Mayo. That is why he called it the Black Triangle.'

When Healy's *Irish Times* articles were published as *Death of an Irish Town*, their originality and power made it immediately recognisable as a unique and brilliant book. When Healy had it reprinted in 1988, he delightfully acknowledged as much in his bold preface.

> For almost twenty years you could not buy, beg, borrow or – eventually – steal this book in Ireland. The public libraries which managed to retain their copies for more than five years were very few. Its pages were photostated illegally. Programme producers in radio and television

kept their own photostated copies under lock and key. It
became the most quoted source book on modern Ireland
in the last two decades.

It probably still is. Irish people no more than thirty years
old will appreciate the feeling and mood evoked by Healy's
portrayal of Charlestown, even though the place as he knew
it has disappeared in the last twenty years. Healy's book is
partly an ode to the values and traditions and comforts of his
staunchly Catholic west-of-Ireland town and partly a tirade
at the acceptance that Charlestown and towns like it should
fall pitifully quiet as the maudlin cycle of emigration played
itself out winter after winter. It was and remains an odd book,
with photographs of the author standing at neglected Bountey
Bridge and in the ruins of a cottage belonging to a relation,
Mike Brett. He found the roll book of the Lowpark Primary
School class of 1944 and tracked down the whereabouts of his
classmates. Of Charlestown's twenty-three wartime kids, only
three were still living in town. Fifteen had left for America or
England. His essay on the big, necessary lie that Irishmen and
women exiled in America perpetrate on themselves, believing
that their new life is superior to the one they fled, is savage
and heartbreaking.

Perhaps the single most poignant image in the book is of
the handball champion Mickey Walsh, described by Healy as
'our last hero' tossing a ball to himself in the dilapidated ball
alley. Today, the ball alley is utterly unplayable. It is located
just a minute's walk from the Healy home but is practically
out of sight behind the bright and impressive town library.
The path up to it is overgrown with weeds and briars, and
the stone-cut gallery seats have also been reclaimed by nature.
A rusting refrigerator sits on what was the alley floor, where
reputations were made in Healy's youth. 'There were years
when the alley would be packed,' Gerry remembers. 'We had
many fine ball players, but I suppose as early as the 1970s it

began to die off. It is an individual kind of sport, and maybe the football took over. Fellas directed their energy into that. The alley just seemed to fall into disrepair. Mickey Walsh would have won plenty more All-Ireland titles, but he had to emigrate. He came back, though, and he is still alive today.'

Neglected though it is, the ball alley would be the feature that John Healy would recognise most easily in contemporary Charlestown. His nephew Stephen grew up in Charlestown during the 1980s. Today he is a teacher in the locality and acknowledges that the town of his youth is gone. Bar the technological advances evident in video shops and jukeboxes in the pub, Stephen's adolescent experiences did not differ greatly from those of his father and uncle. In the last fifteen years, however, the town square has been regulated; traditionally, it was a free-for-all car park. A swimming pool, a gym and a library have appeared, and new housing estates bracket the town, as it is a convenient place to live for people working in the main Mayo towns or in Sligo. The transformation has been radical, and Gerry believes his brother would be stunned by the changes of the past fifteen years.

Stephen Healy did his Leaving Certificate in 1988. Ten years later, a teacher of his drew a classroom-roll graph similar to that which appeared in *Death of an Irish Town*. Of the fifty-two teenagers that Stephen Healy had gone to school with, only seven remained in Ireland. Stephen had flirted with the idea of the American life, heading out to the Charlestown citadels in the Bronx and muddling through the Manhattan construction sites during the muggy summers. He was initially seduced but ultimately arrived at the same conclusion as his uncle.

'I always felt my future was here because I had got my education here. And I suppose I wasn't cut out for the construction game. A lot of my pals were carpenters and plumbers and so on, and there was just no work for them at home. I had a choice. And I am sure it was difficult for them when the likes of me headed home in the autumn. But the one thing that made it easier was that there was such a big crowd over there that they would all meet up in each other's apartments in the evenings, and, to be honest, it felt like being back in Charlestown.'

For years, the Charlestown Sarsfields football team had languished, a peripheral team in the county hierarchy. The great hero of John Healy's youth was Danno Regan, a member of the 1936 All-Ireland team. Healy recalled Regan's status in *Death of an Irish Town*:

> Who can understand now the thrill it was to be taken on Mickey Cullen's lorry, unhooded, sitting on wobbly forms, to travel at a break neck, bone shattering thirty miles an hour to Roscommon to see Danno play. We loaded up in The Square, old and young alike, the rich and the poor and we had the Red and Green flag of Mayo. The Wigner, a walrus-moustached British Army pensioner, always sat dourly with his back to the cab, twiddling his contemplative thumbs while we chugged up Barrack Street singing the rallying song: Up the Sarsfields! Up the Sarsfields! Up the Sarfields every time / When we meet them, we'll defeat them / Up the Sarsfields every time.

It was the slow draining of this community spirit, this fun, that Healy railed against. The football anthem must have sounded like a mockery in his head in the decades when the saying went that the best Charlestown football team was in New York, and the latest generation of kids preferred to stay indoors.

> Your first reaction is a wild impulse to take the kids and kick their backsides hard, to tell them to get up there to The Park and be a real man like Danno Regan was. And then you remember it's not the kids' fault. They never heard us sing 'Up the Sarsfields'; no-one told them about the great

golden glory-days of Danno Regan and of our town and now, in the atmosphere of permanent beal bochtery, of television and its maniacal cry of 'Baaatmaaaann' twice a week fills the void and the vacuum. May Christ pity and spare my sad town. And all our sad towns.

In the 1980s, though, something stirred. In 1982, the town produced a fine minor team featuring Kenny Reilly and Bosco Walsh; but after the Leaving Certificate, most of them left. In 1988, Stephen Healy played centre-forward on another fabulously talented underage team. Brendan Cregg, the national school teacher, had coached them well in their early days, and they began to win everything in sight, culminating in the 1988 minor 'A' title. Three years later, they were county Under-21 champions, although by then several players had emigrated.

Then, out of the blue, they qualified for the senior final. Kenny Reilly had come home from New York and played a great championship. In the week before that 1992 country final against Knockmore, the town was packed with emigrants home for the match. They might have won, too, but for an unforgettably cruel twist when Pádraig Brogan fired a speculative ball that dropped high towards the Charlestown goalmouth and, to the astonishment of everyone, straight into the net. John Casey was playing that afternoon, and although he was inconsolable, he presumed that the town would be playing in plenty of senior finals down the line. But they would not win a senior championship match for the next nine years. After playing with Mayo through the miserable summer of 1993, Kenny Reilly flew to New York again. Plenty of others followed. But at least that brief rising had shown that the spirit that John Healy had pined after was not really departed. It was simply dormant.

And then things turned around. Securing an airport in Knock had become one of John Healy's great obsessions. He had the charm and personality to ally himself to the most dynamic of the Dublin politicians, becoming firm friends with Donagh O'Malley and later Charles Haughey. Healy was a genuine renaissance man. When he visited his brother, he preferred to sit in and drink a bottle of wine rather than tour the saloon bars of Charlestown, and besides writing his chief passions were fishing and painting. He had a small studio in the Achill cottage in which he and his wife, Evelyn, spent the summer months. Healy was close to Monsignor James Horan, who had long voiced his dream of an airport in his parish, and he used his influence in Dublin to try to push the project towards becoming a reality.

Gerry says, 'I remember he took Haughey down once and drove him around to show him exactly how people lived. It was around the time they were threatening to take away the farmer's dole. Charlie was hugely impressed. Anything John ever said or wrote was always to get at the government for neglecting the west of Ireland. And seeing an airport built near Charlestown was hugely important to him.'

John Healy died in 1990, four years after Knock Airport opened. He was only sixty years old and was afflicted with a brain haemorrhage. Gerry cannot recall his ever being ill prior to that day. But at least he had seen the flashing lights of jet planes bringing the young back to Charlestown. Around Christmas of 1994, the first transatlantic flight landed at Knock, and half of the passengers were from Charlestown. The mere fact of landing so close to home rendered the vast separating Atlantic less unfathomable.

'You would always look forward to Christmas,' Stephen Healy remembers. 'Between 1988 and 1995, it was magic because everyone was back from England, Boston, Chicago and New York. You would head down to the pub and you would spend the first hour shaking hands with everyone and talking about the football and who was going well in New

York. The town was alive for those few weeks. And then January was awful. Silent.'

By the mid-'90s, people were slower to leave. Kids were attending college or finding easy work in Dublin. The week nights might be lonesome in the town, but on Friday nights the bus stop was always busy. Confidence was fragile in Charlestown, but at least it was returning. And then John Casey began to light up the football summer, a Charlestown kid oozing with talent and the attitude to match. Casey was young and did not know much about John Healy other than that he was Stephen's uncle, the famous journalist, the man who had written the book. But it was the flight of talented youngsters like Casey and hundreds like him that Healy had been raging against. Here, out of the blue, was the latest in the bloodline of Charlestown heroes that John Healy had despaired of ever witnessing again. And he was sitting in a café the week before the All-Ireland final reading about himself in disbelief, because maybe when you come from a town that has been battered for decades, you can only expect to fly so high.

A decade later, John Casey can look back on the three All-Ireland finals he played with Mayo with enough bravery to admit that they did not go well for him. In the drawn match, he was marked by Darren Fay and when he raced for the first ball, he was astonished to find that the brawny full-back was able to stay on his shoulder. Casey had no gas. He was substituted with three minutes to go. Mayo were two points up. All he had to do was count the seconds down. Tommy O'Malley hugged him fiercely and said to him, 'Case, we are All-Ireland champions.'

'I was crying going into the stands. I didn't care how badly I played. I knew I had contributed all year. I thought we had won the All-Ireland. And I was sitting there watching Colm Coyle's clearance bouncing over the bar.'

In the replay, he was better but could not rediscover the scintillating form of early summer. He scored a point, and then at the death, when Mayo were a point down and on the verge of losing, he had possession and a clear look at the goalposts. He passed it off to Tom Reilly. In the bitter weeks that followed, throughout that long winter of regret, Casey's decision not to shoot was often held against him. 'My excuse was that there was a terrible wind and the shot didn't suit from where I was, so I laid it off, probably hoping we could work a goal or something. It was stupid. I should have had a go. But hindsight is a great thing.'

That autumn, he went to Tralee College on a scholarship. Mark O'Reilly, the young Meath corner-back was also due to start studying there. A potentially awkward meeting was negotiated in a bar when O'Reilly walked up to the Mayo man with a vodka and said, 'Here.'

'We got drunk and didn't talk about the game. That was our first meeting.'

By the following June, Casey was in terrific physical shape, but emotionally he had not fully recovered from the trauma of the 1996 defeat. None of them had. Then, in June, he went to Louisburgh to play a club match. Afterwards, he shook hands with his friend Michael Byrne, who was off to New York for the summer. Casey was driving straight to Letterkenny, and he remembers Byrne stooping down beside the driver's door and saying, 'I'll be back in September for the All-Ireland final, Case'.

The next Tuesday, he drowned in a swimming pool in New York.

'Mickey B. as we called him. I still think about him. He was a terrific football player, in and out for Mayo. Every football player in the county must have been at the funeral. We were due to head off to play a challenge match in Derry, and I remember being collected at the house and trying to get the tears out of my eyes.'

Mayo returned to the All-Ireland final in much the same way as a dog lost in a snowdrift will sense its way home. Casey's form was erratic. He was dropped against Offaly, an All-Ireland semi-final win defined by a series of great saves made by Peter Burke. Casey was restored to the first team for the All-Ireland final. It was a flat day, an occasion stolen by Maurice Fitzgerald. At the official luncheon the following afternoon, Casey wandered over to Fitzgerald and enquired after Billy O'Shea, who had broken his leg early in the game. Fitzgerald said he had been to see him and that he was in bright form. 'No offence, Maurice,' Casey replied. 'But I wish it had been your f***ing leg.'

They both laughed. And two years later, when Casey began to feel pain after matches, he often thought of the flippancy of that remark, of how much he had taken for granted. What began as a persistent bearable pain in his left heel gradually got worse. For the sake of dressing-room bravado, he began referring to his 'Christy Brown'.

'It was the only thing I ever had trouble with. I used to get cortisone injections before league games. I would walk in with a limp and go out like a spring lamb. And I never trained between games. I just pumped iron.' The trouble was elusive. Specialists thought that perhaps the heel of his football boot was aggravating the bone in his ankle, so John Maughan took him to Dubarry to try to get special boots made. On Christmas Day of 1999, Maughan took him to the gym. He played no football throughout the spring and missed the opening round of that summer's Connacht championship. Against Roscommon, he came in from the bench, scored six points and was given the crystal vase by the television people for his starring role. He smiled, but it all felt hollow in comparison to three years earlier. In the Connacht final against Galway, he knew he was struggling, and his last appearance for Mayo was as a substitute in a tame All-Ireland semi-final defeat to Cork.

Through the next winter, he underwent four operations, hanging on to the illusion that he was an still an inter-county football player and even togging out and sitting on the bench against Sligo in the 2000 championship. His last operation took place in St James's Hospital. He remembers talking to the anaesthetist as he lay in the theatre, spoofing about the quality of Mayo fishing. He felt himself drift, woke up again and grabbed a nurse by the arm, shouting, 'Don't cut me yet, I'm not gone.'

'Sir, you had your surgery yesterday,' she replied.

The surgeon came in and breezily informed him that the procedure had been largely successful but passage to the problematic bone had required removing part of the Achilles tendon. It took a few minutes for him to absorb the full meaning of that. He would not be able to run properly again. He would not play for Mayo again. He was twenty-five years old, and he had lost four All-Ireland finals, two at Under-21 grade and those two harrowing days against Meath and Kerry. John Maughan had stepped down as manager, and, unable to train, unable to belong, Casey felt like an outcast. He felt tainted. He had arguments with the county board over medical expenses. He kept driving to see specialists, but the diagnosis was always the same, and his birthdays passed. Occasionally, some of the Mayo boys would call in to say hello on their way through Charlestown. He missed the game terribly. It got so that he would wander up to the pitch to watch the local team training, watching his friends trot laps from the stand. His reincarnation as a goalkeeper was down to circumstance: the regular keeper had a holiday booked, and there was a replay. Casey was asked if he would be interested in stepping in. By accepting, he knew he was acknowledging that his days as a Mayo football player were over. But he played again, a tall, sometimes flamboyant and loud goalkeeper.

In 2001, Stephen Healy was training the team, and,

unexpectedly, they kept on winning. They beat a Crossmolina team that had been crowned All-Ireland club champions just six weeks before. They had the sweetest day against Knockmore, becoming county champions for the first time in ninety-nine years. Once again, the town was full with exiles who could not bear to miss what was a once-in-a-lifetime occasion. Cheques began to arrive in the post to Charlestown, sent by people who had left the town fifty years before. Letters of thanks and gratitude landed on Healy's porch, bearing stamps from all across the United States. Charlestown kept winning, beating Roscommon Gaels and then Annaghdown of Galway in the provincial final. It was a strange winter, electric with hope and optimism. The darkness did not seem so pitch-black or the nights so long. Then they had a long wait to play the mighty Nemo Rangers in the All-Ireland semi-final, and the adventure ended there. That was fine. Charlestown had rediscovered itself as a football town that winter.

Casey attempted to retire a couple of years ago, but somehow or other he always seems to end up back between the sticks. Football matters to him now, but it no longer defines his life. His wife, Rita, has been expecting their first child through the 2007 championship. They built a house near the business, beside where he kicked ball as a child. 'See that blue door? That is dented from me just walloping a ball against it,' he says, as we walk back towards the hardware store, Casey limping slightly as he moves. His leg is still ginger from the Crossmolina game, but he is confident they will beat the champions at the second time of asking. As it turns out, he is right.

Casey has a touch of John Healy's fearlessness about him, an endearing if almost artless compulsion to call things as he sees them. On a football field, that omnipotence is priceless. He rarely misses a Mayo football match now, content to be a fan. Gerry and Stephen Healy are the same. As he got older,

Stephen began to read more and more of his uncle's work. Over time, Charlestown people forgave John Healy, and now he is regarded as a local treasure. There are plans to name the new bypass after him, and if there is a slight irony in that, Gerry is certain his brother would have been touched by the gesture. 'I think he would have been hugely honoured. He would like the town as it is today. And you can be sure he wouldn't by fully happy with it.'

Sometimes when Stephen Healy reads back over his uncle's old books, he sees in them more relevance than ever. There is no question that there is more prosperity and comfort around the Charlestown of today, but the major industry, the factory that John Healy had lobbied for, never arrived. Sometimes, he wonders if the town could be pitched back to the bleakness of the 1970s. And it is a more private town now, too. He has grown used to not knowing everyone when he walks down through the Square. He remembers the huge surge of energy that used to shoot through the town during the last of the old-fashioned emigrant Christmases, when the pubs were crowded and faces were flushed from the rain-lashed night and the sheer thrill of being home. Perhaps the spirit in the town was richer for circumstances being harder. Nothing, except the unbelievable run by the town football team, could match the transitory happiness and wordless pride that 'Charlestowners', as his uncle called them, felt during those short holiday periods.

A few days before the county final, John Casey was sitting in his usual place in the Broadway Café having a cup of coffee. These were the very premises that, in John Healy's youth, had been Jim Mulrooney's shop, where Chamberlain's voice had spoken gravely of the Second World War in the town that raised children who looked west to the neon promise of America. That world had long vanished, and yet John Casey and John Healy were not so far apart. They were both sons of Charlestown. They had both played number one. A man guided his young son up to the table. They asked Casey if he was the Charlestown goalkeeper and, surprised, he agreed that he was. The boy presented him with a match programme for him to put his name on. The child would not even have been born during Casey's storming summers in a Mayo jersey. As John Casey signed his name, images of those madding days crossed his mind. He had not been asked for an autograph in many years, and, for the first time, he had the peace of mind to see it as a pleasure and an honour. 'Thanks,' John Casey called as the young fan exited with his father, leaving him alone to watch the world pass through the Square.

# TWELVE

# HOW SOON IS NOW?

Ballindine is the last town in Mayo on the N17 road to Galway. For many years, motorists familiar with that road would have noticed, about 200 metres inside the Galway border, a small stone shed painted entirely in green and red and bearing the boldest proclamation: 'Mayo. All-Ireland Champs 1951'. Fluttering on a stick tied to the terracotta roof tiles was a small flag of the county.

Located close to the road on a long straight coming just after the county sign for Galway, that shed – that tribute to Mayo football – was impossible to miss. It looked insolent and brave and puzzling, and it seemed the most perfect symbol of the defiance with which people in Mayo keep possession of their football heritage. The paint was so fresh looking and the announcement so brazen and jaunty, it was as though the graffiti artist was either indifferent to or unaware of the fact that an entire half-century had passed since Mayo's last momentous feat. Given that the passion for football in Galway had, in the last ten years, been spectacularly reignited by a Mayo man, the decorated shed, so striking and well tended along the verdant wilds of the country road, was like a demand for acknowledgement. For regardless of the disappointments and disappearances and failures of the past half-century, Mayo football people and Mayo teams are wedded to the belief that they ought to be challenging for All-Ireland glory every year. There is surely something admirable in that.

Lord knows, there have been plenty of dismal match days that have made that abiding ambition seem clownishly deluded and vain. And yet no county in modern times has come as close as often as Mayo has to winning the Sam Maguire Cup. A logical and rigorous examination of all of the big matches that Mayo have played and lost in the decades since last Seán Flanagan raised the cup under the gloomy cover of the old Hogan Stand could arrive at the cold conclusion that in each match, in each separate event, the Mayo teams were either not quite or not nearly good enough to win. That may be true of the most recent All-Ireland-final defeats. But the Mayo men who reached the September weekends of 1989 and 1996 were unquestionably strong enough to have become All-Ireland champions. And trying to square the Mayo side that was so ebullient and dashing against Dublin in August 2006 with the flat and inhibited team that appeared against Kerry just a few weeks later is the stuff of riddle. Few football counties have crashed quite so terribly as Mayo, and equally few appear capable of producing Mayo's unexpected bursts for glory, often flecked with brilliance, campaign summers like those of 1985 or 2006 that may have ended achingly but also left enough lingering joy to convince the 'grassroots' – in the phrase that John Healy minted – that winning the All-Ireland was like finding the right combination for a particularly tricky safe.

The record of those Mayo teams that have performed in All-Ireland finals since 1951 looks all the more woebegone when compared with the counties that seldom make it to the grandest stage but boldly took their chance when it presented itself. Donegal, Derry, Armagh and Tyrone have all won maiden All-Ireland titles since Mayo came close in 1989. Cast against the transcendent joy of those 'new' counties, Mayo's plight has come to seem all the more mystifying and permanent. Mayo football has acquired a sufficiently sturdy archive of heartbreak tales to make it seem as if the gods have been tinkering with their faith.

At a wedding last summer, a former Kerry footballer who had won an All-Ireland playing against Mayo told me that the legend of the 'curse' placed on the heroes of 1951 was going around the drinking dens of the Kingdom. There are several variations on the story, but the bones of it are that during the homecoming celebrations of 1951, a car full of boisterous Mayo footballers interrupted a Mass or a funeral as they passed by a church and that an enraged priest or a fortune teller vengefully swore to the happy band of footballers that Mayo would not be champions again until all of them had left the earth. The origins of the story are obscure, but after matches in which Mayo teams have appeared to have wretched luck, it has inevitably got airings, and it can seem like as logical an explanation as any.

However, the more grounded consolation of statistics shows that for all counties, with the notable exception of Kerry, the All-Ireland football championship is a brutally elusive competition. Becoming the champion football team in Ireland is exceptionally difficult. And yet in Mayo, as successive teams brush tantalisingly against the feeling – and it is the emotion that makes winning the All-Ireland football championship such an enduring and sacred ambition – the belief seems to grow more keen as the memory of the last triumph becomes ever more faint.

That shed near Ballindine has been painted white in the past year. It is possible that the owner grew frustrated after the crushing experiences of the last two Septembers, but it is preferable to imagine that the land changed ownership and that the Mayo colours were made pale by someone whose county allegiance belongs elsewhere. Either way, it is a shame, because that shed was a most simple and powerful commemoration of the latent fervour for the game in Mayo.

At the time of writing, in the deep quiet of the autumnal close season of 2007, Mayo football people are waiting to see who will come back. It seems hard to believe, but the exceptional generation of minor football players that bloomed under Martin Carney at the beginning of the 1990s have reached that lonely place where all athletes must pause and take stock of what has and what has not been achieved and to ask, in all reasonableness, what more they can contribute. In the wounded days and weeks after Mayo's last championship defeat up North, John O'Mahony was tactful and ambivalent about the future of the senior men who have been around since the furious, nearly days of the mid-'90s. It is hard to imagine Mayo football teams without David Brady charging around the field or without the lean and mop-haired figure of James Nallen roaming about the defence. But that day is approaching.

People have begun to recognise too that the sands of time are finite in the case of Ciaran McDonald. When this period of Mayo football has long passed and is subject to distant review, it seems inevitable that the masterless Crossmolina forward will be singled out as the key individual. That is not to say he has been more important than the other players who have poured their souls into the Mayo cause for as long as it was required of them. But McDonald has come to represent something separate and emblematic in the minds of Mayo football people. He has earned that standing the hard way.

Like many players down the years, McDonald has heard the bitter displeasure of unhappy Mayo fans, most seriously after a league match in Enniskillen in the spring of 2003, when the abuse he suffered was sufficiently stinging to persuade him to quit the county scene immediately. There had been several previous such departures. McDonald missed the 1996 All-Ireland run, having moved to America, but returned for the following year's campaign. Famously, he scored a fabulously struck penalty in that year's All-Ireland final against Kerry but also missed a fourteen-yard free. That inconsistency hinted at a fretting soul behind the striking blond image, but he made the practical adjustment of never taking a free from the ground again. For all the incandescence, McDonald is a grafter at heart.

There have been many matches since when McDonald has made elementary errors or underperformed. But there have also been plenty of genuinely special exhibitions of attacking play governed by unique instinct and kicking ability: the two searing goals he fired against Galway in the thrilling 1998 first-round championship match; the 1–09 he conjured against Knockmore in the Mayo championship in June of 1999; the moral courage and grace he displayed in leading Crossmolina to the All-Ireland title against Nemo Rangers in 2001; the unforgettable point he hit in the fourth minute of the 2004 All-Ireland defeat against Kerry; and that deathless point he curled into the sky-blue stronghold of the Hill in the famous semi-final against Dublin, when Mayo – yet again – seemed on the verge of something glorious.

There have been frequent reports of walkouts and reunions between McDonald and several Mayo management teams. The delightful expression of one county-board official, telling the newspapers that McDonald had resumed training after a period of absence – 'He's back, in all his glory' – sums up the mood. Over the years, Mayo people have learned to accept that McDonald is truly different, a lone wolf on the dark plains. Work has generally been the cause of his occasional disappearances from the county scene, and over the years it has become clear that McDonald is absolutely committed to Mayo football, albeit on his own terms. Since becoming an established Gaelic football player, McDonald has operated as a free spirit within the prevailing system. It does not matter that he braids his blond hair or that he has marked his sallow skin with tattoos, that he wears his socks over his knees or often takes the field bearing beaded necklaces, other than the fact that those preferences make him stand utterly alone in a sporting culture that is heavily conservative and uniform in image. It does not matter that there is something of the Native American warrior about McDonald in full flow on the field – the mane of hair whipping about his face, the lean, sinewy frame elusive, the manner of his game gloriously different to everyone else out there, the sheer elegance with which he moves – except that lesser players would risk ridicule for daring to look, to play, so radically different. McDonald has proven himself too good and too mentally and physically tough to earn anything other than the respect of his peers.

And it has been, necessarily, a distant respect. As the years rolled by and the various roles he filled for club and county began to speak for themselves, so did McDonald's public reserve seem all the more remarkable. Even within Mayo, a county where good-natured nosiness is regarded as a personable quality, McDonald has managed to remain marvellously invisible, more of a rumour than a person of substance except when he turns up on match days. He has politely and consistently declined all press requests for interviews down the years, apart from the lone exception when he granted Kieran Shannon of the *Sunday Tribune* an evening watching him practise frees in the dusk at the pitch at Crossmolina. It was a brief but important portrait of an artist, and among the few quotes from McDonald, one sentence seemed to overpower all the others. In talking of what was important to him, McDonald said: 'I just want to play a game of ball the way it is meant to be played.'

It seemed like a reasonable enough call for armistice. That was some six years ago. During that time, surely McDonald has tried to do just that, using the pivotal number-eleven spot to apply his own aesthetic to a team game, with genuinely beautiful passages of play when his ideas have worked out and general frustrations and recriminations when they have not. I questioned practically every Mayo person I met about McDonald. Old coaches and players and acquaintances all speak highly of him as being loyal and easy-going and friendly. But the most common observation was that he is, quite simply, a very private person. The words of one ex-footballer who belongs to McDonald's generation and who played on the same field as him for many years seemed to sum up the combination of awe and bafflement in which Mayo people hold him: 'I played against him many times and shook hands with him, but I never really spoke to the man. He would just play the game and go off. Will he be back for Mayo? I don't know. And I would say whenever he does finish up, we won't ever hear from him again.'

It is, of course, easy to romanticise a player around whom an atmosphere of seclusion and lonesomeness reminiscent of that which surrounded Joe DiMaggio has slowly formed. But when you talk to Mayo football people about Ciaran McDonald, it is as though they are already pining for him even before he has departed the field, perhaps aware that his best chance – and therefore Mayo's best chance – of winning an All-Ireland has passed.

It would, of course, have been fascinating to hear McDonald's voice on the frustrations and disappointments he has endured playing for Mayo down the years. Several loose arrangements were made to meet, but nothing ever came of them. After the last of those haphazard agreements had fallen through and I was driving back through Balla on a splendid autumn Sunday, it suddenly seemed as though McDonald's ongoing silence was completely suitable. What, after all, could he possibly say that had not already been communicated on the football field many times? There was something apt about the contradiction that in a county filled with loquacious and unusually introspective football men, the darling of the current generation has simply played, remaining firmly and nobly silent. Perhaps his silence and his enduring service – thirteen seasons and counting now – is a perfectly eloquent statement on how McDonald feels about Mayo football.

At least that is what I told myself driving through 'Baller' Lavin country and on past The Beaten Path as word came through on the radio sports bulletin that Eamonn Mongey, one of the learned, aristocratic players of the 1950–51 vintage, one of the last of the champions, had died in a Dublin hospital. Another hero departed. Another bonfire quenched. And it was clear then, wondering if Mayo would ever see McDonald in the green and red again and thinking about Eamonn Mongey, that the man who took the trouble to make an emblem out of his country shed had been perfectly right. Time does not matter a damn.

At the Mayo county final on the last day of September, they held a minute's silence in Eamonn Mongey's honour. It was one of those chaotic Irish pre-winter Sundays, with black racing clouds and dazzling sunshine and a brief two o'clock monsoon that drenched the crowd going though the turnstiles at McHale Park. A puddle formed on the concrete pavilion, soaking the tail end of the green-and-red flag that was draped over the table where the Paddy Moclair Cup stood. In the ancient, crumbling press-box, we sat on high stools behind the glass partition, idly watching the insect life caught in cobwebs as the brass band paraded around the field. This winter, a wrecking ball will trash much of the park and the county ground will be modernised. But there was a retrospective mood about this day. Earlier, Ballintubber had played Kiltimagh in the intermediate final, and, in a gripping finale, most of us were glued to the Ballintubber manager, James Horan. This man was probably the best of the luckless group of Mayo forwards of ten years ago, a man who had known double All-Ireland heartbreak. And here he was now, a peaked hat pulled low on the familiar athletic, slouching frame as he gambolled along the sideline, his emotions tethered to the unpredictable play on the field.

His team lost a three-point lead in the last ten minutes, and as we watched Horan mime the gestures of worry and anger and despair, we could not help wonder if the distant frenzy of Croke Park some ten Septembers ago was crossing his mind, if some interior voice was whispering, 'Not again, not again.' It went to the wire, as they say. Ballintubber had a hero when Kevin McGuinness, a substitute, kicked the winning point as if it was no big deal. Then the final whistle went and Horan became lost in the gang of substitutes and supporters who charged onto the field, gripped by the fierce ecstasy of a local victory, ignoring the mild protestations coming from the loudspeaker.

Then it was time for the Mayo senior final. It was no classic, and it followed a familiar theme. Ballina won again. For most of the game, David Brady played full-forward, moving with menace and intent in front of the Charlestown goal, close enough to keep conversation with John Casey. It was Brady's day, scoring one goal and conjuring a further two during a quietly heroic eight-minute spell. Casey could do nothing about the goals. At one point, the old friends got tangled up in the emotion of the game, pushing at each other. The two of them had spent their spare summer time coaching a local Sligo team, Easkey. If they had not been playing against each other that afternoon, they would have been plotting together in the Sligo championship. They shoved each other with the familiar roughness of brothers and walked away. When the final whistle went, Casey shook hands with those nearby and disappeared quickly through the tunnel. Brady stood alone on the edge of the small crowd on the field as the captain made his speech and his teammates celebrated on the podium. He was red-faced and his temple pulsed, and, with a smile, he warned a few pressmen not to even joke about his playing full-forward for Mayo. All he wanted to really talk about was Ronan McGarrity, his friend and teammate, who had recuperated from a serious illness to come back and play a storming final for his club and his town.

'Football isn't as big as what everyone thinks,' Brady said, rubbing his brow with his arm as perspiration steamed from his shirt. Already, the ground was beginning to empty. Over in the clubhouse, a small crowd watched the fading hopes of the Ireland rugby team playing against Argentina in the World Cup in Paris. We could hear the roars of frustration and encouragement drifting through the open window.

On the wall in that clubhouse, there is a framed exhibition of the medal collection belonging to the late Mick Flanagan, the dear friend and teammate of Paddy Prendergast and the other boys of that era. It is a stunning haul: schools, colleges, All-Irelands, the lot, and placed together they look like an unlikely glittering hoard from Tutankhamen's tomb. Flanagan's Celtic Cross from 1951 is placed among school and county medals, no bigger or brighter than the rest. Above the wooden frame stands a black-and-white photograph of Mick. His hair is slicked back and he is wearing a dashing pinstripe suit and looks in fine form. If you had told him, when that photograph was taken, that no Mayo footballer would win an All-Ireland medal in the next half-century, he would have laughed in hearty disbelief.

But that is the reality. Imagine the scene in McHale Park, if, by some magical concoction, all the men who have played senior football for Mayo since 1951 could have assembled out there on that September afternoon, impervious to age. Not just the famous football names, not just the Apollos of their day who dominated the western skies, but those football men who toiled in obscurity for a few brief seasons and then were gone, players who nonetheless belong to this fraternity, who bought into this tradition. Yes, imagine how crowded the field would be if all the football men who wore the green and red in the last half-century could gather for a few moments to see themselves for what they are: a team of many teams, a small army who contributed something of their souls to what was and remains a magnificent idea.

Perhaps those ghosts were all about David Brady as he trooped off the darkening field, battered and happy. Nobody could say for sure if he would be seen playing for Mayo again. When the lights were switched off in McHale Park that night, another football year officially ended. Uncertainty governs the blue fields of Mayo as winter sets in and the long wait continues. They will miss Brady if he goes. They will all be missed. The cause endures.

# Acknowledgements

My sincere thanks to the Mayo football people who graciously gave their time to talk about old games and old times. Your generosity and grace and humour have been humbling and have made working on this story a pleasure.

Thanks to the folks at Mainstream Publishing: Bill for giving the green light, Graeme for keeping things rolling along, Lee for her cover design and Claire, whose conscientious editing means that she has become one of Scotland's leading authorities on Mayo Gaelic football.

Thanks to Malachy Logan, sports editor of the *Irish Times*, for his constant encouragement and help, and for knowing when to ask nothing.

To Mike Finnerty and Denise Horan at the *Mayo News*; Liam Horan, Bernie O'Hara, Henry Wills and Cathy Flynn at the *Western People*; and Margaret Geraghty, Sean Feeney and Joe McDonnell at 21st Century Design: thanks for the help and contacts and advice.

To Carl Duggan and Eoin Duggan, a special thanks for their diligent reading, their patience and their tireless research into Walt Arena.

And with thanks and gratitude to my family: to Siobhan for a million small kindnesses and for keeping me going, and to Rory and Ruby for shouting stop.